CAN DIFFERENT CULTURES THINK THE SAME THOUGHTS?

CAN DIFFERENT CULTURES THINK THE SAME THOUGHTS?

A Comparative Study in Metaphysics and Ethics

KENNETH DORTER

University of Notre Dame Press

Notre Dame, Indiana

University of Notre Dame Press
Notre Dame, Indiana 46556
undpress.nd.edu
Copyright © 2018 by the University of Notre Dame
All Rights Reserved

Title page art: "Confucius, Shankara, and Socrates," by Gloria Wang

Published in the United States of America

Library of Congress Cataloging-in-Publication Data

Names: Dorter, Kenneth, 1940– author.
Title: Can different cultures think the same thoughts? : a comparative study in metaphysics
    and ethics / Kenneth Dorter.
Description: Notre Dame : University of Notre Dame Press, 2018. | Includes
    bibliographical references and index.
Identifiers: LCCN 2017055853 (print) | LCCN 2018003386 (ebook) |
    ISBN 9780268103552 (pdf) | ISBN 9780268103569 (epub) |
    ISBN 9780268103538 (hardcover : alk. paper) | ISBN 0268103534
    (hardcover : alk. paper)
Subjects: LCSH: Metaphysics—Comparative studies. | Ethics—Comparative studies.
Classification: LCC BD111 (ebook) | LCC BD111 .D67 2018 (print) |
    DDC 109—dc23
LC record available at https://lccn.loc.gov/2017055853

To My Brother Ira

CONTENTS

PREFACE

The project of this book has two aims. One is to explore issues in metaphysics and ethics, including the way metaphysics can be foundational for ethics. I approach these issues through the works of major thinkers in the three main philosophical traditions—India, China, and the West—comparing philosophers from two traditions in each chapter. An advantage of this approach is that examining a subject from different directions gives us different perspectives and allows us to see limitations and assumptions that may be inconspicuous otherwise. The comparison may also provide us with a perspective that is more than the sum of its parts. Each of the chapters addresses its theme through the work of a different pair or group of philosophers, while the Conclusion compensates for this diversity of voices with an overview of the book as a whole.

The cross-cultural approach provides the project with a further aim—to consider how far authors from different cultures can be said to have comparable views. At least since Hegel there is an influential view that not only is every culture unique, but the products of those cultures are ultimately incompatible—that the resemblances are superficial and the differences decisive. The issue of the validity of cross-cultural correspondences is addressed in some detail in the Introduction, while the subsequent chapters are devoted to the specific metaphysical and ethical issues. The comparisons that follow have convinced me that there are resemblances that are profound and important, but although the chapters point out commonalities in the different traditions, I make no claim that there is a universal philosophy. On the contrary, in places it is obvious that there are fundamental disagreements among the philosophers studied in different chapters. But within each chapter we see a shared or at least analogous way of looking at things in different cultures.

Philosophers sometimes find it useful to distinguish between "morality" and "ethics," but in what follows the terms are used interchangeably.

I would like to thank Ben-Ami Scharfstein, Lin Ma, and Cristina Ionescu for their very helpful comments and suggestions on an earlier draft.

Earlier versions of chapters 4 and 6 were published, respectively, as "Metaphysics and Morality in Neoconfucianism and Greece: Zhu Xi, Plato, Aristotle, Plotinus," *Dao: A Journal of Comparative Philosophy* 8 (2009): 255–76, and "The Concept of The Mean in Confucius and Plato," *Journal of Chinese Philosophy* 29 (2002): 317–33.

Portions of other chapters were published as follows: "Virtue, Knowledge, and Wisdom: Bypassing Self-Control," *Review of Metaphysics* 51 (1997): 313–43; "A Dialectical Interpretation of the *Bhagavad-Gita*," *Asian Philosophy* 22 (2012): 307–26; "Being and Appearance in Parmenides," in *Metaphysics*, ed. Mark Pestana (Rijeka, Croatia: In-Tech, 2012), 45–64; "The Problem of Evil in Heraclitus," in *Early Greek Philosophy: The Presocratics and the Emergence of Reason*, ed. Joe McCoy (Washington, DC: Catholic University Press, 2013), 36–54; "Indeterminacy and Moral Action in Laozi," *Dao* 13 (2014): 63–81; and "Thought and Expression in Spinoza and Shankara," *Symposium* 18 (2014): 215–35. I would like to thank the respective editors and publishers for permission to reprint this material here.

I would also like to thank Hackett Publishing for permission to use, in Appendix 2 of chapter 3, the contemporary illustration by Liz Wilson of Zhou Dunyi's diagram. The illustration is taken from *Readings in Later Chinese Philosophy: Han Dynasty to the 20th Century*, ed. Justin Tiwald and Bryan W. Van Norden (Indianapolis: Hackett, 2014).

INTRODUCTION

Philosophers in all traditions have argued that our beliefs about how to behave are grounded in our conception of reality, which implies that ethics is ultimately grounded in metaphysics. That view is the connecting theme of the chapters of this book as they examine first the basic issues of metaphysics (the first three chapters) and the relation of metaphysics to ethics (chapters 2–4), then basic theoretical issues of ethics (chapters 5 and 6), and then a fundamental issue in applied ethics (chapter 7). Since these issues are explored cross-culturally through comparisons of philosophers from different traditions, we must also consider the question of whether thinkers from different cultures are genuinely, and not just apparently, able to have comparable thoughts and points of view. Some interpreters believe that the resemblances among these philosophers point to shared experiences that underlie culturally differentiated formulations;[1] others believe that the resemblances are only superficial and that comparable experiences cannot in principle occur within radically different cultures. It is not possible to provide a definitive account of the relation between individual experience and cultural influence— that is, a conclusive demonstration either that all experience is inseparable from cultural factors or that some cognitive experiences transcend such factors—because much depends on the weight given to different elements of the texts. What we can do, however, is examine individual examples to see what the evidence is in each case, both for the role of culture and for the possibility of philosophical thinking that can transcend its cultural origins. Arguments from resemblance and analogy can show how strong the reasons are for believing in a correspondence between different formulations even if they cannot be logically conclusive.

Apart from providing case studies that serve as evidence for the roles of individual experience and cultural influence, cross-cultural comparisons have the value of enabling us to see the particular subjects in different lights: examining a subject from the perspective of more than one tradition enables us to see it from diverse points of view and become aware of alternatives and limitations that may remain hidden from us otherwise. We are led to ask different questions than we would otherwise be likely to do, and to notice by contrast aspects of a text or issue that otherwise may not be apparent.[2] The chapters address some of the major issues in metaphysics and ethics: If our "natural" point of view is practical rather than metaphysical, what can induce us to adopt a metaphysical point of view? If the reality of the world consists in its absolute unity, and the self-subsistence of individuals is only illusory, how is that compatible with the importance we attach to our lives, rather than leading to apathy and fatalism? What is the value of metaphysical models of reality, and how can they provide the basis for achieving a moral point of view? If no absolute point of view is possible, how can some actions be more moral than others? Does virtue follow from knowledge, and, if so, how is it possible to succumb to the temptation of doing something we know is wrong? Does virtuous action consist in finding a mean between extremes, and, if so, how can we locate it? Is nonviolence a realistic goal, and is it compatible with the use of deadly force?

The Problem of Comparative Philosophy

There are striking parallels among the three traditions,[3] such as the view expressed by Plato and Aristotle in Greek philosophy and Confucius in Chinese philosophy that moral goodness requires finding the mean between excess and deficiency, or the view expressed by Shankara in Indian philosophy and Spinoza in Western philosophy of the insubstantiality of individual existence. Even if it were only a question of mapping resemblances among the various traditions, there would still be historical value in such comparisons but not necessarily philosophical advantages. Studying the doctrine of the mean in Confucius and Plato together might not be any more fruitful than studying it in one or the other of them alone. But in fact there are philosophical advantages to the comparisons beyond the tracing of resemblances for its own sake. Not only do the comparisons lead us to different questions and alternative answers, but insofar as philosophers from different cultures may seem to be saying the same thing they remind us of the possibility that an idea might be independent of its particular formulations; and insofar as they differ from one another they make us aware of cultural or personal presuppositions that might otherwise have remained invisible. As Ben-Ami Scharfstein writes:

> The result is that every philosophy is seen in the light of more contrasts, and more contrasts yield a greater variety of interpretations and, it is reasonable to hope, a greater ability to modulate any point of view. . . . By changing your eyes, you see things—meanings, relationships, and values— to which you have so far been blind. A perceptive traveler in philosophy learns to grasp what has been invisible because it is too familiar or, on the contrary, too distant, and is led to take greater care in discriminating exact meanings. (1998, 7–8)[4]

Such comparisons provide us with a basis for considering how far thinkers from different cultures may be said to think the same thoughts, and also to what extent their thinking is limited by cultural constraints and presuppositions.

That comparisons lead us to ask different questions is uncontroversial, but the possibility that philosophers in different cultures may be saying the same thing in different ways has been controversial at least since the time of Herder and especially Hegel, who believed that every culture is unique and that apparent resemblances are arrived at only by abstracting from all that is essential and distinctive in them. That there are at least stylistic differences among the three traditions compared here is unquestionable. Western philosophy is written in the form of treatises or fully composed dialogues with the author's name attached. Traditional Indian philosophy also normally takes the form of fully composed works, but in this case they are based on myth-inflected legends, and they are of usually unknown authorship, although there are occasional exceptions such as Kautilya's *Arthashastra* (Treatise on political economy) from the fourth century BCE. Chinese philosophy, unlike its Western and Indian counterparts, tends to take the form of reported conversations rather than fully composed works, with occasional exceptions like the *Daodejing* by Laozi (*Tao Te Ch'ing* by Lao Tzu),[5] and like Western philosophy it relies on argument rather than myth, but with more weight sometimes given to authority (in the Confucian tradition) or poetic expression (in Daoism and Buddhism).[6] There is, then, no question that cultural differences are a factor in the three traditions. The same is obviously true of linguistic differences. Translations from Sanskrit are difficult enough, even though like English it is an Indo-European language, and translations from Chinese, which is written in pictograms and therefore does not use grammatical forms like conjugation, declension, and tenses, are far more so.[7] Even if we are fluent in the relevant languages, we have to compare them within one language or another, and the language chosen becomes the standard by which the other is judged.[8]

But while there is no possibility of neutrally objective comparisons, the constraints on intercultural comparisons are no greater than those in interpretation generally. Comparable constraints arise whenever we read a text or listen to someone speaking. Even within the same language no two people use words in precisely the same way, and some people are clearly better than others in understanding what another person means. Avoiding misunderstandings is often challenging. The situation is more complicated when a second language is involved, but the problem is not different in kind. A cultural relativist, however, would regard this as an oversimplification: the fact that we can make sense of what is said in other languages does not prove that the sense we make of it is the same as the sense intended. Are similar thoughts impossible in dissimilar languages and cultures, or do these factors affect only the style and method of expression, and not the conception of reality that is expressed?

Hegel argues, as do in different ways contemporary philosophers who have been directly and indirectly influenced by him, that the attribution of conceptual correspondences to different traditions remains at the level of understanding (*Verstand*), which is misled by superficial resemblances, whereas reason (*Vernunft*) sees more deeply and recognizes the unique defining spirit in every culture. He insists that any common features between two cultures only obscure the absolute difference between their underlying spirits and that when the faculty of understanding finds analogies and common denominators among different cultures it does so by abstracting from what is individually distinctive about them. To some extent this was already Aristotle's criticism of Plato's theory of forms, though at the level of individuals rather than cultures, but Hegel extends the criticism historically: the resemblances that we find among structures and ideas in disparate historical cultures are no more than empty forms. Where the understanding sees commonalities, reason grasps the essential differences as moments in dialectical development. He writes:

> It may rightly be said that genius, talent, moral virtues and feeling, piety—all can occur anywhere, in all political systems and conditions; and that there are abundant examples of this. If such assertions are meant to deny that these distinctions are important or essential, then thought has become stuck in abstract categories and is disregarding their specific content. Of course, no distinguishing principles for any such specific content are to be found in these abstract categories. The sophisticated mind that adopts formal points of view of this kind, enjoys a vast field for ingenious questions, erudite views, and striking comparisons, and for seemingly profound reflections and declarations—which can become all the more brilliant the vaguer their subject; and they can be varied and reviewed over and over, in inverse proportion to the certainty and rationality that results from them. . . . Chinese philosophy, by taking the concept of the *One* as its basis, has been held to be the same as the monistic philosophy of the Eleatics and the system of Spinoza. (1988, 69–70)

This last remark cuts close to home, since the second chapter below compares the Eleatic philosophy of Parmenides with the system of Spinoza, even if the third author (Shankara) is taken from Indian rather than Chinese philosophy. The evidence that Hegel gives for his criticism is questionable, however. He says, for example, "To the Chinese, their moral laws are like the laws of nature, expressed as external positive commands, compulsory rights and duties, or rules of courtesy toward one another. What is missing is the element of freedom, through which alone the substantive determinations of Reason become moral conviction in the individual. Morality, for them, is a matter for the state to rule on, and is handled by government officials and the courts"(74–75). Hegel has in mind the Confucian concept of *li*, propriety, which prescribes rituals and practices. Of course, we have such prescriptions as well, but Hegel believes that Chinese morality, unlike ours, was based *only* on external prescriptions. In addition to the external principles of *li*, however, Confucius advocated the internal principle of *ren* (*jen*), humaneness, which is akin to our notion of conscience and therefore "free" in Hegel's sense. Confucius says in the *Analects*, for example: "If you govern them with decrees and regulate them with punishments, the people will evade them but have no sense of shame. If you govern them with virtue and regulate them with the rituals, they will have a sense of shame" (2.3).[9] Similarly, the *Analects* records that "Zi-gong asked: 'Is there one single word that one can practice throughout one's life?' The Master said, 'It is perhaps altruism.[10] What you do not wish for yourself, do not impose on others'" (15.23).

A study of comparative philosophy leads some readers to a very different conclusion from Hegel's: not that philosophies from diverse traditions are different in substance although they may resemble one another formally, but that they may be similar in substance although they differ formally. In other words, their formulations, modes of expression, and cultural references may differ because of differences in the languages and cultures in which they were expressed, but what those formulations point to is a comparable vision of reality. Even if every culture has a unique spirit and expresses truth in its unique way, that does not entail the stronger claim that no identical experience of truth can underlie the differing modes of conceptualization and expression. It does not exclude the possibility that the differences in our thinking may be diverse perspectives of a common preconceptual experience expressed in analogically related ways.

One writer who sees the issue this way is Aldous Huxley, who, in *The Perennial Philosophy*, attempts to demonstrate an underlying unity of the various traditions by showing a correspondence of passages on a wide variety of topics divided into twenty-seven chapters.[11] The book is a monument to erudition and insight into all major traditions and makes an eloquent case for a continuity and parallelism among them, but by quoting these passages in abstraction from their context Huxley leaves himself open to the criticism that he may bring into the foreground only what supports his underlying thesis and leave in the background, however unintentionally, whatever does not. I do not believe that Huxley's anthology distorts the different traditions, but his book cannot convince its skeptics that these resemblances demonstrate more than coincidental similarities within cultures that may be decisively different in their formative experiences. It does not refute the quasi-Hegelian views of Marxists and of postmodernists like Foucault who believe that our spiritual and intellectual life cannot transcend the culture that spawned it. Huxley's documentation is valuable to those who share his point of view but is too selective to satisfy those who do not.

More recently Ben-Ami Scharfstein (1998) and Gene Blocker (1999), among others, have documented in greater detail than Huxley continuities that underlie the differences among philosophers from different traditions,[12] and Scharfstein has subsequently done so in the realm of art as well, concluding that "all the suggested similarities and dissimilarities are best appreciated as belonging to a common universe of discourse in which the humanity of the art is never quite concealed by its locality . . . [and] everyone who takes enough trouble can communicate . . . with everyone else" (2009, 432).[13] Scharfstein's and Blocker's books provide valuable evidence of the connections among diverse traditions, even if such evidence can never be conclusive. The claim that individual experience can transcend its cultural traditions necessarily falls back upon analogy—there are numerous conceptual correspondences among the three major traditions so there must also be an underlying experiential correspondence—but arguments from analogy can never be more than inductive. No matter how many observed similarities may be pointed out, the final inference to an unobservable similarity is always open to question. On the other hand, little in philosophy is demonstrable deductively, or philosophy would long ago have become assimilated to mathematics in the way that Descartes envisioned.

The disagreement is a variation on the old controversy, going back to the Sophists' distinction between *nomos* and *phusis*, convention and nature, often articulated since the nineteenth century as between the

Pavlovians and the Freudians, as to whether there is such a thing as human nature. If there is constancy of human nature across diverse cultures, then we would expect there to be substantial parallels in philosophical worldviews; if not, then the resemblances are more likely to be only superficial. Thus Scharfstein and Blocker both make a case for universal features of human nature. Scharfstein writes that "there is a level at which the differences between traditions grow less isolating and comparisons grow genuinely illuminating. I say this for the simplest of reasons: the biological likeness between human beings, the similarity of their social needs, and their similar ways of fulfilling themselves, intellectually and otherwise" (1998, 36). Blocker quotes the contemporary Ghanaian philosopher Kwame Gyekye: "The universality of philosophical ideas may be put down to the fact that human beings, irrespective of their cultures and histories, share certain basic values; our common humanity grounds the adoption and acceptance of some ideas, values, and perceptions, as well as the appreciation of the significance of events taking place beyond specific cultural borders" (1999, 38). These are important considerations but not decisive ones. Hegel, for example, accepts that there is a human nature—*Geist* or spirit—but believes that historical cultures create a second nature that makes comparisons specious.

The relationship between thought and the linguistic and cultural forms in which it is expressed is deeply problematic. If we conceive of thought and its expression in terms of content and form, there can be just as little content without form as there can be form without content—as for Aristotle in the physical world there can be just as little matter without form as form without matter—which might be taken to imply that there can be no thought without its linguistic expression.[14] While this seems to be true of *conceptual* thought, it does not preclude that there is a kind of thinking that is preconceptual. In every culture those who claim to have experienced a reality that underlies the one we perceive physically testify that the experience is formless as well as contentless (at least as far any anything conceptual is concerned) but afterwards is given form and content in the attempt to reflect on and communicate it. On that view it is conceivable that fundamental experiences may be intrinsically similar even if never the same in expression. More than linguistic expression is involved here, more than the problem of translation from one language to another, which has been carefully examined by philosophers as diverse as Walter Benjamin (1968) and Donald Davidson (1973–74).[15] It is not only a matter of how successfully Shankara can be translated into Latin, or Spinoza into Sanskrit, for example, but also a question of how far two models of reality very different in their particulars can be considered parallel in their meaning.[16] The issues of translation and interpretation have recently been given an encyclopedic examination by Lin Ma and Jaap van Brakel, who support the legitimacy of intercultural comparisons while also addressing the difficulties and limitations inherent in such comparisons.[17]

The view that every culture has a unique spirit, and that this spirit expresses our experience of reality in a unique way, can be designated "perspectivism," as opposed to "cultural constructivism," the stronger claim that not only does the expression of our experience differ from one culture to another but even the experience itself is essentially different. According to perspectivism, as I am using the term, the differences in our thinking are diverse perspectives of a common prelinguistic experience that is expressed in analogically related ways, while according to cultural constructivism no experience can be common to the thinking that takes place within differently constructed cultural or linguistic frameworks; there may be only one reality, but it would be more like Kant's noumenal reality, which can never be experienced as it is in itself (although the constructivist view would be more radical than the Kantian view that all rational beings experience the same phenomenal representation of reality regardless of their culture). The term *perspectivism* originates with Nietzsche, who wrote, "There is *only* a perspective seeing, *only* a perspective 'knowing'; and the *more* affects we allow to speak about one thing, the *more* eyes, different eyes, we can use to observe that thing, the more complete will our 'concept' of this thing, our 'objectivity,' be."[18] Where the cultural constructivist would emphasize the plurality of eyes, the perspectivist would emphasize the implied unity of what is seen: "one thing" (*eine Sache*), "that thing" (*dieselbe Sache*), "this thing" (*dieser Sache*). Other perspectivists go beyond Nietzsche in regarding perspectival knowledge as capable of leading to transcendence of perspective, which is no longer "knowing" in the previous limited sense. In Zhuangzi (Chuang Tzu), for example, as McLeod puts it: "There is *also*, however, perspective-independent truth, most often having to do with features of the *dao*, and to have *knowledge* of these truths requires seeing the limitations of our individual perspectives and gaining distance from these perspectives. . . . This is not just *another* perspective, the 'perspective of the *dao*,' if you will, but rather is a transcendence of perspective" (2016, 111).

Points of View

I am attributing the possibility of common experiences only to the specific philosophers who are compared in each chapter. I am not claiming that there is a universal experience that all philosophers share. For example, I argue that Laozi and Heraclitus articulate a similar worldview, but I would not claim that this view is shared by Confucius or Socrates. I believe that there are cross-cultural commonalities on particular issues explored by particular thinkers from different traditions, but not that there is such a thing as a single universal philosophy, even within the same tradition. On the contrary, in every tradition there are exponents of every possible point of view. How could one claim that Spinoza and Hume, for example, express comparable experiences of reality? Even if there is a single reality underlying all our experiences, that reality can be perceived in multiple ways depending on our temperament and our priorities, the kinds of questions that interest us;[19] even if there is a single reality experienced by all people in all cultures, we each, for whatever reason, are especially aware of or care about some aspects at the expense of others. But each of these ways of experiencing reality may occur in comparable ways in different cultures.

Given the undoubted fact that there are real differences among the three traditions, if comparative philosophy is capable of discovering truths that transcend those differences, where do interpreters stand when we make comparisons? If we compare the three traditions from within the standpoint of our own, we risk imposing the categories of our tradition onto the other two, however inadvertently and involuntarily.[20] On the other hand, if we discuss each of the three entirely from within its own perspective it is hard to see how we can compare them. The only way out of this dilemma would be if interpreters could stand outside all three traditions in some neutral area, but in that case we would have no point of view at all, since traditions alone can give us ways of talking about reality, even if those ways are necessarily subject to the limitations of finitude and the need to make choices. Looked at in this way the problem would seem to be insoluble, but it is no more or less insoluble than any act of interpretation. Western philosophers do not generally consider the act of interpreting Plato or Aristotle to differ significantly from that of interpreting Kant or Hume because Greek philosophy is the foundation of Western philosophy, but the world within which Plato and Aristotle wrote is almost as alien to us now as the worlds of Chinese and Indian philosophy—its religious beliefs, social practices, political institutions, and way of life generally, all entirely alien to ours. Even Kant and Hume lived in a different world from ours. L. P. Hartley's words "The past is a foreign country," referring to a time barely fifty years earlier, have become almost proverbial because we recognize the truth in them. The difficulty of interpreting previous philosophers in one's own tradition differs only in degree from a Western reader's difficulties of interpreting Chinese or Indian philosophers. Even the interpretation of our contemporaries presents analogous difficulties, given the uniqueness of every individual thinker. In short, the problem of comparative philosophy is a special case of the problem of hermeneutics generally, and Gadamer's explanation that there is a fusing of the conceptual horizons of the writer and interpreter applies as much to comparative philosophy as to interpretation generally.[21] There is no interpretation without bias, just as there is no interpretation without a point of view, but whatever its limitations the interpretation of the thoughts of others is indispensable to philosophy and to rational life in general.

The Example of Heidegger

I have limited the cross-cultural comparisons to philosophers who, as far as can be ascertained, arrived at their views independently of one another, so I do not include Schopenhauer's relationship to Buddhism, or any subsequent philosophers, all of whom have meanwhile become aware of Indian and Chinese philosophy to varying degrees (and vice versa). Although not included in the following chapters, examples of the *influence* of Eastern philosophy on Western philosophers (and vice versa) show in their own way that the same thinking can occur within different cultures. The development of Heidegger's philosophy provides an illustration. Heidegger had knowledge of Chinese Daoism at least from 1930,[22] but at first his views were far from Daoist in important respects. In *Introduction to Metaphysics* (1935), for example, philosophy is a violent undertaking, rather than the *wei wuwei* (doing by not doing) of Daoism: "Only by undergoing the struggle between Being and seeming did [the Greeks] wrest Being forth from beings, did they bring beings into constancy and unconcealment" (Heidegger 2000, 80).[23] Our weapon in the struggle is *logos* (which Heidegger takes in its etymological root as "gathering" rather than the more usual translation of "reason" or "speech"): "This *logos* had to determine the essence of thinking and bring thinking into opposition to Being" (94–95). Over against *logos* is *phusis*, which Heidegger interprets not as nature but as "emerging sway" (*aufgehende Walten*, 96). Because *phusis* holds sway over us, "the true [i.e., unconcealment] is . . . only for the strong" (102), it is like troops bringing the enemy to a standstill (105). Where our engagement with Being takes the form of techne, "*Techne* characterizes the *deinon*, the violence-doing, in its decisive basic trait; for to do violence is to need to use violence against the over-whelming" (122). The Greeks "used only violence and . . . thus they won for themselves the fundamental condition of true historical greatness" (125).

Nothing could be further from Daoism (or from the Upaniṣads, in which we humbly try to make ourselves worthy of the grace of the hidden to reveal itself) than this violent antagonism[24]—a conception presumably influenced by the contemporary Nazi cult of violence. Heidegger goes on to say that humans engaged in this confrontation, as uncanny (*unheimlich*), "on all ways have no way out, they are thrown out of all relations to the homely [*heimlich*], and *atē*, ruin, calamity, overtakes them" (116). Here the goal sought by the Upaniṣads and Daoism, the effacement of the individual self in the face of what had been hidden from us, is not a consummation but a calamity. In this sense Heidegger is indeed an existentialist (although not a humanist, given his conception of Being, as he makes clear in his *Letter on Humanism*).

In *The Origin of the Work of Art*, written about the same time as *Introduction to Metaphysics*, there is a comparable duality between the self-closing nature of earth and the intrinsic openness of world. "To be a work [of art] means to set up a world. . . . The work moves the earth itself into the Open of a world and keeps it there" (Heidegger 1975, 44, 46). Here too the duality is represented as a struggle, although without the language of violence; enmity between the two is balanced by mutual interdependence: "The more the struggle overdoes itself on its own part, the more inflexibly do the opponents let themselves go into the intimacy of simple belonging to one another" (49). Although the *Origin of the Work of Art* lacks the rhetoric of violence of *Introduction to Metaphysics*, here too we must strive against what is radically *other*, rather than being patiently receptive to what is in fact our true self.

This changes, however, twenty-four years later in 1959 with Heidegger's publication of *Gelassenheit*.[25] *Gelassen* means relaxed, calm, patient, and here Heidegger's hermeneutic of Being shows a kinship to the hermeneutics of receptivity in the Upaniṣads and Daoism. Instead of the violent striving and struggle of the previous works, here we have patience and the suspension of willing. The following passages are condensed from the second of the two essays in *Gelassenheit*, "Conversation on a Country Path about Thinking," beginning with the second page (p. 59) and ending with the final words (p. 90). The ellipsis marks in brackets at the end are in the original but without brackets.

> *Scientist:* Then . . . thinking is something other than willing.
> *Teacher:* And that is why . . . I want non-willing.
> *Scholar:* And the term non-willing means, further, what remains absolutely outside any kind of will. . . . So far as we can wean ourselves from willing, we contribute to the awakening of releasement [*Gelassenheit*].
> *Teacher:* Say rather, to keeping awake for releasement. . . . Because on our own we do not awaken releasement in ourselves . . . but let it in. . . . We are to do nothing but wait Waiting . . . but never awaiting, for awaiting already links itself with re-presenting and what is re-presented. . . . Man of himself has no power over truth. . . .
> *Scholar:* Man is he who is made use of for the nature of truth. And so, abiding in his origin, man would be drawn to what is noble in his nature. . . . Noble-mindedness would be the nature of thinking and thereby of thanking.

Teacher: Of that thanking which does not have to thank for something, but
   only thanks for being allowed to thank. . . .
Scholar: Then wonder can open what is locked?
Scientist: By way of waiting [. . .]
Teacher: [. . .] if this is released [. . .]
Scholar: [. . .] and human nature remains *appropriated* to that [. . .]
Teacher: [. . .] from whence we are called.

We can see how Heidegger became more influenced by Eastern philosophy as earlier influences waned.[26] That this was possible shows the compatibility between different traditions where ways of thinking did not
arise independently of each other, while the chapters below document
the extent of compatibility even where they do arise independently.

The Scope of the Book

To keep the book within reasonable bounds I have limited myself to
metaphysical and moral issues. Consequently I have not included political writers, although there are promising comparisons to be made between Mozi (Mo Tzu) and the Utilitarians (or Marx); Xunzi (Hsün Tzu)
and Hobbes; and Sunzi (Sun Tzu) and Machiavelli. Nor have I explored
comparisons of Indian Carvaka or Lokayata with Western materialism,
or between the logicians in the three traditions, whether the more systematic logicians like Aristotle with the Indian school of Nyaya, or the
more deconstructive Zeno and Gorgias with their counterparts in the
Chinese School of Names, such as Hui Shi (Hui Shih) and Gongsun
Lung (Kung-sun Lung).
   There are various ways that Buddhism might be compared with
Western philosophy. First, a comparison is sometimes made between
Buddhism (especially Nagarjuna) and Greek skepticism. Both are fundamentally interested in attaining peace of mind, and both are cautious
about conceptual knowledge. This is obvious in the case of skepticism and
also in the Buddhist "middle way" concepts of *anicca* (no constancy) and
anatta (no self). *Anicca* is the view that we are not the same person at different moments, since we have always changed to some degree, and yet

we are not really different persons; we can only describe ourselves as in between the same and not the same, to which no concept can correspond, in violation of Aristotle's principle of the excluded middle. *Anatta* is the view that the self reduces to its parts, so that there is no self left over after the parts have been deducted, yet on the other hand there is a unity to the parts; we can only say that we are in between having a self and not having a self, to which again no concept can correspond. But the differences between Greek skepticism, which eschews all forms of assent, and Buddhism, which affirms the middle way and the four noble truths, seem to me to be significant enough that a chapter comparing the two movements would not be sufficiently productive for our purposes. Comparisons have also been made between Buddhism and the skepticism of Hume in certain respects, but, once again, the differences seem to me to outweigh the resemblances. Second, a fruitful comparison can be made between the Buddhist concept of maya—that spatiotemporal distinctions among individuals have no intrinsic reality—and Kant's concept of the limitations of the phenomenal realm, but the fundamental issues are dealt with in the chapter on Parmenides, Spinoza, and Shankara, whose own concept of maya is similar in the relevant ways (but not in all ways) to the Buddhist version, although Shankara was not a Buddhist,[27] so a chapter on this comparison would be largely redundant. Third, I also considered a comparison between the apparent idealism of Yogacara Buddhism and the apparent idealism of Leibniz, but in the end the disanalogies were more significant than the parallels. Fourth, a comparison can also be made between Buddhist atomism and Greek atomism, but it seemed that such a comparison would take us more in the direction of the history of philosophy and science than in the direction of the kinds of issues dealt with in the following chapters. In the end Buddhism did not become the focus of any of the following chapters, even if it often hovers in the background. Although the comparisons adumbrated above are not fleshed out into chapters, they further contribute to the documentation of the ways the same themes recur in the three major traditions.

The chapters move from issues in metaphysics (chapters 1 and 2) to the way that metaphysics can provide a basis for ethics (chapters 3 and 4) to issues in theoretical and in applied ethics (chapters 5, 6, and 7). Because the chapters take the form of cross-cultural comparisons, with different philosophers compared in each chapter, the terminology changes from chapter to chapter, but the viewpoints addressed are fundamentally compatible, so that the book as a whole offers something like a consecutive argument. At this point it may be helpful to anticipate the results and conclusions of the individual chapters.

The first chapter, "Going beyond the Visible: Zhuangzi and the Upaniṣads," explores ways that metaphysical thinking can arise out of our ordinary thinking, tracing six means of evoking wonder within us and making us open to an awareness of the fundamental unity and indivisibility of reality: namely, paradox, humor, allegorical or evocative stories, bodily comportment, mentoring, and reasoning. Because Western philosophy pays less attention to the alternatives to reasoning, the primary comparison in this chapter is not between Asian and Western philosophers, as in the later chapters, but between the Chinese philosopher Zhuangzi and the Indian Upaniṣads. Zhuangzi uses humor far more than do the Upaniṣads, while the Upaniṣads use religious language far more than does Zhuangzi. But these are differences of emphasis and technique. Despite the differences, both agree on the importance of achieving a metaphorical awakening and on the general ways that this can be achieved.

The three philosophers of chapter 2, "Appearance and Reality: Parmenides, Shankara, and Spinoza," represent not only two different geographical traditions, India and the West, but also two different historical eras within Western culture, and despite the more than two thousand years that separate Parmenides and Spinoza they more recognizably belong to the same tradition, a tradition very different from that of Shankara. I would not claim that this is true of traditions generally, since there are vast differences within each of the three major traditions, but it is true in this case. Parmenides, as far as we can tell from fragment 8, the one substantial piece of his writing that survives, was, like Spinoza, a linear thinker who supported his claims with logical arguments; in fact he is considered by many to be the founder of Western logic. The works of Shankara, by contrast, are nonlinear in organization and appeal to our intuitions rather than to logical inferences. Again, although Parmenides sometimes uses the language of religion, especially in speaking through a goddess, he makes use of none of the traditional mythology of his culture, just as Spinoza (unlike

Philo or Maimonides) makes no use of his Jewish heritage in propounding his ideas. Shankara, on the other hand, makes his Hindu traditions the scaffold of his formulations. Also, Spinoza, in his appropriation of the Cartesian shift from objectivity to subjectivity and epistemology, formulates his ideas very differently from the objective ontological categories of Shankara (e.g., *sattva, rajas, tamas,* and causal body, subtle body, gross body). Parmenides stands between the two poles of Spinoza and Shankara, giving epistemological rather than ontological explanations of our misperception of unitary reality as a multiplicity, like Spinoza, but from an objective rather than subjective point of view, like Shankara. Again, Spinoza stands opposed to both of the others in his doctrine of the noninteractive parallelism of thought and extension, while Shankara stands apart from the other two in his views on reincarnation and karma (although even for Shankara these exist only in the realm of maya). Despite these differences there are substantial areas of agreement: all three believe that reality is a timeless unity; all three believe that the way to overcome the illusion of multiplicity is to subordinate our passions, or our identification with our body, to our rationality; and all three identify the whole with goodness, a goodness that is the natural object of desire rather than created by desire. These similarities outweigh the differences in the three philosophers' approaches and modes of expression. They point to a cross-cultural correspondence of thought, rather than to merely superficial and formal resemblances between essentially different worldviews.

Chapter 3, "Metaphysics and Morality: Zhu Xi, Plato, Aristotle, Plotinus," is more complex than the others because it compares four philosophers who resemble and differ from one another in a variety of ways. I suggest at the beginning of the chapter that Zhu Xi's (Chu Hsi's) philosophy reads like a synthesis of Plato's theory of forms (without his dualism between rational and irrational principles), Aristotle's connection between form and empirical investigation (without his dualism between form and matter), and Plotinus's self-differentiating holism (without his indifference to the empirical world). All four have in common a belief that the goodness of the highest principle provides a basis for individual morality. In the end the philosopher that Zhu Xi most resembles is Plotinus, because of the way they both derive the whole of reality from a single principle, and because the dualisms of Plato and Aristotle are more alien to him than was Plotinus's relative indifference to the physical world. The philosopher most unlike the other three turns out to be Aristotle, because of the difference between his "bottom-up" teleology and the "top-down" self-differentiation advanced by the other three (see Appendix 1 at the end of the chapter). We see then that individual differences can be more decisive than cultural differences and that individual resemblances can cut across and override cultural divides—in which case cultural traditions, although essential to the expression of ideas, need not be decisive to the arising of those ideas in the minds of individual thinkers.

In chapter 4, "Indeterminacy and Moral Action: Laozi and Heraclitus," Laozi and Heraclitus are so individual in both their thinking and their modes of expression that cultural factors are relatively inconspicuous apart from the examples they use and the obvious fact that Laozi addresses himself primarily to the ruler and Heraclitus to the citizen. Because of their idiosyncratic writing it is also more difficult than in other chapters to estimate the correspondence of their thinking, especially as they both warn of the inadequacy of words and emphasize the inseparability of opposites. However, there are also areas of doctrinal agreement as well as semiotic ones. They agree in emphasizing the relativism of viewpoints and speak against dualistic thinking that divides points of view into right and wrong, and both nevertheless provide definite prescriptions for right and wrong thought and behavior, founded on a distinction between whole/part thinking and part/part thinking. This agreement strikes me as particularly significant in its emphasis on achieving what Heraclitus calls an awakened state, or what Laozi calls the perception of the world as an uncarved block. There is a fundamental resemblance in their thinking that transcends their cultural differences, and the significant differences in their modes of expression are products not of their respective cultural traditions but rather of their distinctive personalities.

Chapter 5, "Virtue Is Knowledge: Socrates and Wang Yangming," is more straightforward than its predecessors. The views of Socrates (as reported by Plato) and Wang Yangming (as quoted by his students) sound very much alike. Although Socrates speaks in terms of virtue and Wang speaks in terms of actions, it does not seem that this was more than a verbal difference, since for Wang actions are inseparable from character (virtue). For both, the principal views coincide: (1) If what we call knowledge does not result in virtuous action, then it is not fully knowledge but only opinion. (2) Moral knowledge cannot simply be abstract knowledge but must be knowledge by acquaintance; we must practice it in order to know it. Thus both thinkers were wary of formalizing their views by putting them into writing lest knowledge by description be mistaken for knowledge by acquaintance. (3) To truly know the good is to love the good with a love that leaves no room for *akrasia*, weakness of will. (4) We have within us the power to recognize the good. The views of the two philosophers are expressed differently and defended differently, and the examples used reflect the differences between the priorities of their cultures—for example, mathematics in the case of Socrates and filial piety in the case of Wang Yangming—but the messages themselves are virtually indistinguishable. In this chapter more than any of the others, cultural differences play little or no role in the philosophies formulated.

In chapter 6, "The Ethical Mean: Confucius and Plato," Confucius and Plato approach the issue of the moral mean very differently. Confucius applies the golden rule and asks, "What would be the right action taken toward me from the point of view of my self-interest?" and then takes that action toward someone else. Plato, on the other hand, asks what the right action would be from the standpoint of techne toward its object rather than from the standpoint of self-interest. These differences can be traced at least in part to the fact that Greek culture had a strong interest in techne as a phenomenon, while Chinese culture did not. We can mitigate the difference by noting that the two aspects of techne—knowledge of principles and sensitivity to kairos—correspond to the extension of knowledge and the golden rule in Confucian philosophy; but they are hardly identical. Again, Plato's account in the *Republic* refers to a distinction between sensible reality and intelligible reality (traceable back at least to Parmenides), to which nothing in Confucius explicitly corresponds. Although the influence of culture here is unmistakable, both philosophers saw, independently of any demonstration, that virtue consists in finding the correct balance between not going far enough and going too far and then used the concepts at hand within their culture to justify that conclusion. Common to both philosophers is the view that the mean cannot be achieved without self-knowledge, and the evidence provides no reason to doubt that our ability to know ourselves can rise above cultural constructions.

If chapter 5 shows the least influence of the different cultures within which the two philosophers worked out their ideas, chapter 7, "Nonviolent Warriors: The Bhagavad Gita and Marcus Aurelius," shows significant differences between the respective cultures of the writers. On the basic questions there is substantial agreement: both the Bhagavad Gita and Marcus Aurelius agree about rising above personal interest to achieve a disinterested perspective; both believe that to do so we must devote ourselves to reason instead of the appetites; both believe that selfless action and religious devotion contribute to the life of reason; both believe in forgiving our enemies because God works through us all and their actions have been fated by providence from the beginning of time; both are compatibilists with respect to free will; and both believe that warfare is compatible with a purified, that is, nonviolent, state of mind. But where Marcus believes that reason is the highest state we can achieve, and is equivalent to divinity, the Gita holds reason (*sattva*) to be only the highest condition of nature (*prakriti*), which is only a spatiotemporal representation of true divinity—timeless, spaceless *puruṣa*. Hence there is no reference to mystical union in Marcus Aurelius or any indication that he practiced meditation as Krishna advises in the Gita. The closest Marcus comes to a conception of mystical union is in his belief that "there is one soul, though it is distributed among infinite natures and individual circumscriptions (or individuals). There is one intelligent soul, though it seems to be divided" (*Meditations* 12.30).[28] The difference between the two authors is that the *Meditations* is written in the context of a rationalist tradition and the Gita in the context of a religious tradition. It is a difference that explains not only their diversity with regard to a reality beyond nature but also their diversity with regard to duty: the religious scriptures within which the Gita was written resulted in conflicting duties, but for the rationalist Marcus Aurelius duty could no more be inconsistent than could reason itself. Nevertheless, whatever religious and cultural differences they have, they agree on the essentials—nonviolence, providence, and the other issues mentioned above—so the conclusions correspond despite the difference in their cultural origins.

CHAPTER ONE

GOING BEYOND THE VISIBLE

Zhuangzi and the Upaniṣads

In the next three chapters we will see how metaphysical thinking can have ethical implications, but here we will address the preliminary question of what is meant by metaphysics and how it arises out of our usual practical way of thinking. Although the term etymologically means "after the physics," a reference to the sequence of Aristotle's writings, it has come to mean "beyond the physical," a kind of thinking that recognizes a reality beyond the world of our senses. Metaphysical thinking is often organized into a systematic interpretation of that reality, but it need not be systematic as long as it concerns itself with a reality beyond the sense-perceptible. We will be concerned in this chapter with metaphysics in this more general sense.

Since our customary point of view is to regard the world in empirical terms as equivalent to what the senses perceive, what moves us to acknowledge a radically different reality? Even in religion there is a tendency to conceive the unseen world as an extension of the physical world: God is a father, heaven is above and hell below, tangible rewards and punishments are meted out for good and bad behavior, et cetera. This is religion in Plato's cave. How do we become free of the self-reinforcing attitude that "seeing is believing"? The dominant response of Western philosophy has been to offer arguments showing the limitations of our normal way of thinking and the need for a different kind of thinking, like the efforts of Plato's Socrates to undermine our usual opinions by reference to the timeless nonsensible truth of mathematics (a strategy not used by traditional Asian philosophers as far as I know) or by *reductios ad absurdum* that paralyze our customary thought and leave us in a state of wonder.[1] Philosophy begins with wonder, as Plato (*Theaetetus* 155d) and Aristotle (*Metaphysics* A.2.982b12–19) attest.[2] One way that Western philosophy differs in emphasis from Asian philosophy is in this relative prominence of intellectual arguments to change our perspective. There is more emphasis in Asian philosophy than in the West on nondemonstrative techniques for bringing our customary thinking to a halt and redirecting it into other channels, most dramatically in the koans of Zen Buddhism. For that reason in this chapter we shall primarily compare philosophers from the two Asian traditions, although there will be briefer comparisons with some Western philosophers.

Awakening

Zhuangzi begins with a striking image: "In the northern darkness there is a fish and his name is Kun [roe, fish egg]. The Kun is so huge I don't know how many thousand *li* he measures. He changes and becomes a bird whose name is Peng [roc, a mythical bird]. The back of the Peng measures I don't know how many thousand *li* across, and when he rises up and flies off, his wings are like clouds all over the sky. When the sea begins to move, this bird sets off for the southern darkness, which is the Lake of Heaven" (chap. 1, p. 1).[3] The image suggests a double transformation in a single direction. The name "Kun" reminds us that even the biggest fish started out a miniscule egg.[4] The egg is transformed into a living creature submerged in darkness, but through a second transformation it flies up from the depths of the northern darkness into the light of the sky. It cannot do this without support, however: "If wind is not piled up deep enough, it won't have the strength to bear up great wings" (chap. 1, p. 2). What does all this signify? At first it may seem to be an image of the transformation of yin into yang,[5] but there is no suggestion that Peng subsequently metamorphoses back into Kun, like yang into yin, so we must look elsewhere.[6] In chapter 2 Zhuangzi mentions two kinds of awakenings: "While he is dreaming, he does not know it is a dream, and in his dream, he may even try to interpret a dream. Only after he wakes does he know it was a dream. And someday there will be a great awakening when we know that this is all a great dream" (chap. 2, p. 16).

This can be read as a demythologization of the Kun-Peng story. Just as the egg metamorphoses into the darkness-dwelling Kun, who in turn transforms into Peng that flies into the bright sky, our dreaming self awakens first from sleep into the ontological darkness of the material world and may subsequently awaken again into the brightness of mental illumination. How Zhuangzi helps us to achieve the second transformation is the hermeneutical dimension of the book. As Kuang-ming Wu writes: "Understanding Chuang Tzu is not a matter of mere academic curiosity, but nothing short of a life enlightenment and conversion . . . like that envisioned by Plato in the myth of the cave. . . . Since Chuang Tzu seems to insist that a proper understanding of him entails a rejection of usual understandings of understanding, he demands nothing less than a transvaluation in hermeneutics" (1982, 31). As we have seen, the comparison with Plato's cave is apt. The prisoners' inability to see anything when they turn from darkness to light, and their subsequent refusal to believe in any reality beyond the shadows on the wall, has its corresponding image in Zhuangzi: When Peng rises up ninety thousand *li* and prepares to journey to the southern darkness, "the cicada and the little dove laugh at this, saying, 'When we make an effort and fly up, we can get as far as the elm or the sapanwood tree, but sometimes we don't make it and just fall down on the ground. Now how is anyone going to go ninety thousand *li* to the south!' What do these two creatures understand? Little understanding cannot come up to great understanding; the short-lived cannot come up to the long-lived" (chap. 1, pp. 1–2).[7] Peng flies from the northern darkness in which Kun lives, and which is tantamount to simple ignorance, to the brightness of the sky, which corresponds to the light of conceptual understanding, and then finally to the southern darkness, which must be not the darkness of ignorance but the darkness of ineffability.[8]

The Upaniṣads offer a parallel analogy. Like Zhuangzi, the *Kena* tells us that our goal is reached not by ordinary ("little") understanding but only by awakening:

It is conceived of by him by whom It is not conceived of.
He by whom It is conceived of, knows It not.
It is not understood by those who understand It.
It is understood by those who understand It not.
When known by an awakening, It is conceived of.

(2.3–4)⁹

One feature of awakening from a dream is that normally we cannot achieve it by our own effort because we do not realize we are dreaming; we must be awakened by something other than our will. That is true also for the higher kind of awakening. The *Katha Upaniṣad* speaks of the need for grace:

One who is without the active will beholds Him, and becomes freed from
    sorrow
When through the grace of the Creator he beholds the greatness of the
    Self [*Atman*]. . . .
This Self is not to be obtained by instruction,
Nor by intellect, nor by much learning.
He is to be obtained only by the one whom He chooses;
To such a one that Self reveals his own person.

(2.20–23)¹⁰

This also seems to be the meaning of Zhuangzi's remark that Peng can fly only if enough wind is piled up under his wings. The implication is that we cannot achieve this awakening by our own efforts alone. Similarly, not until "the sea begins to move [does the bird Peng] set off for . . . the Lake of Heaven" (chap. 1, p. 1).

But the Upaniṣad also reverses the metaphor of awakening: "Truly everything here is Brahman; this self (*atman*) is Brahman. This same self has four fourths. The waking state . . . is the first fourth. The dreaming state . . . is the second fourth. If one asleep desires no desire whatsoever, sees no dream whatsoever, that is deep sleep, . . . the third fourth. . . . The state of being one with the Self . . . is the fourth" (*Mandukya Upaniṣad*, verses 2–7). Here the dreaming state is higher than the waking state. How is that possible? The *Brihadaranyaka Upaniṣad* explains: "When one goes to sleep, he takes along the material of this all-containing world, himself tears it apart, himself builds it up, and dreams by his own brightness, by his own light. Then this person becomes self-illuminated. There are no chariots there, no draft-animals, no roads. But he projects from himself chariots, draft-animals, roads. . . . For he is a creator" (4.3.9–10). Dreaming, then, is an echo of maya, the illusory projection of individuated things: "This whole world the illusion-maker (*mayin*) projects out of this [*Brahman*]. . . . Nature (*Prakriti*) is illusion, and . . . the Mighty Lord is the illusion-maker" (*Śvetaśvatara Upaniṣad* 4.9–10).

Zhuangzi does not exalt the dream state over the waking state, but he does point to comparable consequences. The most famous passage in his book is also about dreaming and waking: "Once Zhuang Zhou [Zhuangzi] dreamed he was a butterfly, a butterfly flitting and fluttering around, happy with himself and doing as he pleased. He didn't know he was Zhuang Zhou. Suddenly he woke up, and there he was, solid and unmistakable Zhuang Zhou. But he didn't know if he were Zhuang Zhou who had dreamed he was a butterfly or a butterfly dreaming he was Zhuang Zhou. Between Zhuang Zhou and a butterfly, there must be *some* distinction! This is called the Transformation of Things" (chap. 2, p. 18). To see the point of the story we need to ask ourselves what difference it makes to our consciousness whether we are awake or dreaming. If we think we're a butterfly we do what a butterfly does, if we think we're a person we do what a person does. It's futile to ask whether the form we find ourselves in is our true form. Our true form is the Dao, and we express it in whatever form we find or imagine ourselves:[11]

The Perfect Man has no self. (chap. 1, p. 3)

Yan Hui said, "Before I heard this, I was certain that I was Hui. But now that I have heard it, there is no more Hui. Can this be called emptiness?" "That's all there is to it" (chap. 3, p. 25)

The clansman Tai . . . sometimes he thought he was a horse; sometimes he thought he was a cow. His understanding was truly trustworthy; his virtue was perfectly true. (chap. 6, p. 54)

The implication of this absence of self is that there is no ultimate difference between things. As the *Katha Upaniṣad* says:

> Whatever is here, that is there.
> What is there, that again is here.
> He obtains death after death
> Who seems to see a difference here.
>   (4.10)

If there is no ultimate difference among things, then all things reduce to a singularity. Zhuangzi is explicit about this:

> This man, with this virtue of his, is about to embrace the ten thousand things and roll them into one. (chap. 1, p. 4)

> Heaven and earth are one attribute; the ten thousand things are one horse.[12] (chap. 2, p. 10)

> The Way makes them all into one. . . . No thing is either complete or impaired, but all are made into one again. (chap. 2, p. 11)

> If you were to hide the world in the world, so that nothing could get away, this would be the final reality of the constancy of things.[13] (chap. 6, p. 45)

The Hermeneutics of Awakening

Heraclitus remarks that "for the waking there is one common world, but when asleep each person turns away to a private one" (B89), the world of dreams. Even in our waking world, however, we are asleep in a metaphorical sense: "People fail to notice [*lanthanei*] what they do when awake, just as they forget [*epilanthanontai*] what they do while asleep" (B1). In Zhuangzi and in the Upaniṣads we saw that we must awaken not only from our private dreams but also from the public dream of maya in which we see all things as self-subsistent individuals instead of transitory moments of the One, whether conceived as the Dao or as Atman.

How can authors bring about this transformation in their readers? I suggested earlier that "the southern darkness" is the darkness of ineffability. Zhuangzi uses the wheelwright's art as a metaphor: "You can get it in your hand and feel it in your mind. You can't put it into words" (chap. 13, p. 107). How can words awaken us to what cannot be put into words? I just spoke of "the One, whether conceived as the Dao or as Atman," but *Atman* means "self," and according to Zhuangzi "The Perfect Man has no self" (chap. 1, p. 3). If the ineffable can be named in antithetical ways, what efficacy can speech have to raise our minds to this thought?

The Upaniṣads and Zhuangzi both recognize this issue.[14] The *Kena Upaniṣad* says:

> There . . . speech goes not, nor the mind.
> We know not, we understand not
> How one would teach It.
> Other, indeed, is It than the known,
> And moreover above the unknown. . . .
> That which is unspoken with speech,
> That with which speech is spoken—
> That indeed know as Brahman.
> (1.3–4)

And Zhuangzi writes: "Words are not just wind. Words have something to say. But if what they have to say is not fixed, then do they really say something? Or do they say nothing? People suppose that words are different from the peeps of baby birds, but is there any difference, or isn't there? What does the Way rely on, that we have true and false? What do words rely on, that we have right and wrong? How can the Way go away and not exist? How can words exist and not be acceptable?" (chap. 2, pp. 9–10). Not surprisingly, this has been a contentious passage and has been taken by some as evidence that Zhuangzi is a skeptic or relativist.[15] If words are like the peeping of baby birds, however, are they really meaningless? The peeps of baby birds are demands for food or cries for help. The sounds made by older birds may be mating calls or warnings. The utterances of animals are means of communication, they are not meaningless. If Zhuangzi wanted to suggest that words are meaningless he could have chosen inanimate sounds like the rustling of leaves or the splashing of water. Instead the simile suggests a distinction between conceptually determined verbal meanings and language that is intended to be provocative rather than descriptive. Zhuangzi seems to be suggesting that words are signals rather than mirrors, not that words (and therefore his own writings) are intrinsically meaningless. Later he writes: "Words are like wind and waves; actions are a matter of gain and loss. Wind and waves are easily moved; questions of gain and loss easily lead to danger. Hence danger arises from no other cause than clever words and one-sided speeches" (chap. 4, p. 28). This implication that words influence actions shows the affinity between words and the peeping of birds, which is also meant to influence actions. Actions are not only physical but also mental: words can produce understanding, an experience of truth, knowledge by acquaintance (like the wheelwright's art) where knowledge by description is no longer possible.[16]

> A little earlier Ziqi Yan said to Cheng Ziyou:
> "You hear the piping of men, but you haven't heard the piping of earth. Or . . . the piping of Heaven! . . . The Great Clod belches out breath, and its name is wind. Then ten thousand hollows begin crying wildly. . . . And when the fierce wind has passed on, then all the hollows are empty again. . . ." Ziyou said, "By the piping of earth, then, you mean simply [the sound of] these hollows, and by the piping of man, [the sound of] flutes and whistles. But may I ask about the piping of Heaven?" Ziqi said, "Blowing on the ten thousand things in a different way, so that each can be itself—all take what they want for themselves, but who does the sounding?" . . . In sleep, men's spirits go visiting; in waking hours, their bodies hustle. With everything they meet they become entangled . . . certain that they are the arbiters of right and wrong. . . . Music from empty holes, mushrooms springing up in dampness. . . . Without them, we would not exist; without us, they would have nothing to take hold of. . . .[17] It would seem as though they have some True Master, and yet I find no trace of him. He can act—that is certain. Yet I cannot see his form. He has identity but no form. (chap. 2, pp. 7–8; insertions by translator)

Here again we have three levels: the piping of men, of earth, and of heaven. The piping of men—flutes and whistles—is analogous to our dream world in which we each have our own private reality ("In sleep, men's spirits go visiting"). The public world, however, speaks to us with the same set of voices ("[the sound of] these hollows"), but we cannot hear them independently of our individual biases ("Without us, they would have nothing to take hold of") but only subjectively, so we each become "arbiters of right and wrong."[18] But there is a third level, the piping of heaven, "blowing on the ten thousand things in a different way, so that each can be itself." The wind that sets all these hollows to their piping is necessary to them in the same way that the wind is necessary to support the wings of Kun (chap. 1, p. 2).

The metaphor of piping is a transition between the metaphor of the peeping of birds and the metaphor of the three levels of dreaming, waking, and awakening. The piping is the way the levels are expressed in sound. In the first level, flutes and whistles, we are not necessarily trying to communicate, and we are isolated individuals like sleepers. The piping of the earth, however, is the same for all of us, although it is not perceived as the same by each of us because it is perceived subjectively. Our goal then, like the goal of the second awakening, is to hear the piping of heaven, the unrelativized source of the whole, but this piping is inaudible and ineffable: "They have some True Master, and yet I find no trace of him. He can act. . . . He has identity but no form."

The *Katha Upaniṣad* says:

An intelligent man should suppress his speech in his mind (*manas*).
The latter he should suppress in the Understanding-Self (*jñana-atman*).
The understanding he should suppress in the Great Self (*mahat-atman*).
That he should suppress in the Tranquil Self (*śanta-atman*).
Arise! Awake!

(3.13–14)

Here too we see that speech must be overcome and is only a way to awaken the mind. The mind, in turn, should ultimately be concerned not with formulaic knowledge that can be articulated in speech but with a deeper knowledge, understanding, which eventually leads beyond the individual self of speech and conscious thought to the Great Self and finally the Tranquil Self, in both of which our particularity, our discreteness from

all other individuals, disappears into the tranquility of undivided oneness. The passage also shows that the disagreement between Zhuangzi
and the Upaniṣads over whether the sage has a "self" is only semantic.
When Zhuangzi says that "the Perfect Man has no self" (chap. 1, p. 3) he
means no discrete self, no self that sees itself as separate from and in competition with all other beings. This is the view of the Upaniṣads as well.
Even though *Atman* literally means "self" (or "soul"), it is the self that
we all share rather than the one that sets us apart from one another. The
word for the individual soul is usually *jiva*, although terminology varies
among writers. What the Upaniṣads mean by *Atman* is what Zhuangzi
means by *Dao*. In all cultures technical terms are appropriated from ordinary language, as for example our word *matter* derives from the Latin
word for lumber (*materia*). Similarly Zhuangzi and the Upaniṣads took
words that were already familiar in their culture. Confucius, for example,
often speaks of the *dao* (the right way), although not in the sense that the
Daoists intend it, and *atman* was a familiar term from Hindu religion.
In their ordinary use the meanings of the two terms are quite different,
but in their appropriation by Zhuangzi and the Upaniṣads their meanings converge to name the unity and reality that we experience when we
awaken from the perception of apparently discrete particulars.

The Way (*Dao*) and the Self (*Atman*) are metaphors for what cannot
be put into words but only experienced, and very different metaphors
can point to the same experience. We may say the experience of looking
into the eyes of our beloved is like looking into a deep pool, or we may
say it is like looking at luminous stars. The fire of stars is incompatible
with the water of pools, but in both cases we are trying to evoke the same
ineffable experience.[19] Metaphors force us to make connections between
completely different things. When Plato uses the sun as a metaphor for
the Idea of the good, we do not think of the good as something spatial
and fiery. Metaphors force us to look beyond the concepts themselves to
some common quality that is not itself a concept; if it were a concept we
could simply define it and we would not need a metaphor. This does not
mean Zhuangzi and the Upaniṣads never use concepts and reasoning—
they would not count as philosophy otherwise. It simply means that
concepts and reasoning are only one component. Their limitations are
regularly brought to our attention by other devices such as the following.

Paradox

Zhuangzi writes, for example,

> Good fortune is as light as a feather, but nobody knows how to pick it up. (chap. 4, p. 32)

> Hide the world in the world. (chap. 6, p. 45)

> You can hand it down, but you cannot receive it. (chap. 6, p. 45)

And the *Īśa Upaniṣad* says,

> It moves. It moves not.
> It is far, and It is near.
> It is within all this,
> And It is outside of all this.
> (verse 5)

At a literal level these are or imply logical contradictions. This means, not that they are logical nonsense, but that they are not to be taken as logical propositions at all. They are meant to force us into a nonbinary way of thinking. We will see other examples in subsequent chapters. Zen koans take this practice to its purest level.

Humor

Because conceptual reasoning may easily seduce us into mistaking the words for the experience behind them, and paradoxical formulations may produce only bafflement, the two techniques are regularly supplemented with evocative stories. One of the hallmarks of Zhuangzi's stories is that they are often humorous. A famous example is "Three in the Morning": "To wear out your brain trying to make things into one without realizing that they are all the same—this is called 'three in the morning.' What do I mean by 'three in the morning'? When the monkey trainer was handing out acorns, he said, 'You get three in the morning and four at night.' This made all the monkeys furious. 'Well, then,' he said, 'you get four in the morning and three at night.' The monkeys all were delighted" (chap. 2, p. 11). What is the point of this whimsical presentation? Why not simply say that people who try to discover the oneness of things ("to make things into one") are wrong to think that some things are better than others? They think this because some things provide immediate gratification (four in the morning) while the benefits of other things are more distant (four in the evening) and therefore less evident.[20] People need to realize that if everything is a manifestation of oneness, then proximity in time and place is irrelevant. Again, when carpenter Shi's apprentice praises the incomparable beauty of an enormous tree near the village shrine, and Shi dismisses the tree as a useless kind of wood that serves no purpose, the tree replies in Shi's dream, "You and I are both of us things. What's the point of this—things condemning things? You, a worthless man about to die—how do you know I'm a worthless tree?" This is followed by the story of Ziqi of Nanbo, who also comes upon an enormous tree. "'It turns out to be a completely unusable tree,' said Ziqi, 'and so it has been able to grow this big. Aha!—it is this unusableness that the Holy Man makes use of!'" (chap. 4, pp. 30–31).[21] These stories go beyond "Three in the Morning": We fail to realize the oneness of things not only because we judge them by their immediate benefit (four in the morning) but because we judge them by their benefit at all. Benefit is measured by the partial point of view of the one benefited and thus prevents us from passing beyond partiality to the universality of the One. That is why the first useless tree is located in a religious shrine and the second is dear to the Holy Man.

Why present this message in a comical form, like "Three in the Morning"; why not put it conceptually? As Bergson points out, the comic requires "a soul that is thoroughly calm and unruffled. . . . Its appeal is to intelligence, pure and simple" (1911, 4–5).[22] Another factor is evident in a joke's loss of effectiveness when explained. To hear a joke explained is to receive a set of concepts; to "get" a joke is to have an experience of discovery, a pedestrian analogue of awakening. Kierkegaard writes: "Humor is not yet religiosity, but lies on its surface. . . . The humorist . . . sets the God-idea into conjunction with other things and evokes the contradiction" (1941, 41, 51).[23] That is why jokes can function hermeneutically in

the *Zhuangzi*. Few other philosophers, however, use humor as a hermeneutical tool. Even stories that are not humorous, like the stories of the
useless trees, give us a kind of experience rather than a bare conceptuality,
although without the piquancy of the comic.[24]

The Upaniṣads too are full of stories, although rarely as fanciful as
the most whimsical of Zhuangzi's. In the *Chandogya* when Indra and
Virocana ask Prajapati for the true nature of "The Self [*Atman*], which is
free from evil, ageless, deathless, sorrowless, hungerless, thirstless, whose
desire is the Real, whose conception is the Real," Prajapati replies, "Make
yourselves well ornamented, well-dressed, adorned, and look in a pan
of water. . . . That is the Self, That is the immortal, the fearless. That is
Brahman." But this joke, unlike those in Zhuangzi, is explained: "Indra,
even before reaching the gods, saw this danger: . . . '*That* one [the reflec-
tion in the water] is blind when this is blind, lame when this is lame,
maimed when this is maimed. It perishes immediately upon the perish-
ing of this body.'"[25]

Another passage in the *Chandogya* has more in common with
Zhuangzi's provocative humor. Six men come to Aśvapati Kaikeya to ask
what Atman is. He asks each what they think Atman is, and the six identify it, respectively, with sky, sun, wind, space, water, and earth. Aśvapati
Kaikeya replies to each in turn that (1) sky "is only the head of Atman,
and your head would have fallen off if you had not come to me"; (2) the
sun "is only the eye of Atman, and you would have become blind if you
had not come to me"; (3) wind "is only the breath of Atman, and your
breath would have departed if you had not come to me"; (4) space "is
only the body of Atman, and your body would have fallen to pieces if
you had not come to me"; (5) water "is only the bladder of Atman, and
your bladder would have burst if you had not come to me"; (6) the earth
"is only the feet of Atman, and your feet would have withered away if
you had not come to me" (5.11 18). The absurd images of the suppli-
cant's head falling off, et cetera, challenge our understanding. The picture of Atman as having a head, eyes, breath, body, bladder, and feet,
which correspond to the natural features of the world (sky, sun, wind,
space, water, earth), depict the world as the outward form of a living
self, just as our own body is the outward form of the "little world," the
microcosm. Aśvapati Kaikeya concludes by warning his guests against

"knowing this Universal Atman as if something separate. He, however, who meditates on this Universal Atman that is of the measure of the span—thus, [yet] is to be measured by thinking of oneself—he eats food in all worlds, in all beings, in all selves." To thus identify with Atman is to become immortal, not in the sense of indefinite continuance, but in the sense of identifying with the timeless: he exists "in all worlds, in all beings, in all selves." By contrast, if we identify only with our mortal body then "we" are mortal and die. And after we die our head falls off, we are blind, our breath stops, our body falls to pieces, our bladder bursts, and our feet wither away.

Stories

We can write paradoxically and humorously without telling stories. What does the storytelling of Zhuangzi and the Upaniṣads add to the experience? What Zhuangzi says evocatively in his stories about the useless sacred trees, Aristotle says more directly (and, needless to say, not whimsically): "We do not seek [wisdom] for the sake of any other advantage; but as the man is free, we say, who exists for himself and not for another, so we pursue this as the only free science, for it alone exists for itself. . . . And such a science either God alone can have, or God above all others. All the sciences, indeed, are more necessary than this, but none is better" (*Metaphysics* A.2.982b25–983a11).[26] "[Contemplation] alone would seem to be loved for its own sake; for nothing arises from it apart from the contemplating" (*Nicomachean Ethics* 10.7.1177b1–2). If Aristotle can say the same thing conceptually that Zhuangzi says imaginatively, what advantage do stories offer that compensates for abandoning the clarity of direct affirmation?

Aristotle's account remains abstract, intellectual. That is not a fault, it is the foundation of almost all philosophy, but consider the difference between intellectual assent and Plato's conception of "conversion" that he illustrates by our liberation from the cave. Previously his model of the tripartite soul illustrated how commonly our intellectual beliefs are defeated by our emotions, as does Aristotle's doctrine of incontinence (*akrasia*). Since time-lapse photography would show all things rising out of and eventually falling back into the world, we may believe *intellectually* that individuals are as insubstantial as waves in the sea, and therefore that our true self is the whole, not the part. But to accept this *emotionally*, to *fully* perceive ourselves as nothing but moments of the whole and thus not to feel at all competitive toward others, requires a different kind of seeing and feeling, as well as a different kind of conceptual thinking, a complete awakening.[27] That is why we need what the Upaniṣads call "grace" (*prasada*).

To be emotionally as well as intellectually convinced is what Plato calls the conversion, the turning around of the soul. Socrates compares true learning to an eye that cannot be turned to the light from the darkness except by turning the whole body. In the same way the intellect must be turned around from the realm of becoming together with the entire soul until it is able to endure the contemplation of what is, and what is brightest of what is, namely the good (*Republic* 7.518b–c). The turning of the entire soul means that the seats of the emotions—appetite and spiritedness, which were contending against rationality in book 4—are now in agreement with it. To understand in this way is to convince the emotions as well as the intellect. When the converted guardians return to the cave and see what kind of goods the prisoners pursue, they would "go through any sufferings, rather than share their opinions and live as they do" (516d).

How can stories reach us at an emotional level and persuade us more completely than intellectual arguments alone? Aristotle writes: "With a view to action experience seems in no respect inferior to art [*techne*], and men of experience succeed even better than those who have theory without experience. The reason is that experience is knowledge of individuals, art of universals, and actions and productions are all concerned with the individual. . . . But yet we think that knowledge and understanding belong to art rather than to experience . . . because the former know the cause, but the latter do not" (*Metaphysics* A.981a13–27). While arguments are effective because they appeal to our rational nature with universal concepts, stories are effective because they appeal to our emotional nature by giving us an experience of individuals in action. Aesop's stories are effective in just this way. Rational arguments for the superiority of long-term benefit over immediate gratification may receive intellectual assent but fail to impart the necessary self-control. The popularity of Aesop's story of "The Grasshopper and the Ant" is due to its ability to give us a vicarious experience of what the argument presents to us abstractly. It is in our nature to identify vicariously with individuals we hear or read about, something in us responds to and is influenced by the stories on a preconceptual level. Hence one of the axioms of literature is "Show, don't tell." In the *Republic* Plato describes how this phenomenon can influence us either for good or for ill (3.386a–402a). By using both arguments and stories Zhuangzi and the Upaniṣads reach us on both levels.

Bodily Influence

Zhuangzi also tries to reach us at the level of our *body*, as when he writes: "The True Man of ancient times . . . ate without savoring; and his breath came from deep inside. The True Man breathes with his heels; the mass of men breathe with their throats. Crushed and bound down, they gasp out their words as though they were retching. Deep in their passions and desires, they are shallow in the workings of Heaven" (chap. 5, p. 42).[28] To achieve the universal standpoint we must rid ourselves of attachments, and to do that we must eat for nourishment rather than pleasure. We must also learn to overcome the anxiety and worry that accompanies attachment. When we worry we become tense, we clench our abdominal muscles and breathe shallowly from our throat and chest instead of deeply from our diaphragm and abdomen. By reversing the symptoms we can sometimes mitigate the underlying condition. I once saw a dog who was afraid of everything and always kept its tail between its legs. A trainer suggested that the owner attach the end of the leash to the dog's tail so he could hold up the tail while he walked the dog. The result was almost instantaneous. The posture of the tail signaled confidence to the dog, and the dog responded by displaying confidence. In the same way, when we breathe deeply we signal to our body that we are relaxed, and we feel more relaxed as a result. The more relaxed we feel, the less anxious we are about things and therefore not as attached to their fates. Aristotle writes: "A slow step is thought proper to the great-souled man, a deep voice, and a level utterance; for the man who takes few things seriously is not likely to be hurried, nor the man who thinks nothing great to be excited, while a shrill voice and a rapid gait are the results of hurry and excitement."[29] However much Aristotle's great-souled man may differ from Daoists in other ways, we can see here how physical behavior is inseparable from state of mind. Reversing the symptoms of an emotional state can help reverse that state itself. In the same work Aristotle points out that "we become just by doing just acts, temperate by doing temperate acts, brave by doing brave acts" (2.1103b1–2). By the same principle we become calm by acting in a calm manner, and so on. As with the passage from Zhuangzi, what are described as symptoms of great virtue may also function as a means to attaining it. If we force ourselves to move unhurriedly and speak with a deep (i.e., calm) voice, our body sends a signal to our mind that we are relaxed and relatively unattached to results, taking "few things seriously." Reforming our bodily habits will help reform our mental habits, as well as the other way around.

The Upaniṣads are especially sensitive to this dimension: they abound in references to proper comportment and to the importance of the bodily activities that facilitate the attainment of Atman in meditation. The Śvetāśvatara, for example, says:

> Holding his body steady with the three upper parts erect, and causing the senses with the mind to enter into the heart, a wise man with the Brahma-boat should cross over all the fear-bringing streams. Having repressed his breathings here in the body, and having his movements checked, one should breathe through his nostrils with diminished breath. Like that chariot yoked with vicious horses, his mind the wise man should restrain undistractedly. In a clean level spot, free from pebbles, fire, and gravel, by the sound of water and other propinquities favorable to thought, not offensive to the eye, in a hidden retreat protected from the wind, one should practise Yoga. . . . Lightness, healthiness, steadiness, clearness of countenance and pleasantness of voice, sweetness of odor, and scanty excretions. These, they say, are the first stage in the progress of Yoga. (2.8–13)

Mentoring

A passage from Plato's Seventh Letter says, "There is no way of putting [the object of philosophy] into words like other studies. Acquaintance with it must come after a long period of attendance on instruction in the subject itself and of close companionship, when suddenly, like a blaze kindled by a leaping spark, it is generated in the soul and becomes self-sustaining" (341c–d, cf. *Phaedrus* 276a–277a). The Upaniṣads abound in accounts of this kind of teacher-disciple mentoring, and we find it in Zhuangzi as well, for example in Woman Crookback's mentoring of Buliang Yi (chap. 6, p. 46). Although teachers cannot hand wisdom over to their students in so many words, they can use all of the above techniques to bring about a fundamental change of perspective in their students. All of the authors discussed in this book are teachers. The effort they put into their writings is for the benefit of the rest of us.

However effective these hermeneutical techniques may be, their success is subject to the limitations of individual natures, as Zhuangzi affirms. "'Can the Way be learned?' asked Nanpo Zikui. 'Goodness, how could that be? [replied Woman Crookback.] Anyway, you aren't the man to do it. Now there's Buliang Yi—he has the talent of a sage but not the Way of a sage, whereas I have the Way of a sage but not the talent of a sage'" (chap. 6, p. 46). Talent is a component of what the Upaniṣads call "grace," and a prerequisite for emotional awakening. If one of the "outer chapters" can be trusted, even Zhuangzi was not beyond backsliding:

> Zhuangzi's wife died. When Huizi went to convey his condolences, he found Zhuangzi . . . pounding on a tub and singing. [Huizi said,] ". . . It should be enough simply not to weep at her death. But pounding on a tub and singing—this is going too far, isn't it?" Zhuangzi said, "You're wrong. When she first died, do you think I didn't grieve like anyone else? But I looked back to her beginning and the time before she was born. Now there's been another change and she's dead. It's just like the progression of the four seasons. . . . If I were to follow after her bawling and sobbing, it would show that I don't understand anything about fate. So I stopped." (18.140–41)

Only after he resurrected an argument to set himself back on course was he able to accept fate with equanimity. In a similar vein, the Dalai Lama has said that when he first thinks about what's happening in Tibet he becomes upset, but when he reminds himself that those who are destroying Tibetan culture act from hate and ignorance he feels calmer. Another story, from an unknown source, concerns a Zen master whose disciple found him in tears and asked why he was crying. "My wife died," was the answer. "But you told us that all earthly things are illusions." "It's true," he replied, "but she was the greatest illusion."

Both Zhuangzi and the Upaniṣads share a vision of awakening to the unity of all things and employ similar hermeneutic devices to give us the guidance of words and at the same time to prevent us from mistaking the words for the experience itself: paradox, humor, allegorical or evocative stories, bodily comportment, and mentoring, as well as reasoning. At the same time there are obvious differences. Zhuangzi uses humor far more than do the Upaniṣads, while the Upaniṣads use religious language far more than does Zhuangzi. Despite these differences the basic views about the nature of things and ways of communication are very compatible between the two, however much they may differ on the surface because of the cultural contexts in which they must be expressed.

CHAPTER TWO

APPEARANCE AND REALITY

Parmenides, Shankara, and Spinoza

The previous chapter construed metaphysics in its most general sense as the thinking of a reality that eludes our senses, a timeless, placeless realm apprehensible by thought rather than sense. In this chapter and the next we shall look at metaphysics of a more systematic kind. The oldest metaphysics in Western and Indian philosophy is the dual-aspect model: the world can be understood either as a unity or as a multiplicity, depending on the adequacy of our understanding. Thus for the earliest Western philosophers the true nature of the world was a unity metaphorically conceived as water or air, by Thales and Anaximenes respectively, or non-metaphorically by Anaximander as "the indefinite" (*apeiron*) and by Parmenides as "it is" (*estin*). In Indian philosophy it is most often conceived as Atman (self), whose unity is hidden from us by maya. Maya leads us to misperceive timeless, placeless unity as spatiotemporal individuality. Although this view is ancient it has continued to be influential, returning in Vedanta, Buddhism, Spinoza, Kant, Schopenhauer, Whitehead, and others, in which the fundamental dichotomy is between the world as it appears to us and as it is in itself, in reality.

Parmenides in fifth-century BCE Greece, Shankara in early ninth-century CE India, and Spinoza in late seventeenth-century CE Holland all saw the world as ultimately a single substance that they equated with God (although this equation is less certain in the case of Parmenides) and proposed ways of disciplining our thinking to overcome our initial perception of the world as an aggregation of individual substances.[1] The ways that these philosophers converge and diverge in their thinking indicate that philosophy can never completely escape its culture but also suggest the possibility of comparable experiences within cultures that developed from different roots—so that philosophers from radically different cultures, not only writing in different languages but using entirely different conceptual frameworks, could have comparable perceptions of the nature of reality and wisdom.

Interpreting Parmenides

It will be helpful to begin with some remarks about Parmenides because even though his writing is far more direct and literal than that of Heraclitus, whom we will look at in chapter 4, for various reasons, including that it survives only in fragments, its interpretation is no less problematic.[2] Virtually every sentence has become a bone of contention among his interpreters because the relative weight given to them leads to antithetically different pictures of his thought. The following interpretation is a variation of the "aspectual" view, the view that the unchanging One and the changing many are two aspects of the same reality: the timeless, placeless aspect and the spatiotemporal, related to what Parmenides calls the way of truth and the way of opinion. Seen in this way, the distinction parallels, although with significant variations among the three thinkers, Spinoza's distinction between *natura naturans* (substance as a timeless, placeless unity) and *natura naturata* (spatiotemporal modes of substance, i.e., individuals), and Shankara's concept of "superimposition" in which we impose temporality and spatiality onto timeless, undifferentiated reality.

Part of the problem with the interpretation of Parmenides is that, "like the thought, so too the language is new and it was created as the language of this thought. The individual term, as a linguistic expression, is thus to a great extent unknown and unprecedented" (Hölscher 1968, 90).[3] Parmenides has been read as a materialist on the strength of descriptions like "It is complete on all sides, like the bulk of a well-rounded ball, evenly balanced in every way from the middle; for it must be not at all greater or smaller here than there" (B8.43–45).[4] But he has also been read as an idealist, or as a phenomenological ontologist, in the light of statements like "The same thing is for thinking and for being" (B3).[5] Again, he is read as a logician who believes we can discover the truth about reality only through abstract reasoning, by following the implications of the laws of noncontradiction ("In no way may this prevail, that things that are not, are," B7) and excluded middle ("It is or it is not," B8.16).[6] Or he is seen as a philosopher of linguistic predication, on the basis of statements like "That which is there to be spoken and thought of must be" (B6).[7] And he has been read as a mystic for whom we can know the truth only by the grace of a divine revelation, like that of the goddess who addresses to him the words of his poem.[8]

Cutting across these differences, interpretations are also divided by the variety of strategies for reconciling the two apparently inconsistent parts of Parmenides's book. The most influential strategy in the twentieth century, which continues to be defended today, regards Parmenides as distinguished both by the rigor of his logic and by the naïveté of his judgment: on one hand he is the father of Western analytic philosophy, the first to use explicit logical reasoning in the service of philosophical inquiry, subtle enough to have anticipated Descartes's *cogito* demonstration (although in the service of "it is" rather than "I am"),[9] yet on the other hand a rigorous adherence to inadequate logical principles is believed to have led him unknowingly toward a conclusion that is neither reasonable nor Cartesian, namely that nothing ever changes and that he himself, along with the rest of the world, does not exist.[10] It is widely believed that although this is a fatal difficulty, Parmenides's failure to recognize it can be excused by his early date,[11] but we do him no favor by excusing his lapses until we have done our best to make certain that they really are lapses. In the case of a work so incompletely preserved we may need to look more intensively than usual at the possible implications of what remains, which we are less likely to do if we are too ready to excuse any difficulties.

In John Palmer's terminology, the view of Parmenides as unable to account for multiplicity and change is the strict monist interpretation. Prior to it, the most widespread view, going back to Parmenides's earliest interpreters, was the aspectual view, the view that being and appearances are two aspects of the same reality.[12] Fragment B16 in particular lends itself to the aspectual interpretation more readily than to the others:

> For as each person has a mixture of much-wandering limbs,
> so is mind present to humans. For that which thinks—
> the nature of the limbs <combined in the body>—is the same
> in all people and every one; for the full is thought.[13]

The first sentence presents us with an analogy: mind is present to human beings the way people are related to their body parts: diverse human beings are unified within the same mind the way diverse limbs are unified within a single body. The second sentence explains: although our limbs themselves differ from one person to another, their nature is the same in each of us, and that nature manifests itself in mind ("that which thinks"), which is therefore the same in all of us. The phrase "the same in all people and every one" makes the point both collectively and distributively. Distributively it means that each of us has the same mental nature as every other. Collectively it means that all humans together are unified and have their nature as parts of the same rational nature, the way our limbs are unified and have their nature as part of the same person. In the same way that hands and feet have their function only as part of a body, each of us has our function only as part of the rational whole. And in the same way that what unites the limbs of our body is life, what unites all individuals in being is rationality.[14] All of this is summed up in the final clause, "For the full is thought," which recalls B4: "Things which although absent are securely present to the mind. For you will not cut off what is from clinging to what is." This explains what the goddess means at the end of B1 when she says, "The things that appear must be in an acceptable sense because they permeate all things completely."[15] Just as there is no body without its constituent limbs, there is no being without the things that appear and permeate everything. And just as our limbs lose their separateness in the realm of life as part of a living person, all things that appear to our senses lose their separateness in the realm of the timeless and spaceless.[16]

   On the basis of the aspectual interpretation we can say that for Parmenides, as for Shankara and Spinoza, the world is ultimately a single substance, closely associated with divinity (the goddess), and that he too proposed ways of disciplining our thinking to overcome our initial perception of the world as an aggregation of individual substances. But to say that the being of the world is closely associated with a divinity is not the same as saying that it *is* God. Does Parmenides go as far as to identify being with the divine, as Spinoza and Shankara do? Although such an identification is nowhere explicit, it seems to be implied by analogy. The goddess, like being, is portrayed not only as eternal but also as beyond time, since her abode is beyond the gates that separate night from day (B1.11–22).[17] And like being she is beyond space as well as time, for the road that leads to her goes through all cities (B1.2–3) and yet is "far from the beaten path of humans" (B1.27).[18] The road is an image of the reality that is dispersed yet immediately present, "things which although absent are securely present in thought" (B4). It is far from the beaten path of humans because the beaten path is the way of sense perception, not the way of thought. The goddess then, beyond time and space, seems to be a personification of being and not just a vehicle of its description. In one sense she is a personification of the intellectual experience in which the characteristics of being disclose themselves to Parmenides. In another sense she is a personification of being itself.

Parmenides, Shankara, Spinoza

The main points of comparison among the three philosophers will be their respective methods and their conceptions of God, knowledge, freedom, and immortality.

Method

On the surface two writers could hardly be more dissimilar than Spinoza and Shankara, the former presenting his *Ethics* in the most linear possible way, beginning with definitions and axioms and deriving its conclusions with every effort at rigorous logical precision, while Shankara's major works are commentaries on the Upaniṣads and especially the *Vedânta-Sûtras*. Even his two most systematic works of undoubted authenticity, the first 121 brief paragraphs of the *Upadeśa Sāhasrī* (Thousand teachings) and the 68 brief paragraphs of the *Atma Bodha* (Knowledge of the self)—as well as the longer but less certainly authentic *Vivekachudamani* (Crest jewel of discrimination)—are nonlinear in organization.[19] Where Spinoza's *Ethics* claims to demonstrate its conclusions with logical and even mathematical rigor, Shankara employs no obvious arguments but relies on his readers to recognize the truth of his claims from their own inner experience—more like the direct evidence of phenomenology than the indirect evidence of logical inference. Again, while Spinoza aims to clear the decks of the traditional beliefs that prejudice his readers against what he believes would be clearly seen to be true by an unbiased intellect, Shankara explicitly builds on the traditions established by the Upaniṣads and Bhagavad Gita, and his most important writings are sympathetic commentaries on classical texts.[20] Parmenides straddles these differences, as we have seen, with some passages establishing him as a pioneer in abstract logic and others tending toward the mythic and mystical.

The multivalence of Parmenides's writing becomes apparent in the two other thinkers as well when they are looked at in more detail. Despite Shankara's use of traditional texts when they provide a conceptual framework for his ideas, he has no hesitation in departing from them when he disagrees.[21] For example, "Anything that is eternal cannot have a beginning despite a hundred texts (to the contrary)," and "The deluded fools, believing the rites inculcated by the Vedas and the Smrtis to be the highest, do not understand."[22] So Shankara's appeals to the inner experience of his audience have nothing to do with religious faith where doctrines are accepted on the basis of an external authority. As for Spinoza's turning of his back on tradition, although this is true in the way his ideas are presented, the ideas themselves are often indebted to his predecessors,[23] if less evidently than in the case of Shankara, and his recommendation that people who have not yet become rationally self-sufficient should follow the "sure maxims of life" (Vp10s) is meant in much the same spirit as Shankara's recommendation of scripture for those who have not yet grasped the nature of reality for themselves.

The centrality of the geometrical method to Spinoza's philosophy is a matter of controversy, although there is general agreement that it "certainly does not represent the way and order in which Spinoza *discovered* his truths" (Nadler 2006, 39).[24] His earlier *Short Treatise on God, Man and His Well-Being* (1660), written in an Aristotelian style (but with a brief appendix that summarizes his argument in geometrical fashion), and his *Treatise on the Emendation of the Intellect* (1662), presented as an intellectual autobiography, show that the geometrical method of the *Ethics* (1677) may function more as a device of presentation than a device of discovery.[25]

God

There is an obvious difference between the three conceptions of God, insofar as Spinoza's God is conceived rationalistically, Shankara's in terms of Hinduism, and Parmenides's as a Greek goddess, but in this they are using the modes of expression available to them. If we focus on the experiences that their words point to rather than the terminology itself, we can see how the formulations may be related perspectivally as different cultural expressions of what may be a comparable underlying conception.

The most evident convergence among the three thinkers is in their monism. Spinoza's conclusion, "Whatever is, is in God, and nothing can be or be conceived without God" (Ip15), is based on his preliminary definition of God as "a being absolutely infinite, that is, a substance consisting of an infinity of attributes, of which each one expresses an eternal and infinite essence" (Id6); the infinite leaves no room for anything else.[26] For Shankara too there exists only God, whose inner nature is an absolute unity that can never be fully comprehended by us.[27] Parmenides is more ambiguous. The goddess of B1, who speaks throughout, may represent the timeless unity of the whole, as was suggested earlier and will later be argued, but she also speaks of a goddess in the middle of the temporal world "who governs all things. For she rules over the hateful birth and union of all things" (B12). In that case the world of becoming, perhaps no less than the timeless reality spoken of in B1 to B8, has a divine quality. Perhaps this is compatible with the views of Spinoza and Shankara insofar as the temporal appearance of what is timelessly divine must have its own reflected divinity as well, but they never express it so.

Knowledge

If the intrinsic nature of reality is an absolute unity but is perceived by us as a multiplicity because of our cognitive limitations, how are these limitations conceived?

For Spinoza the most common species of knowledge is also the least adequate, namely imagination, which is made up of individual sense perceptions and memories that are "mutilated, confused, and without order." Imagination is the mind's capacity to form images, which are "the affections of the human body whose ideas present external bodies as present to us" (IIp17s). When our body is affected by another body, our mind forms an image of that other mode (i.e., individual), which it regards as present until some other idea arises in the mind that excludes the presence of that mode.[28] Our knowledge of external bodies can never be adequate because adequate knowledge of an individual mode involves knowledge of the mode that was the cause of that mode, which in turn involves knowledge of the mode that was the cause of the latter, ad infinitum (IIp9 and IIp25). So the occasion for error is part of a more general situation: since the ideas of the affections of the body are *in infinitum* rather than adequate, they can never be clear and distinct and can only be confused (IIp28). By contrast the second species, rational knowledge, comprises not individual perceptions but "common notions and adequate ideas of the properties of things"—the kind of reasoning with which the *Ethics* is composed.[29] Rational knowledge sees regularity in multiplicity where imagination sees only diversity.

The third species, intuitive knowledge, takes the next step, from seeing regularities and commonalities to seeing the essence of things with immediacy. It "proceeds from an adequate idea of the *formal* essence of certain attributes of God to the adequate knowledge of the essence of *things*" (IIp40s2, emphasis added). In Spinoza's example, given the numbers 1, 2, and 3, there are two ways (three, if we count the rote learning of rules by imagination) to find a fourth that is to the third as the second is to the first. Rational knowledge would apply the common property of proportionals demonstrated in Euclid 7.19, but intuitive knowledge immediately sees the fourth proportional number is 6; "We see this much more clearly because we infer the fourth number from the ratio which, in one glance, we see the first number to have to the second" (IIp40s2). The operative phrase is "in one glance" (*uno intuitu*): intuitive knowledge is the immediate perception of how things fit together. In the mathematical example it is the common proportionality; in the case of reality as a whole it is to see all individuals as modes of God—the *natura naturans* ("nature naturing," nature as unitary substance) of *natura naturata* ("nature natured," nature as the multiplicity of things that appear in time and place). The desire for the third kind of knowledge can arise from the second kind (reason) but not from the first (imagination), since clear and distinct ideas cannot follow from confused ideas (Vp28),[30] so we need first of all to replace imagination as far as possible with reason, the second kind of knowledge, which, in turn, may ultimately lead to intuitive knowledge, the rarest species of knowledge, won only with the greatest effort (Vp20s).

Here the difference in formulation between Shankara and Spinoza is especially evident. Where Spinoza uses the language of epistemology under the influence of Descartes's recasting of philosophy on a subjective basis and distinguishes among faculties of thinking, Shankara uses the language of ontology, tracing our misperception of reality to the "causal body," which misrepresents the unity of God as a spatial and temporal multiplicity, "superimposing" multiplicity onto unity and creating *maya*, a word cognate with *make* that originally referred to the creation of the world by the gods but came to mean "illusion" among Hindu and Buddhist philosophers for whom our division of reality into individuals is the product of unenlightened thinking.[31] This is also the cause of our own misperception of ourselves as individual substances who act on and perceive other things as separate from ourselves.[32] The world is thus a kind of illusion, not in the sense that instead of a world there is nothing, but rather in the sense that the self-subsistence of individuals is illusory, the same way that there is no intrinsic difference between space inside and outside of a jar.[33] What is illusory is not the existence of the world but its appearance of being *saguna*, intrinsically possessed of differentiating attributes, whereas in itself it is *nirguna*, without such attributes. For Spinoza, by contrast, we perceive the unity of *natura naturans* as the diversity of *natura naturata* because of our imagination, the first kind of knowledge. Since the imagination is based on individual perceptions, it can never discern their unity, unlike reason, which is based on "things which are common to all, and which are equally in the part and the whole" (IIp38). Thus imagination necessarily but inadequately perceives the unity of *natura naturans* as the multitude of *natura naturata*.

Parmenides's answer is closer to Spinoza's:

> Do not let habit born from much experience compel you along this way
> to direct your sightless eye and sounding ear and tongue,
> but judge by reason the heavily contested refutation spoken by me.
>
> (B7)

In other words, because in our experience the things that appear to our senses seem to come into being, change, and be destroyed, we are in the habit of thinking that all existence is characterized by transience. We fail to recognize that there is another sense of reality, perceived by reason rather than the senses, for which this is demonstrably false.[34] On the usual view, to be is to be an individual. But although individuals appear to sense perception they do not appear to reason, and they cannot be defined but only described.[35] But if, as Hegel later put it, "the real is the rational and the rational the real," then individuals are no longer real in the precise sense of the word (knowable by reason); they have mere existence (*bloße Existenz*). It is clear from B7 that what Parmenides means by "to be" is what is there for reason, not what is there for the senses. But what is there for the senses is not the same as what is not there at all (nonbeing). When the goddess says in B2 that there are only two ways of inquiry, she adds the words, "for thinking," as she does again when she tells Parmenides to restrain his thought from this way of inquiry. This does not exclude the possibility that there exists something that appears to the senses but is not intelligible, not knowable by reason.[36]

That is how Parmenides was interpreted by Aristotle, who had the entire book before him: "For, claiming that, besides the existent, nothing non-existent exists, [Parmenides] thinks that of necessity one thing exists, viz. the existent and nothing else (on this we have spoken more clearly in our work on nature [*Physics* 1.3], *but being forced to follow the observed facts*, and supposing the existence of that which is one in definition, but more than one according to our sensations, *he now posits two causes and two principles*."[37] That is, according to reason all things are one, but according to the senses there is multiplicity and opposition, so Parmenides developed a two-level ontology. Simplicius too, who like Aristotle had the whole book before him, and to whom we are indebted for preserving most of the text that remains, says: "He calls this discourse 'appearance' and 'deceitful,' not as outright false, but because the sensible world has fallen from the intelligible reality into the domain of manifestation and appearing."[38]

Despite the substantial differences in their formulations, the three models serve the same function. Shankara's recommendation that we overcome the causal body by recognizing our identity with God corresponds to Spinoza's recommendation for overcoming our perception of the world as *natura naturata* through intuitive knowledge of our identity with God, as modes of *natura naturans*, and to Parmenides's warning about being misled about the ultimate reality of spatiotemporal individuals by "habit born from much experience."

Freedom

Spinoza's compatibilist determinism allows for freedom from affects or passions because when we are guided by reason rather than passion our choices follow from our own nature and are deliberately chosen for what they are, whereas we can never have adequate understanding of passions, which are the effects of what is alien to us.[39] Because of the parallelism between extension and thought, the *idea* of anything that increases the body's power of acting increases the mind's power of thinking, raising us to a higher level of perfection and causing us to be affected by joy (IIIp11&s). This is freedom in the fullest sense, self-determination, but we can attain this freedom only by accepting determinism: since everything happens necessarily (Vp6s) and follows from the nature of God (Vp14), the cause of our affects is God rather than the individual modes, which are only intermediaries (Vp32). "If we separate emotions, or affects, from the thought of an external cause, and join them to other thoughts, then the love, or hate, toward the external cause is destroyed, as are the vacillations of mind arising from these affects" (Vp2). In much the way that the Buddhist doctrine of *anatta* (things have "no self" because they cannot be absolutely distinguished from their parts) is meant to destroy the power of externals over us by denying their substantiality, Spinoza's claim that they are no more than modes of God aims at the same result. Here too the problem is conceived in epistemological terms, with the imagination as the basis: as long as we act from passions, we inevitably choose lesser goods over greater goods when the lesser goods can be achieved quickly and the greater goods require patience, because the images of what is present or can soon become present have more power than the others (IVp8–IVp10).[40] Consequently, if a free person is one who acts on the basis of adequate knowledge (reason) and thus "complies with no one's wishes but his own, and does only those things he knows to be the most important," then the person who acts instead on the basis of affects is a slave and, "whether he will or not, does those things he is most ignorant of" (IVp66s).

On this issue Shankara takes his terminology from the traditional metaphysical system of Samkhya (in the monistic version of the Bhagavad Gita rather than the pluralistic version of Ishvara Krishna), which here too gives an ontological rather than epistemological explanation. Like Spinoza (preface to IV and IVp4), Samkhya conceives of the inner person (*puruṣa*), that is, God, and outward nature (*prakriti*) as ultimately the same; and as for Spinoza God is *natura naturans* while the universe is *natura naturata*, for Shankara there is a comparable distinction between the all-encompassing unity of God as *puruṣa* (person) and the multiplicity of the universe as *prakriti* (nature).[41] But Shankara's *prakriti* has an ontological structure that *natura naturata* lacks: as it applies to us it consists of three "bodies":[42] the gross body is the visible parts of our body; the subtle body our organs of perception, action, speech, and thought; and the causal body the cause of our distorted view of the world, woven out of the three modes *sattva*, *rajas*, and *tamas*—reason, passion, and dullness.[43] *Tamas* has only a privative counterpart in Spinoza: a deficiency of the *conatus* (striving) that is the essence of an individual mode, "by which each thing strives to persevere in its being" (IIIp7); in accordance with the original meaning of *virtue* as "power," Spinoza identifies the *conatus* with virtue and power (IVd8).[44] *Rajas*, in turn, corresponds to Spinoza's concept of *passion*, while *sattva* is comparable to reason in Spinoza, the second kind of knowledge, and like the second kind of knowledge it can become an end in itself instead of pushing us on to the third kind of knowledge: "*Sattva* binds the Self [*Atman*] by attachment to knowledge"[45]—it prevents us from attaining the most complete knowledge by leading us to believe that we already have all the access to truth that we need. For Shankara the ultimate goal is to pass from the conceptual knowledge of *sattva*, which is still at the level of nature (*prakriti*), to the direct experiential knowledge that goes beyond nature to its source and true self, *puruṣa* (God). This is also the ultimate goal of the third kind of knowledge in Spinoza, *scientia intuitiva*, knowing in one glance (*uno intuitu*). Here too a direct immediate experience, knowledge by acquaintance, is superior to the conceptual knowledge of reasoning, which is essentially descriptive. In Spinoza this kind of knowledge is not confined to knowledge of God, as is the knowledge of *puruṣa* in Shankara, but is the species within which the knowledge of God finds its adequate manifestation (5p27, 5p31s). Here again we find a correspondence between the goals of the two thinkers but a difference in their models. In Shankara's case the model is essentially an ontological one, since *prakriti* and *puruṣa* represent distinct ontological stages. But for Spinoza the ontological difference arises out of an epistemological one: the third kind of knowledge is not limited to a different order of being, like the difference between *prakriti* and *puruṣa*, but applies to any immediate grasp of the essence of things, including mathematical relations (2p40s2). The difference between our direct knowledge of God and our indirect rational knowledge of common properties is in the first instance due, not to a difference in nature of these objects, but to a difference in the type of knowledge we make use of, since all three kinds of knowledge can be directed at the same objects, as Spinoza's mathematical example shows. The ontological difference between *natura naturata* and *natura naturans*, unlike that between *prakriti* and *puruṣa*, is arrived at in Spinoza's approach only subsequently to the epistemological division of ways of knowing.

If the models are different in approach—epistemological in one case, ontological in the other—the underlying implications are again the same. For Shankara as for Spinoza, the goal is to use knowledge to overcome our bondage to the passions and achieve freedom: "The mind is the only cause that brings about man's bondage or liberation: when tainted by the effects of *rajas* it leads to bondage, and when pure and divested of *rajas* and *tamas* it conduces to liberation."⁴⁶ As with Spinoza, bondage is due to ignorance, which is burned up by knowledge,⁴⁷ and our liberation from it is accompanied by love and joy.⁴⁸ Spinoza's explanation is epistemological. We are obscured, not by an ontological mode like *rajas* and *tamas*, which together with *sattva* is constitutive of nature (*prakriti*), but by a confusion in our ideas: "The passions depend on inadequate ideas alone" (IIIp3). Thus "An affect which is a passion ceases to be a passion as soon as we form a clear and distinct idea of it" (Vp3); "All the appetites, or desires, are passions only insofar as they arise from inadequate ideas, and are counted as virtues when they are aroused or generated by adequate ideas" (Vp4s). Again, for Spinoza as for Shankara, the final liberation from the passions, which results from our recognition that the adequate cause of all things is God, is inseparable from love and joy (Vp27).

On this subject there is nothing precisely comparable in Parmenides. The concept of emotional bondage and rational liberation does not appear explicitly in ancient Greek philosophy before Plato, or possibly Socrates. For Parmenides there is intellectual bondage to appearances, and liberation from it, but it is not also conceived as emotional bondage and liberation. The distinction between ourselves as active and as in thrall to passion has not yet made its appearance in Western philosophy. Nevertheless, there is something analogous in Parmenides to the idea of liberation. Why did Parmenides put his teaching into the mouth of a goddess instead of speaking in his own voice like his predecessors? Is the goddess simply a literary device with no further significance than to give to Parmenides's words an aura of authority, like an invocation of the muse, or is there a connection between the eternal being that the goddess speaks of and the immortal goddess herself? But why personify this experience, and why choose a divinity? Is anything added to the concept of being by calling it divine? When Xenophanes said that "Homer and Hesiod have ascribed to the gods all deeds which among men are a reproach and a disgrace: thieving, adultery, and deceiving one another" (B11), he was taking exception to the earlier view that divinity was compatible with immorality; and by the time of Heraclitus the divine was explicitly connected with wisdom, beauty, goodness, and justice (B32, B48, B102). An identification of Parmenides's conception of being with the goddess has a significance that is more than literary if it is meant to suggest that being is the source of value as well as existence. Existence alone has no moral significance, no connection with value. Parmenides conceives of being and the goddess, however, in terms of value as well as existence. The keys to the doors that lead to the goddess's realm are controlled by Justice (Dike) (B1.14), and the goddess tells Parmenides that "it was not an evil destiny that sent you forth to travel this road . . . but Right [Themis] and Justice" (B1.26–28). Dike and Themis reappear in the context of being itself: "Justice [Dike] has permitted it neither to come to be nor to perish" (B8.13–14), and "Mighty Necessity holds it in the bonds of a limit . . . since it is not right [*themis*] for what is to be incomplete" (B8.30–32).[49] In light of the moral qualities that complement the ontological qualities of being, the connection that Parmenides draws between being and the divine has more than a literary purpose, and his poem has more than an ontological purpose.[50] This moral dimension brings Parmenides into line with Shankara's and Spinoza's conception of wisdom as a liberation from the passions that drag us to immorality and unhappiness, although these connections, so emphatic in Shankara and Spinoza, have to be teased out in the case of Parmenides, and it is unlikely that they were more explicit in the missing parts of his text.

Immortality

For Shankara, when we attain intuitive knowledge of the divine we become in a sense identical with the divine and immortal.[51] Spinoza's conclusion is similar—"The third kind of knowledge is possible only insofar as the mind itself is eternal" (Vp31). If mind and body are two aspects of the same thing (IIp6, IIp7), it is sometimes wondered how Spinoza can maintain that "the human mind cannot be absolutely destroyed with the body, but something of it remains which is eternal" (Vp23).[52] In fact mind and body are both destroyed in the same way and eternal in the same way. The mind does not survive temporally when the body is destroyed—its eternality is not continuance in time but timelessness as a mode of eternal substance: "What is conceived through God's essence itself . . . [and which] pertains to the essence of the mind will necessarily be eternal" (Vp23). The same is true of the body: although the individual body does not survive temporally as a mode of *natura naturata*, it too is conceived through the essence of *natura naturans*—it is a mode of God's timeless, placeless extension, the eternal universe—and is in that sense eternal: "In God there is necessarily an idea that expresses the essence of this or that human body, under a species of eternity" (Vp22).[53] In this sense we are all equally immortal, but in another sense, for both Shankara and Spinoza, we can achieve something more through the knowledge and love of God. The more one achieves the third kind of knowledge, "the more he is *conscious* of himself and of God, that is, the more perfect and blessed he is" (Vp31s, emphasis added). To the extent that our mind is considered under the aspect of eternity, its "intellectual love of God is the very love by which God loves himself" and by which he loves us (Vp36&c).[54] Although we are all equally eternal in the entirely impersonal sense of being modes of eternal substance, and no one can achieve immortality in the sense of individual temporal survival, our eternality can become a living part of our lives to the extent that our consciousness dwells in what is eternal within us (*natura naturans, puruṣa* /Atman) rather than what is transient and other than ourselves (*natura naturata, prakriti*).[55] Aristotle too was an advocate for this possibility even though he was not a monist: "We must not follow those who advise us, being men, to think of human things, and being mortal, of mortal things, but must, so far as we can, make ourselves immortal, and strain every nerve to live in accordance with the best thing in us. . . . This would seem, too, to be each man himself, since it is the authoritative and better part of him. It would be strange, then, if he were to choose not the life of himself but that of something else."[56]

This theme, again, does not appear explicitly in Parmenides, but it may be implicit. There are references to immortality, but they are not extended to Parmenides himself. The goddesses in B1 and B12 are of course immortal by definition, and the charioteers who bring Parmenides to the goddess are also immortal (B1.24), but nowhere is it said that wisdom confers a kind of immortality in the way that it does for Shankara and Spinoza. However, if the wisdom that Parmenides commends takes us beyond place and time, then implicit is a timeless sense of immortality no longer limited to the continuance in time that is characteristic of the immortality of reincarnation found in Orphism, Pythagoreanism, and Empedocles. For Parmenides, as for Spinoza and Shankara, corresponding to the epistemological difference between truth and appearance, where truth is perceived by reason and appearance by the senses, there is an ontological difference according to the presence or absence of place and time. The senses tell us that reality is composed of innumerable individuals spatially and temporally separate from one another, but

> On this way there are signs
> exceedingly many—that being ungenerated it is also imperishable,
> whole and of a single kind and unshaken and complete.
> Nor was it ever nor will it be, since it is now, all together
> one, continuous.
>
> (B8.2–6)

When we distinguish time as past, present, or future, we designate the present as "now," but that distinction is rejected here, because we would never say of the past "nor was it ever" or of the future "nor will it be." The now that is "all together one, continuous" collapses the distinction between the parts of time into a timeless present: since what-is as a unity never changes, past and future have no meaning for it; it is beyond time, as in B7 it was beyond space.[57] Appearances are the manifestations of being to our senses in space and time. But space and time, whatever they are in themselves, are not intrinsic to being, which is simply "now" and indivisible. The Way of Truth is to use reason to see beyond the particularity of temporality and spatiality to the timeless unity of what is.[58]

If being is beyond time and space, apprehensible only by reason, and appearances are spatiotemporal manifestations of being, apprehensible only by our senses, what is the status of space and time themselves? They cannot be features of being, since it is clear from B8 that what-is is without internal distinctions. Nor can they be separate principles (as for Plato the Receptacle is distinct from the formative principle of the Good), since B2 insists that anything apart from what-is is nothing. For Parmenides as a monist the one path open would be some form of self-differentiation, in which the first principle, although undifferentiated in its original nature, differentiates itself in a metaphysical analogue of atomic decay or the dispersal of light, the result of which is a logical or ontological hierarchy rather than a temporal sequence. This is evidently Simplicius's interpretation when he says, "The sensible world has fallen from the intelligible reality into the domain of manifestation and appearing."[59] But the fragments afford no clue to Parmenides's answer, or even whether he considered the question.

Disanalogies

That Spinoza's affirmation of immortality and Parmenides's apparent affirmation of it gave rise to interpretive difficulties that do not arise in Shankara is due this time, not to the difference between the languages of epistemology and ontology, but to a difference within the ontologies themselves. For Spinoza the distinction between thought and extension is not, like the difference between *natura naturans* and *natura naturata*, a consequence of our imagination (or in Shankara's case the causal body); rather, these are intrinsically different attributes of God (IIp1–3)—although it is possible to interpret them otherwise.[60] Since our minds and bodies are these attributes at the level of individual modes (IId1, IIp11), and since attributes are simply aspects of God's essence (Ip16), our mind and body are only different aspects of our modality and have no causal connection with one another (IIp6). There is nothing comparable in Shankara, or in Parmenides, in whom this issue is never more than implicit. Where for Spinoza the mind cannot affect or be affected by the body even at the level of *natura naturata*, for Shankara the soul is conceived as an independent reality that can move and be affected by the body, at least in the maya world of superimposition. In Shankara there is nothing like Spinoza's conception of mind and body as modes of noninteracting parallel attributes of thought and extension, although he does not disagree in principle with Spinoza's claim that our mind is merely a mode of God's thinking nature. Conversely, since there is no concept of soul in Spinoza, there is also no concept of the reincarnation so often referred to by Shankara, and no concept of either one in Parmenides. But this difference too is not as definitive as it appears: even for Shankara individual souls belong to the illusoriness of *prakriti*: "Brahman appears to be a 'Jiva' [individual soul] because of ignorance. . . . The ego-centric-individuality is destroyed when the real nature of the 'Jiva' is realised as the Self [Atman]."[61]

Despite the difference between the conceptions of the mind-body relationship in Shankara and Spinoza—a relationship that is only implicit in Parmenides—there may be a *functional* correspondence between their views in the way both models shield subjectivity from materialistic reductionism. One consequence of Spinoza's mind-body parallelism is to rule out the Cartesian conception of a soul that acts independently of the body, and this has understandably led some readers to interpret Spinoza's view as materialistic in its implications (this is emphasized by the direction of Spinoza's explanations, from body to idea rather than from idea to body). But another consequence of the parallelism is to preserve the self-sufficiency of mind from the kind of reductionism by which Hobbes and others make it merely an attribute of organized bodies (in a way not unlike the Indian materialism of Carvaka). On the reductionist view, at least in its extreme form as eliminative materialism, consciousness and mental events are merely supervenient qualities arising from what happens in the body and have no intrinsic reality. Spinoza's insistence that "as long as things are considered as modes of thought, we must explicate the order of the whole of Nature . . . through the attribute of Thought alone" (2p7s) implies that eliminative materialism fails to provide an adequate picture of reality. The evenhandedness of Spinoza's denial that either thought or body can influence the other retains (against the Hobbesians) the integrity of the mind even as it sacrifices (against the Cartesians) the mind's independence. In the appendix to Part I Spinoza illustrated a point about teleology with the example of a stone falling from a roof onto someone's head and killing him. If rather than killing its victim the stone merely hurt him, what would be the cause of the pain? The conventional reply, that the pain was caused by impact of the stone, would be ruled out by Spinoza's model of non-interactive parallelism, since it would imply that a bodily event is the cause of a mental event. On Spinoza's view the stone falling on someone's head is the cause of damage to that person's body, but the pain experienced in the victim's mind is caused not by the stone but by the *idea* of the stone striking the body. The materialist and idealist accounts are present here side by side.[62]

How Parmenides conceived of these issues cannot be determined on the basis of the remaining text and testimonies. The concept of reincarnation was already present in Greek thought, and the mind-body problem was preparing its entrance, but neither makes an appearance in the Parmenidean fragments.

The conceptual and rhetorical worlds of Parmenides, Shankara, and Spinoza are radically different. The abstractness of Spinoza's formulations results not only from the modeling of his approach on geometric demonstration but also from the influence of Descartes's recasting of philosophy from an objective to a subjective footing. Where for Aristotle "first philosophy" was metaphysics and began with investigation into the ultimate nature of reality, for Descartes first philosophy becomes epistemology and begins with an investigation into the conditions of knowledge. For Spinoza, following Descartes, it is not enough to say that actions are what we do and passions are what are done to us. He must address the epistemological issue of how, given that all our experience is encountered within our consciousness, we can distinguish within our consciousness between what we are the cause of and what is caused in us by something else. His answer is that in the former case we have adequate, clear and distinct, ideas of what transpired, and in the latter case only confused ideas: "Our mind does certain things and undergoes other things, namely insofar as it has adequate ideas it does certain things, and insofar as it has inadequate ideas it necessarily undergoes other things. . . . The actions of the mind arise from adequate ideas alone; the passions depend on inadequate ideas alone" (IIIp1&3). Thus actions are ideas that the mind can perceive clearly and distinctly through itself, while passions are ideas that the mind cannot perceive clearly and distinctly through itself. This epistemological way of thinking is alien to Shankara, as also to Western philosophy before Descartes, including Parmenides. Even Spinoza's conception of God as infinite substance is formulated subjectively, since the traditional ontological conception of substance is here assimilated to an epistemological one: "By substance I understand what is in itself and is conceived through itself, that is, that whose concept does not require the concept of another thing from which it must be formed" (Id3); the first conjunct, "what is in itself," represents the traditional view, while the amplification, what "is conceived through itself," is an epistemological reinterpretation of that view.

Not all of the differences between the three thinkers are reducible to the distinction between ontology and epistemology or are mere forms of expression. In no sense do Parmenides and Shankara share Spinoza's belief that extension and thought are parallel noninteracting realms, nor do Parmenides and Spinoza share Shankara's belief in reincarnation, even at the level of *natura naturata*. In the latter case there is no doubt that cultural differences play a part, since Shankara comes from a tradition in which reincarnation is accepted as a matter of course, while for Spinoza the reverse is the case, and for Parmenides the conception was present only in the mystery religions rather than mainstream Greek polytheism. Thus for Shankara our tendency toward superimposition is a karmic consequence of our past lives,[63] while for Spinoza it is a consequence of the fact that our individual mind is the idea of our body and thus looks first to the body and the faculty of imagination.

Moreover for Spinoza, since the attributes are "that which the intellect perceives of substance as constituting its essence" (1d4), *natura naturans* refers not only to God or substance but to its attributes as well (1p29s), and therefore extension (2p2), whereas for Shankara extension would almost certainly count as part of maya,[64] and similarly for Parmenides it would belong to the world of the senses. This difference is, however, more verbal than substantive, since extension is an attribute of God only under the aspect of eternity and cannot include any finite extended thing: "We conceive things as actual in two ways: either insofar as we conceive them to exist in relation to a certain time and *place*, or insofar as we conceive them to be contained in God and to follow from the necessity of the divine nature" (5p30s, emphasis added). The attribute of extension is the abstract (timeless) possibility of extended modes. Any particular mode would be a modification of *natura naturans*, which corresponds to Parmenides's "habits" born of sensory experience and Shankara's mode of maya.

Again, Shankara describes the person who attains enlightenment as "thoroughly inebriated with drinking the undiluted elixir of the Bliss of the Atman."[65] Spinoza's intuitive knowledge of God is comparable to what Shankara means by enlightenment, and Spinoza agrees that the experience is bliss (*beatitudo*, 5p42), but it is hard to imagine Spinoza comparing this calm blissfulness with the religious fervor of inebriation (*pace* Novalis's description of Spinoza as God-intoxicated). In meditative philosophies like Buddhism there is usually a sequence of experiences that the meditator passes through before reaching the highest level, the earlier of them intoxicating, the later sober.[66] So it is conceivable that Shankara is describing only an early level when he compares it to intoxication, but there is no indication that the state of mind that Spinoza describes in part 5 is ever experienced as inebriating rather than calmly blissful, as would be the case for Parmenides as well.

Such rhetorical differences may make us feel as though we are in an altogether different world in each case: in a world of reason and science in the case of Parmenides and Spinoza, and in a world of religion and faith in the case of Shankara. However, despite the differences in methodology and rhetorical tone between Parmenides's Greek rationalism, Spinoza's immersion in the scientific and logical culture of the European Enlightenment, and Shankara's immersion in the Vedantic tradition of classical India, their views have an underlying affinity. For all three, reality has a double aspect, on one hand as a collection of apparently self-subsistent individuals (the world of the senses, *natura naturata*, or maya) and on the other hand as a single substance within which all individuality is merely a transient feature (what-is, *natura naturans*, or Atman). The latter is the former perceived adequately. For Spinoza and Shankara again, and for Parmenides by extension, the passions impede our liberation from the inadequate view of reality, and in all three cases this is because of our identification of our self with our individual body rather than with our underlying unity with all things, and our consequent identification of good and evil with pleasure and pain. Thus Spinoza says that in the case of the passions we do not desire something because we think it is good, but we think it is good because we desire it (IIIp9s, IIIp39s). The desire is a product of our belief that something is favorable to our body (IIIp12): that is, for ourselves conceived as members of *natura naturata*, a collection of competing individuals. And Shankara writes, "We indeed observe that a person who imagines the body, and so on, to constitute the Self, is subject to fear and pain, but we have no right to assume that the same person after having . . . comprehended Brahman to be the

Self, and thus having got over his former imaginings, will still in the same manner be subject to pain and fear whose cause is wrong knowledge."[67] These passages are reminiscent of Parmenides's warning against becoming habituated to the objects of sense perception.

For all three there is also another sense of goodness that is not simply relative to our desires, whereby we *do* desire something because it is good, rather than calling it good because we desire it—namely what Spinoza calls "a desire which arises from a true knowledge of good and evil" (IVp15–17), so that it turns out that pain may sometimes be good, and pleasure or joy sometimes evil (IVp43). To the extent that we can overcome the standpoint of the individual body (*natura naturata*) in favor of intuitive knowledge that sees the whole "in a single glance" (*natura naturans*), this second sense of goodness appears that is noncompetitive: "Knowledge of God is the mind's greatest good" (IVp28). When we act from passions we are in competition for the same external things (IVp32–34), but when we act from reason we are acting in accordance with the common nature of all: "The greatest good of those who seek virtue is common to all, and can be enjoyed by all equally" (IVp36). To put it differently, in order for us to live by reason it is desirable that our fellow human beings also live by reason, so "we necessarily strive to bring it about that men live according to the guidance of reason," which is the true meaning of morality (IVp37&s1). Therefore our treatment of others, even those who injure us, will be motivated by love rather than hate (IVp46). "Acting absolutely from virtue is nothing else in us but acting, living, and preserving our being (these three signify the same thing) by the guidance of reason, from the foundation of seeking one's own advantage" (IVp24), and the only thing that reason regards as in its advantage is what leads to understanding (IVp26). Thus "We know nothing to be certainly good or evil, except what really leads to understanding or what can prevent us from understanding" (IVp27), and the knowledge that achieves this to the greatest extent is knowledge of God, infinite substance (IVp28). To achieve this is to achieve what Spinoza calls self-esteem (*aquiescentia*) (IVp52).

This nonrelative sense of goodness is evident in Shankara as well: "The ignorance characterised by the notions 'I' and 'Mine' is destroyed by the knowledge produced by the realisation of the true nature of the

Self."[68] If we can eliminate superimposition and discover our true self that is eternal and unchanging within, we will recognize—like those who attain intuitive knowledge of God in Spinoza and recognize that their substantial nature is identical with God—that although "the individuality in us delusorily thinks he is himself the seer and the knower . . . the oneness of the individual soul and the Supreme Soul . . . has to be realised."[69] Both thinkers agree that the only way to achieve this is to overcome the hold on us of the passions, since the importance that we attach to them is an affirmation of the primacy of our bodily existence and comfort. Thus for Spinoza the strategy was to replace our inadequate ideas (passions) with adequate ideas (action, reason), and for Shankara it was to overcome passion (*rajas*) and dullness (*tamas*) with reason (*sattva*). In Parmenides the nonrelative sense of goodness was implied in the references to Justice (*Dike*: B1.14, B1.26–28, B8.13–14) and Right (*Themis*: B1.26–28, B8.30–32).

How does the world appear to us if we reach the goal of liberation? For Spinoza, since the dichotomy is essentially an epistemological one, having intuitive knowledge of God and experiencing the world as *natura naturans* seems to be no obstacle to our perceiving the world at other times as *natura naturata*, as long as we can do so dispassionately. The same with Parmenides: through our senses and our reason we seem to be able to retain both aspects of the world, as particularity and unity. For Shankara, because the distinction is ontological rather than epistemological, the relation between the two realms is presented more radically: the individuality of *prakriti* ceases to exist when we overcome the delusion: "Where is the universe gone, by whom is it removed, and where is it merged? It was just now seen by me, and has it ceased to exist? It is passing strange!"[70] But this cannot be a permanent condition even for Shankara, or we would not have his writings.

CHAPTER THREE

METAPHYSICS AND MORALITY

Zhu Xi, Plato, Aristotle, Plotinus

The previous chapter focused on metaphysical writings and metaphysical issues, but issues of morality were also visible less centrally as consequences of the metaphysics, most obviously the connection between divinity and morality, which becomes fully explicit in Spinoza. Here in chapter 3 the connection between metaphysics and morality will become an explicit theme.

The reason for bringing Zhu Xi together, not with Plato, Aristotle, or Plotinus alone in this chapter, but with all three is that if he had been a Western philosopher we would say that he synthesized their philosophies: that he took from Plato the theory of forms, from Aristotle the connection between form and empirical investigation, and from Plotinus self-differentiating holism.[1] But to combine different philosophies a synthesis has to leave aside the incompatible elements that distinguish them from one another, so a synthesis involves rejection as well as inclusion. Thus, while Zhu Xi champions a theory of forms, he does not accept the dualism by which Plato opposed to the rational forms an irrational material principle, a "receptacle" for the forms.[2] And while he shares Aristotle's emphasis on the investigation of things, Zhu Xi does not share Aristotle's irreducible dualism between form and prime matter, or his teleology. Finally, while he shares with Plotinus a holistic ontology and a self-differentiating cosmology, he does not share Plotinus's indifference to the empirical world and strongly opposes that tendency in Buddhism (which he regards as having contributed to North China's subjugation by Jurchen "barbarians" from Manchuria).[3] Understanding these differences will help us discover what is at stake in their various commitments.

Like Plato, Zhu Xi and Chinese philosophers generally did not compartmentalize philosophy into separate areas such as metaphysics, ethics, and politics but combined as many aspects of philosophy as necessary to answer the question they happened to be addressing. Even Aristotle, who first divided philosophy into its various species, made it clear how they were all related within the enterprise of philosophy as a whole. In our own study of philosophers it has been helpful to emulate Aristotle's example and gain clarity by narrowing our focus to a particular aspect of their thought; but it has also been helpful to see how the aspects are connected and to notice how the various areas of a philosopher's interest do not merely coexist in juxtaposition with each other but also mutually inform each other—that our metaphysical beliefs, for example, have consequences for our moral beliefs. The present chapter will pursue this double objective by looking at the metaphysical, ethical, and empirical aspects of these philosophers' work with a view to seeing how these areas are connected.

Metaphysics

For a schematic comparison of the four metaphysics discussed below, see Appendix 1.

Zhu Xi

Zhu Xi shares the view of Zhou Dunyi (Chou Tun-i) that the meaning of all things is to be found in their source, which is itself beyond being. He writes: "[Zhou Dunyi said,] 'The operations of Heaven have neither sound nor smell.' And yet this is really the axis of creation and the foundation of things of all kinds. Therefore [Zhou Dunyi identifies] 'the Ultimate of Nonbeing and the Great Ultimate [*wuji* and *taiji*].'"[4]

Elsewhere he says, "Without mention of *Wuji*, *Taiji* becomes only a thing [among other things] and cannot be the root of myriad transformations."[5] The operations of heaven are not beings if beings are what can be perceived by the senses; therefore they can be considered nonbeing. Thus too, the Great Ultimate, which is prior not only to sensible qualities but even to differentiation, is the ultimate of nonbeing. Neo-Confucianism shares the view that Plato articulates when he writes that the ultimate principle is "beyond being" (*Republic* 509b): the *reason* why there are beings cannot itself be a being.[6] Similarly for Plotinus, "There is the One beyond being."[7] Because Zhu Xi accepts the identity of the Ultimate of Nonbeing and the Great Ultimate, he believes that Daoism goes too far when it not only connects being with nonbeing but derives being from nonbeing. "Lao Tzu said that being comes from nonbeing. He is wrong."[8] Even to separate the two is wrong: "It does not mean that outside of the Great Ultimate there is an Ultimate of Nonbeing."[9]

In all this it should be borne in mind that the distinction between prior and posterior for all these thinkers is one not of temporal priority but of logical or ontological priority, as for us the laws of nature are logically prior to the physical world that embodies them but did not exist at a time before physical reality existed. That is what Zhu Xi means by saying, "One can't speak of principle [*li*] and material force [*qi*] in terms of first and later. But when we look into it, it seems as if principle exists first and material force later"[10]—it is conceptually prior but not temporally prior. For all four thinkers the ontological structure of the world is eternal and its cosmological genesis is one of logical or ontological priority, not temporal priority. The One in Plato and Plotinus did not first exist by itself and then proceed to generate the forms: both are eternal and unchanging (emanation is a metaphor for ontological—not temporal—self-differentiation). Nor did Aristotle's physical world exist for a time before it began to love God.

Aristotle

For Aristotle, to be is to be an individual, a "this" (*tode ti*), so the ultimate principle must be conceived as an individual being, God, rather than an originally undifferentiated principle. Like the ultimate principles in the other three philosophies, Aristotle's God is beyond "being" understood as "physical being": (a) God is beyond the scope of physics because God is eternal, unmoved, and separable;[11] (b) God is without magnitude or parts and is indivisible;[12] (c) in God alone subject and object coincide.[13] But because Aristotle's principle is an individual distinct from other individuals, its cosmological creativity does not take the form of self-differentiation like neo-Confucianism's derivation of the world from the Great Ultimate, Plotinus's derivation of it from the One, or Plato's derivation of the forms from the Idea of the Good. For Aristotle the meaning of the world is to be found not in its source but in its goal, not in emanation or self-differentiation but in teleology. The ultimate principle, Aristotle's God, is entirely self-contained and at rest. Unmoved and unmoving, God cannot create by taking action. God's creativity is the metaphysical equivalent of a gravitational pull by which the natural world is brought into a rational order. It is a motion *toward* God rather than *from* God or a first principle. Like Plato, Aristotle shares the Greek dualistic view that creation does not occur ex nihilo: rather, it occurs by bringing order and purpose to preexisting material that is otherwise random and chaotic—although for Plato and Aristotle, unlike the religious tradition, *preexisting* means ontologically distinct rather than temporally prior.[14] Aristotle argues that (1) anything that seems good moves others through their desire (*orexis*) for the good; (2) insofar as God exists by necessity, God's mode of being is good; (3) therefore God moves all things by being the object of *orexis* or eros.[15]

This is hard to conceive. How can we make sense of a claim that seems to imply that plants grow and rivers flow because they love God? Aristotle's God is not loved as a person, like the God of religion. God is pure rationality. Like Plato, Aristotle sees rationality as the fundamental principle of reality, and since for Aristotle this principle must be an individual the rational principle becomes a pure mind whose "thinking is a thinking on thinking."[16] This still does not seem very helpful if it now implies that plants and rivers love rationality. The *Metaphysics* begins with the words, "All human beings have by nature a desire to know." The word translated by "desire" is *orexis*, the same word used in

Book Λ when Aristotle says that anything that seems good moves others through their desire (*orexis*) for the good. Our desire to know is our desire for the ultimate good, pure rationality, God. We are not normally aware that this is the goal our desire is pulling us toward. We are aware at first only that we enjoy sense perception, especially sight, even when no practical advantage is involved. Since sense perception is the beginning of knowledge, our love of sense perception is just the most immediate manifestation of our love of knowledge and rationality: "For this reason waking, perception, and thinking are most pleasant" (*Metaphysics* Λ7.1072b17). Our enjoyment of sense perception leads beyond itself to a love of more advanced forms of knowing: memory, experience, and conceptual knowledge (*Metaphysics* A.1). Beyond these is a kind of thinking that is higher still, *theoria* or contemplation, in which we can briefly experience the rationality that is God.[17] Thus our love of lower forms of knowledge is really an intimation of our love of God, our love of the pure nonrelational rationality that is the goal and purpose and meaning of the universe.

This may explain the roots of human motivation, but how does it explain nonhuman activity? The opening words of the *Metaphysics* say that our innate desire to know is not only insofar as we are human beings but insofar as we are *natural* beings: "All human beings have *by nature* a desire to know." Our desire is an expression of the fundamental teleological movement of nature as a whole. At the beginning of Λ.10 Aristotle says that just as an army contains its good both in its leader and in its order, the universe contains its good both in its object of desire, God, and in its order, which is analogous to that of a household.[18] The head of a household in Aristotle's day is the only one who directly contributes to civic society, through his political participation. In an analogous way the human race is the only one that directly contributes to achieving nature's goal of rationality. But the head of the household can accomplish his ends only with the support of the entire hierarchy of family, servants, and animals that enable the household to function. In the same way, human beings could not fulfill the goal of nature if we were not supported by the animal, plant, and mineral realms.[19] It is not that plants grow and rivers flow out of love for the mind of God but that nature as a whole does what is necessary for its highest manifestation, human beings, to achieve that goal. We are like the fruit of a tree, which could not exist without all the other parts. Only human beings are capable of reaching the goal and achieving consummate happiness (*Nicomachean Ethics* 10.8.1178b24–32), but lower forms of life, in seeking to thrive, seek to emulate the actualization of God as far as their nature allows. Their efforts to survive are a love of life, and implicitly of the most actualized life, which is God (*Metaphysics* Λ7.1072b26–30), and they emulate God's eternality in their desire to reproduce themselves through procreation (*De anima* 2.4.415a–26–b2). In the case of nonliving phenomena like rivers, which lack not only the human ability of reasoned choice but even the animal drive toward survival and procreation, their love of God takes the form of a tendency—that by analogy we might call a striving—toward regularity. The laws of nature are the initial manifestation of rationality, the most elemental emulation of the perfect mentality that is God. As Aristotle puts it, "It is on such a principle that the heavens and nature depend."[20]

Plato

Plato's relationship to Zhu Xi's view of cosmology as the self-differentiation of the highest principle is more complex, neither as removed from it as Aristotle's teleology nor as parallel to it as Plotinus's emanationism. In the *Republic* Plato writes that just as the sun furnishes visible things not only with their visibility but also with their genesis, growth, and nourishment, the Idea of the Good, which is beyond being, provides the forms with their intelligibility, existence (*einai*), and being (*ousian*).[21] There is good reason why Neoplatonists like Plotinus saw this passage as prefiguring their emanationism. If intelligible things (the forms) receive not only their intelligibility but also their existence and being from the Good, which is itself beyond being, then being (the forms) can be regarded as emanating from what is beyond being (the Good).[22] Again, since the sun too is the offspring of the Good (508b), and visible things receive not only their visibility but also their genesis, growth, and nourishment from the sun (509b), we can regard first the intelligible realm, and then the visible one (beginning with the sun), as following from the Good in an emanationistic way. As with the self-differentiating principle of neo-Confucianism, I take emanation to be a matter of logical or ontological priority rather than temporal priority, a metaphor for timeless self-differentiation.

The *Timaeus*, introduced as the sequel to the *Republic*, also hints at emanationism. According to the *Timaeus*'s mythic account, the world is created by a divine craftsman or "demiurge": "He was good, and for one who is good no jealousy can ever arise about anything. And being free from jealousy he desired that everything should be as much like himself as possible" (29e). The demiurge represents the transition from unchanging being to the realm of change, beginning with soul, as he looks to the former to create the latter.[23] If we see this transition as a stage of emanation it would explain why his motivation in creating the changing world is given only in privative terms: "being free from jealousy." The world comes about not because the creator has a reason for creating it but because he has no reason *not* to create it. The implication is that unless a restraining force like jealousy operates to prevent it, creation follows automatically from the nature of the creator. Although these passages imply a kind of emanationism, it is not the full emanationism or self-differentiation of the neo-Confucianists or Neoplatonists, since the *Timaeus*, like Greek cosmology generally (at least before Plotinus), regards creation not as the bringing into existence of a world ex nihilo but the bringing of order to an ontologically independent disorderly material. Unlike complete emanationism, the emanationism implied by the *Republic* and *Timaeus* does not create the receptacle into which the rest of creation is deposited (49a); it is a dualism rather than a monism.[24]

Plotinus and Zhu Xi

It is Plotinus who most resembles Zhu Xi in the area of cosmology. Both derive all the phenomena of the world from a single formative principle that, like Plato's Good and Aristotle's God, is the source of goodness:[25] the One for Plotinus, and the Great Ultimate (*taiji*) or Principle (*li*) for Zhu Xi, who endorses the famous saying associated with Zhang Zai's

Western Inscription, "Principle is one but its manifestations are many."[26] The problem for both is how the one differentiates itself into many. For Zhu Xi, following Zhou Dunyi, within principle is the differentiation between motion and rest: "The Great Ultimate [*taiji*] through movement generates yang. When its activity reaches its limit, it becomes tranquil. Through tranquility the Great Ultimate generates yin."[27] Next, yin and yang, combining in different proportions, generate the five agents of material force or *qi* (*ch'i*), namely water, fire, wood, metal, and earth. Given material force and its five agents, all the phenomena of the world can be accounted for.[28] Here again, "generate" refers to a logical or ontological sequence rather than a temporal one. Yin and yang, for example, did not exist at a time before material force existed, since they *are* material force. As we saw earlier, not even principle is temporally prior to material force, nor is material force or the myriad things numerically distinct from principle.[29]

The terminology sounds alien to modern ears, but the basic ideas are not unfamiliar. In modern science too the distinction between positive and negative forces, which correspond to yang and yin, is one of the most fundamental.[30] Again, it is on the basis of various combinations of positive and negative charges that the atomic structures of all the elements are differentiated, just as the five elements of classical Chinese physics are distinguished by the proportions of positive yang and negative yin. And all our elements taken together constitute the totality of matter and energy, as for neo-Confucianism they constitute material force or *qi*. Zhou Dunyi continues: "When the reality of the Ultimate of Nonbeing and the essence of yin, yang, and the Five Agents come into mysterious union, integration ensues. Heaven constitutes the male element, and earth constitutes the female element. The interaction of these two material forces engenders and transforms the myriad things. The myriad things produce and reproduce, resulting in an unending transformation." This distinction between heaven and earth corresponds to modern concepts of universal laws of nature ("heaven") and the material basis of existence that is subject to them ("earth"). There is nothing primitive about the thinking behind neo-Confucian cosmology, however differently it is expressed, and however much modern science has been able to fill in details that were beyond the scope of older science.

For Plotinus too the initial distinction is between rest and motion. In a fuller citation of a passage quoted earlier he says, "[First] there is the One beyond being, . . . [second] Being [*to on*] and mind [*nous*], and [third] the nature of Soul."[31] The duality that immediately follows from the One is a single principle but with an objective and subjective side: being and mind (a partial prefiguration of Spinoza's double aspect theory). Both aspects, being and mind, are at rest. But soul, the next in descent, is the principle of motion (5.2.1.16–22). The second and third principles, then, exactly correspond to the tranquility and activity of neo-Confucianist principle.

The crucial difference between neo-Confucian and Plotinian cosmology involves the difference between the role of material force in neo-Confucianism and the role of matter in Plotinus. We saw that material force or *qi*, embracing the five agents, is third in order of descent, after principle and yin/yang. For Plotinus the issue is more complicated. For him matter is distinct from the principle of motion, soul, whereas for Zhu Xi *qi* comprises *both* matter and the principle of motion, as the translation "material force" implies.[32] Plotinus makes not only a distinction within what neo-Confucianism calls material force (i.e., the distinction between matter and motion) but a further distinction within the concept of matter itself. Matter has two characteristics: (1) it is an unchanging substratum that receives forms and thereby produces differing manifestations of them (*Enneads* 2.4.4.4–8)—for example, two chairs have the same form but different matter), and (2) it makes change possible, since change is the addition or subtraction of forms from various levels of matter (2.4.6). The presence of both characteristics—substratum and potentiality for change—in corporeal matter leads to a problem. As the substratum that makes individual things possible, matter must come *before* the individual things into which it is differentiated.[33] But in its other characteristic as pure potentiality it must come *last* because potential existence is less real than actually existing things. In other words, although matter is *cosmologically fourth* and prior to individual things, it is *ontologically last* and posterior to individual things. But the degree of reality of anything (its ontological position) should correspond to its distance from the source of all reality, the One (its cosmological position). For matter to be fourth in distance cosmologically and last ontologically is a serious difficulty in Plotinus.

For Zhu Xi this is not a problem because the corresponding concept, material force, is not pure potentiality devoid of any actuality, as is matter in Aristotle and Plotinus. Like the modern concept of matter-energy, it combines activity with receptivity, and it can even be said to be the total manifestation or being of the Great Ultimate. But if Plotinus's emanationism encounters an aporia at the level of matter, Zhu Xi's self-differentiation encounters its own aporia in the transition from principle to the yin/yang duality. Yin and yang result (ontologically, not temporally) from the repose and movement of the Great Ultimate, but the point of identifying the Great Ultimate with the Ultimate of Nonbeing was to indicate that the principle that explains why anything exists must itself be prior to existence and without differentiation of its own. Without internal differentiation, however, there does not seem to be anything by which it can set itself into motion. Nonbeing is neither in motion nor at rest.

Traditional metaphysics is a way of taking our conceptualization of the world to its limits. Eventually conceptual coherence breaks down and we are faced with a first principle that is beyond conceptualization. Neo-Confucianism tacitly acknowledges this by identifying the Great Ultimate with the Ultimate of Nonbeing, a claim that from a strictly analytical point of view is incoherent since it identifies affirmation with negation. Plato insists on a similar limitation in the first part of the dialogue *Parmenides* when he shows that the theory of forms cannot replace its metaphorical approximations with precise concepts without breaking down in aporia.[34] Thus too in the *Republic*, when Glaucon asks for an account of the highest principle, the Idea of the Good, Socrates replies: "You will no longer be able, my dear Glaucon, to follow me, although for my part I would not willingly omit anything. But you would no longer see an image of what we are saying, but the truth itself. . . . And [we must insist that] the power of dialectic alone can reveal it to someone who is experienced in the things we just went through, and it is not possible in any other way" (533a). Zhu Xi too, another dialectical thinker, says regarding the concept of heaven, "One must see such a thing for himself. It is not something that can be fully explained in words."[35] In the case of Aristotle we need only recall that the highest principle, God, is described as a "thinking [that] is a thinking on thinking" (*Metaphysics* Λ.9.1074b34–35). From an analytical point of view this makes no sense, as if we could talk about a seeing that is nothing but a seeing of seeing. Perhaps that is why Aristotle says that the answer to the question "What is being [*to on*]?" "was sought for long ago and is sought for now, and is always sought for and always aporetic."[36] To say that the answer is always aporetic is to say that a definitive conceptual explanation is impossible in principle.

If metaphysics aims to take conceptualization to its limits, and ends for at least some of its most prominent authors by giving us something that can no longer be conceived, what is accomplished? Why not say at the outset, with skeptics throughout history, that it is pointless to ask such questions because the answers can never be verified or even clearly conceptualized? For the thinkers we have been discussing, the point of metaphysics is not to give definitive answers to elusive questions or to provide a complete classification and ordering of all the levels of reality between primal being and sensible phenomena, although attempts at both of these may be made along the way. It is to make us aware of the unseen foundation on which empirical reality is based. But what is to be gained by alerting us to a mysterious quality of existence if the mystery can never be definitively explained? The purpose of this kind of thinking is not to satisfy our desire for information but to transform our way of seeing the world—what Plato calls a conversion or turning around of the self (*Republic* 518b–c, 521b–c). Something similar is implied by Zhu Xi's statements that "scholars who can get it in words are shallow; those who can get it in images are profound" and that "penetration will come as a sudden release."[37] A sudden switching of perspective takes place. Like Plato (as well as Zhuangzi, the Upaniṣads, and Heraclitus), Zhu Xi compares this with awakening from sleep: "When our mind-and-heart is not clear and bright, we may be compared to someone in deep sleep. . . . I see that the essential task is in awakening."[38] For both thinkers the immediacy of realization may require many years of patient effort.[39] The goal is not primarily intellectual, like discovering the answer to a theoretical question, but moral in Aristotle's sense: by bringing our distinctive human potential to its consummation it makes us good in every sense. It nurtures in us a happiness that is also moral goodness, a happiness in which we see that we are "one body" with the world as a whole, as Cheng Hao put it;[40] or in Plato's words, when we achieve that way of seeing and look at those whose lives are given over to pettiness and rivalry, we would "go through any sufferings rather than share their opinions and live as they do" (*Republic* 516d). Let us see how this happens.

Morality

The connection between metaphysics and morality is easiest to see in Plato and Aristotle because of their dualisms between rational form and irrational matter and their identification of moral behavior with rationality and immoral behavior with irrationality. This dualism is the basis of Plato's doctrine of the virtues in the *Republic*, where justice means being governed by rationality.[41] In Aristotle it is evident in the opposition between form and matter, including the opposition between God as pure form and nature as formed matter.[42] Aristotle does not connect matter with evil as explicitly as Plato and Plotinus do, but the connection is implied: matter, as pure potentiality, permits every possible kind of existence, bad as well as good, so only an imperfect and unstable presence of rational goodness is possible in the material world.[43]

If metaphysical thinking makes us aware of a pure rationality that underlies the imperfectly rational material world and gives that world its meaning, and we become aware that our own lives are more meaningful the more they are governed by rational thought and behavior, we grow in moral virtue. *Rational* here means unbiased (truth-loving), not simply logical; it is what *The Great Learning* means by "rectification of the mind" or what Zhu Xi means by "to have the mind in all things and to be in accord with all creation."[44] When we understand that goodness resides in form rather than matter, we will value the rewards of the mind above those of the body, and rationality above the satisfaction of corporeal appetites. For Plotinus the issue is more complicated because he derives all of reality from a single principle rather than from independent contrasting principles, so there is no separate basis of evil. But by making physical matter cosmologically fourth, so that its influence is felt throughout the empirical world, and ontologically last, so that it contains no trace of goodness (*Enneads* 1.8.7.21–23), Plotinus's position on this question ends up very much like those of Plato and Aristotle: because metaphysical thinking leads us to see the unworthiness of corporeal reality as compared with intelligible reality, it is a corrective against the belief that happiness can be found in corporeal pleasure, power, or wealth, and it undermines the temptations of immorality.

Zhu Xi's position is more difficult because there is no clear contrast between form and matter. As we have seen, what the Greeks called matter is for him an aspect of *qi*, material force, which is not opposed to rationality the way matter is for his Greek counterparts.[45] Not only does Zhu Xi derive everything from principle, but also he says that "what is received from Heaven is the same nature as that in accordance with which goodness ensues, except that as soon as good appears, evil, by implication, also appears. . . . But it is not true that there is originally an evil existing out there, waiting for the appearance of good to oppose it. We fall into evil only when our actions are not in accordance with the original nature."[46] Zhu Xi's explanation as to how we can depart from our original nature and introduce evil into the world is that the goodness of principle can be obstructed: "If there is obscurity or obstruction . . . [then] the Principle of Heaven will dominate if the obstruction is small, and human selfish desire will dominate if the obstruction is great."[47] The source of the obstruction, not surprisingly in view of what we have seen in the Greeks, is material force: "Man loses his original nature and beclouds it by habits engendered by material force."[48] But how is that possible when material force arises ontologically directly out of principle, immediately after yin and yang? In the absence of anything that does not arise entirely from principle, what can prevent material force from being entirely faithful to principle? Zhu Xi explains that material force (unlike the Greek conception of matter) is opposed to goodness not by nature but only when it is impure or turbid.[49] But what can compromise the purity of material force if everything derives from principle and there is nothing outside of it? According to Zhu Xi: "When physical nature that is clear and balanced is received, it will be preserved in its completeness. This is true of man. When physical nature that is turbid and unbalanced is received, it will be obscured. This is true of animals. . . . Men have mostly clear material force; hence the difference between them and animals. However there are some whose material force is turbid, and they are not far removed from animals."[50] To be turbid or impure is to be unbalanced. Material force can be obscured and impure even though it is simply the self-manifestation of principle, because the impurity is not the presence of an external element but the lack of an internal balance. Thus "Evil cannot be said to come directly from goodness. There is evil when one . . . falls on one side"; conversely, "Only when the mind attains its proper balance is it capable of appreciating the goodness of human nature."[51]

Material force is the totality of the five agents, and turbidity is a metaphor for a lack of balance among them:

> Although nature is the same in all men, it is inevitable that [in most cases] the various elements in their material endowment are unbalanced. In some men the material force of Wood predominates. In such cases, the feeling of commiseration is generally uppermost, but the feeling of shame, of deference, and compliance, and of right and wrong are impeded by the predominating force <and so on with the others>. . . . It is only when yin and yang are harmonized and the five moral natures (of humanity, righteousness, propriety, wisdom, and good faith) are all complete that a man has the qualities of the Mean and correctness and becomes a sage.[52]

Apart from the technical details, the connection that Zhu Xi draws between virtue and the balance or harmony of our internal elements not only is similar to the views of Plato and Plotinus but also is not very different from our own way of speaking.[53] When we describe immoral people as unbalanced we do not mean it only metaphorically. In the past such talk referred to the four humors and their respective temperaments that corresponded to the four elements. Today when we speak of chemical imbalances in the brain we have a more sophisticated model in mind, but the basic idea is unchanged.

What can we do to achieve this balance when it is absent and preserve it when it is present? Zhu Xi takes his cue from *The Great Learning*, which tells us that the way to rectify our mind is ultimately through the investigation of things:[54] "We must eliminate the obstructions of selfish desires, and then [the mind] will be pure and clear and able to know all. When the principles of things and events are investigated to the utmost, penetration will come as a sudden release."[55] But how can empirical investigation of things eliminate selfish desires? Scientists seem no more or less selfish and no more or less well balanced than the rest of us. Instead of resolving the question of how we can remove the obstruction within our mind, we are now left with the additional question of what empirical knowledge has to do with morality.[56]

The first part of Zhu Xi's answer is that the principle of mind is the same as the principle of things, and even of the Great Ultimate itself: "The principle of mind is the Great Ultimate. The activity and tranquility of the mind are the yin and yang."[57] The connection between mind and the Great Ultimate extends also to our individual minds: "Things and the principle in my mind are fundamentally one. . . . Things and mind share the same principle."[58] I do not know any place where Zhu Xi gives reasons for connecting the principle of our mind with that of the universe, but he would probably accept the reasons that Plato gives. Most explicitly in dialogues like the *Meno* and *Timaeus*, and implicitly in other places like *Republic* 7, Plato shows that mathematical principles not only underlie the workings of the world but are also intrinsic to the workings of our mind. We can use mathematics to discover the laws of nature, and we can work out mathematical truths within ourselves rather than having to take someone else's word for them the way we do with other kinds of information, so the principle of the workings of nature and the principle of the workings of our mind must be the same. For Zhu Xi, since the principle of mind and of the Great Ultimate are identical we can even speak of something like consciousness in plants. When he was asked whether plants have consciousness, he replied: "Yes, they also have. Take a pot of flowers, for example. When watered, they flourish gloriously, but if broken off, they will wither and droop. Can they be said to be without consciousness? . . . But the consciousness of animals is inferior to that of man, and that of plants is inferior to that of animals."[59] "Consciousness" here simply means an inward principle that accounts for outward behavior. It is like Schopenhauer's calling the inwardness of all things "will," without implying that it is the kind of deliberate will that we experience within ourselves.[60] This becomes clearer in a later passage: "Heaven and Earth reach all things with this mind. When man receives it, it then becomes the human mind. When things receive it, it becomes the mind of things (in general). And when grass, trees, birds, animals receive it, it becomes the mind of grass, trees, birds, and animals (in particular). All of these are simply the one mind of Heaven and Earth. Thus we must understand in what sense Heaven and Earth have mind and in what sense they have no mind. We cannot be inflexible."[61]

If mind is principle, by removing obstructions to our mind we will automatically know principle. In his *Treatise on the Examination of the Mind* Zhu Xi says that we must "investigate things and study their principles to the utmost, to arrive at broad penetration, and thus to be able fully to realize the principle embodied in the mind . . . . Therefore one who has fully developed his mind can know his nature and know Heaven, because the substance of the mind is unbeclouded and he is equipped to search into Principle in its natural state" (Chan 1963a, 604). If we can avoid trying to impose our will on things, and can simply rest in harmony with the whole, our mind will see things clearly.[62] This is what Zhu Xi means by "having no mind": "When the myriad things are born and grow, that is the time when Heaven and Earth have no mind <because they are simply in accord with principle>. When dried and withered things desire life, that is the time when Heaven and Earth have mind <because they are resisting the natural order>."[63] Or: "The four seasons run their course and the various things flourish. When do Heaven and Earth entertain any mind of their own?

As to the sage, he only follows Principle. What action does he need to take? This is the reason why Ch'eng Hao said, 'The constant principle of Heaven and Earth is that their mind is in all things and yet they have no mind of their own. The constant principle of the sage is that his feelings are in accord with all creation, and yet he has no feelings of his own.' This is extremely well said."[64] If we achieve this state of mind of letting things be, without imposing our will on them, we become able to recognize the underlying principle that otherwise eludes us. Zhu Xi adopts Mencius's term for this, "seeking the lost mind," which corresponds to Plato's metaphor of recollection or seeking lost knowledge.[65]

To understand principle is to understand that the world is not absurd and blindly mechanistic but ordered and harmonious when looked at as a whole rather than from the point of view of individual parts. To be guided by desires that privilege our own part within the whole, rather than acknowledging the primacy of the whole, is a failure to understand the world. Accordingly Zhu Xi says, "Thoughts that are not correct are merely desires. If we think through the right and wrong, and the ought and ought-not of things, in accordance with its principle, then our thought will surely be correct."[66]

To answer our earlier question, what gives empirical investigation a moral dimension for Zhu Xi that it does not have for modern science is that his search for factual knowledge is not for the sake of knowledge as information,[67] and especially not to give us the means to impose our will on nature through technology. Its goal is to understand the natural world and see that the natural world has an inner meaning, of which the meaning of our own life is an extension. Thus "One who has preserved the mind can nourish his nature and serve Heaven" (Chan 1963a, 604). Because of the moral dimension of such knowledge, it is inseparable from our behavior: "Knowledge and action always require each other. . . . As one knows more clearly, he acts more earnestly, and as he acts more earnestly, he knows more clearly. . . . When one knows something but has not yet acted on it, his knowledge is still shallow. After he has experienced it, his knowledge will be increasingly clear, and its character will be different from what it was before."[68]

Empirical Investigation

Zhu Xi's belief that understanding the principles of all things helps us understand and act on moral principles leads him to an interest in empirical phenomena that is comparable to Aristotle's:

> If we wish to extend our knowledge to the utmost, we must investigate the principles of all things we come into contact with. . . . It is only because all principles are not investigated that man's knowledge is incomplete. For this reason the first step in the education of the adult is to instruct the learner, in regard to all things in the world, to proceed from what knowledge he has of their principles, and investigate further until he reaches the limit. . . . [Eventually] the qualities of all things, whether internal or external, the refined or the coarse, will all be apprehended.[69]

He even developed a theory of causality.[70] He does not, however, share an interest in empirical knowledge as an end in itself. For Zhu Xi, such knowledge should always be a means to moral insight and improvement: "What we call clarifying the good is nothing more than in careful contemplation and handling affairs to distinguish between impartiality and selfishness and between the heterodox and the orthodox, and nothing more. This is the reality of the exhaustive investigation of things."[71] He was interested in using particular phenomena more as clues to moral principles that they illustrated than as clues to the laws of nature that they exhibited. To take an example from Yung Sik Kim: "Zhu Xi frequently said that pushing a cart requires exertion of force at the beginning to start the motion, but that once the motion has started, force is no longer needed because it keeps moving of itself. . . . But he did not go on to infer a general notion of inertia applicable to all motion. . . . His interest was not in the general tendency of motion to continue but in showing that study requires a strong exertion of effort only at the beginning after which it is easy to continue" (Kim 2000, 297–98). As Kim points out, this is not an isolated example; Zhu Xi frequently uses "natural phenomena in discussing analogous moral problems" (316).

There is a kind of complementarity between Aristotle and Zhu Xi in this area. Zhu Xi explicitly believes that the investigation of empirical matters is a means to moral development, but he does not seem to have undertaken systematic investigations of the whole natural world (apart from astronomy and geography) the way Aristotle did, and it can be questioned whether his investigations would count as science in our sense.[72] Aristotle, on the other hand, explicitly embraced the practice of thorough investigation of the particulars of nature in all their diversity, but there is no direct evidence that he regarded them as bearing any relationship to moral virtue. Nevertheless, although Aristotle did not make an explicit connection between empirical investigation and inner transformation, as Zhu Xi does, there is an implicit connection. We saw that for him all nature is organized toward one end—the attainment of a condition that is as God-like or rational as possible—the way all the elements of a household are organized for a single highest purpose. In *De anima* Aristotle purports to show how the principle of life (*psuchē*) forms a kind of continuity from its lowest manifestation to its highest, culminating, with human beings, in a God-like principle within us.[73] Moreover, to adequately understand any part of nature requires us to understand not only its form, its material, and the activity that produces it but also its purpose (*Physics* 2.3.194b16–195a3). This holds true for natural science even more than for the study of human works: "In the works of nature the good and the purpose is still more dominant than in works of art."[74] For Aristotle, as for Plato, the clearest evidence of this is astronomy. The first motion produced by the unmoved mover will be that of the heavens; it is therefore the most perfect motion, circular motion,[75] and it contains "not the faintest sign of chance or of disorder" (*Parts of Animals* 1.1.641b23–24). As in Plato, this is more difficult to establish with more complicated kinds of beings, and Aristotle acknowledges that in such cases it is not "possible to trace back the necessity of demonstrations of this sort to a starting-point, of which you can say that, since this exists, that exists" (*Parts of Animals* 1.1.640a7–9). Nevertheless, the more our investigation of natural phenomena demonstrates the rational basis of their existence, and the more we appreciate the underlying rationality and goodness of the world, the more we will recognize the truth of the claim that the fulfillment of our own nature lies in rational and moral thought and behavior (*Nicomachean Ethics* 1.7). Anyone who can then take the next step and see that the consummate form of rational thought is that which approximates divine thought will see the insubstantiality of the rewards of pleasures and power and will be protected against the lure of immorality.

Plotinus takes little interest in matters of empirical investigation, although there are some exceptions.[76] The case of Plato is more ambiguous. He never devotes the kind of detailed attention to empirical matters that Aristotle does, but he shows serious interest in a range of empirical matters in a way that Plotinus does not. In the *Phaedo* Plato's Socrates says that he studied empirical science as a young man but was disillusioned because it was concerned only with the "how" of causality and not with the "why," which for Socrates was the true cause (96a–99c). He proceeds to recommend the theory of forms because it is "safe" from the difficulties of mechanistic explanations, but he also admits that mechanistic explanations are at least sophisticated and informative (100c) while those based on the theory of forms are not. Explanations such as "Things are beautiful because of beauty," are simplistic, artless, foolish, and ignorant, he says (100d, 105c). Accordingly he proceeds to give a more sophisticated version of the theory of forms, which incorporates mechanistic explanations as well: "I see a safety beyond the first answer . . . not safe and ignorant . . . but [safe and] subtle" (105b). Here he is concerned not only with formal causes like heat but also with mechanistic causes like fire that make the formal causes possible. In context such empirical observations seem to have the same kind of moral consequences as they do for Zhu Xi.

The connection becomes clearer in the *Republic* when Socrates shows how mathematical sciences can be used to lift us out of the cave of mere opinion and raise us toward a view of the Idea of the Good that corresponds to principle in Zhu Xi (7.521d–531d). He says, "In these studies a certain instrument of learning in everyone's soul is purified and rekindled after having been destroyed and blinded by our other pursuits" (7.527d–e).[77] The clearest resemblance to Zhu Xi appears near the end of Socrates's ascending series of mathematical studies, when he argues that the science of astronomy can help lead us to the conversion experience of perceiving the good. The importance of empirical facts here lies not in the facts themselves but in their manifestation of mathematical order, which helps us recognize the rational reality that underlies the visible one (530a–c).

It is in the *Republic*'s sequel, the *Timaeus*, that this aspect of his thought is most evident. The *Timaeus* is a mythic account of the creation of the world to illustrate how the world's governing principle may be conceived as rational and good despite the irrationality of many of its phenomena. To establish the plausibility of his claim Plato shows how the whole range of physical phenomena and biological organisms can be explained consistently with the presumption of underlying goodness. Looking at it from the other direction, it means that an investigation of things can lead us to an appreciation of the goodness inherent in them and consequently can lead us to appreciate how the nurturing of the goodness within ourselves leads to the most complete fulfillment of our existence and the stabilization of what is unbalanced within us.[78] The stabilizing of our fundamental rationality precisely parallels Zhu Xi's talk of restoring our internal balance. What Plato says here of the heavenly bodies applies to all the other phenomena that are investigated in the *Timaeus*, even if the rational basis of their functioning is less obvious than that for the orbits of the stars and planets.

For all four thinkers, metaphysics is a powerful instrument of morality, indeed the only instrument that can show us the relationship between existence and goodness. The empirical investigation of things, on the other hand, becomes important as a way of confirming the existence of this relationship by showing the rational basis of the various kinds of existents. Plotinus, however, like the Cheng Hao and Wang Yangming traditions of neo-Confucianism, regards that kind of investigation as a distraction from the higher things—our own nature and the nature of goodness. For one who is already convinced of the fundamental goodness and meaningfulness of reality, their approach may be all that is necessary.[79] For those who are not yet convinced, even though an investigation of physical phenomena does not guarantee success, it does provide as much evidence as the subject permits.

Appendix 1: Schematic Comparison

These diagrams are only to facilitate comparisons. For Zhou Dunyi's own diagram, see Appendix 2.

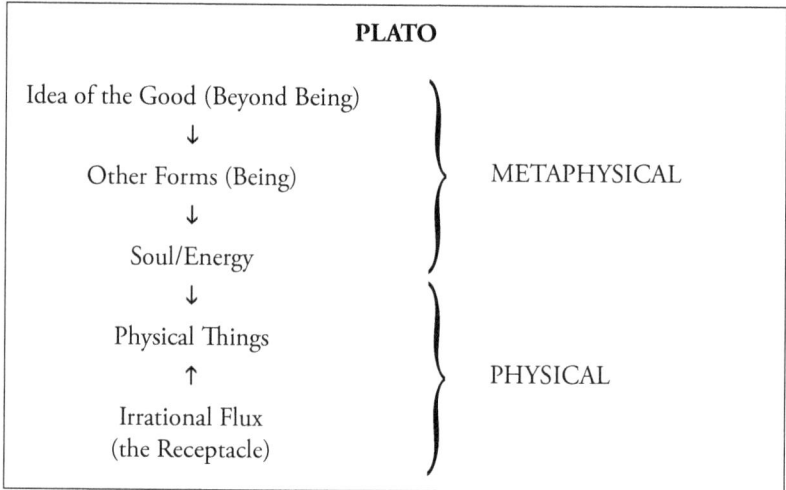

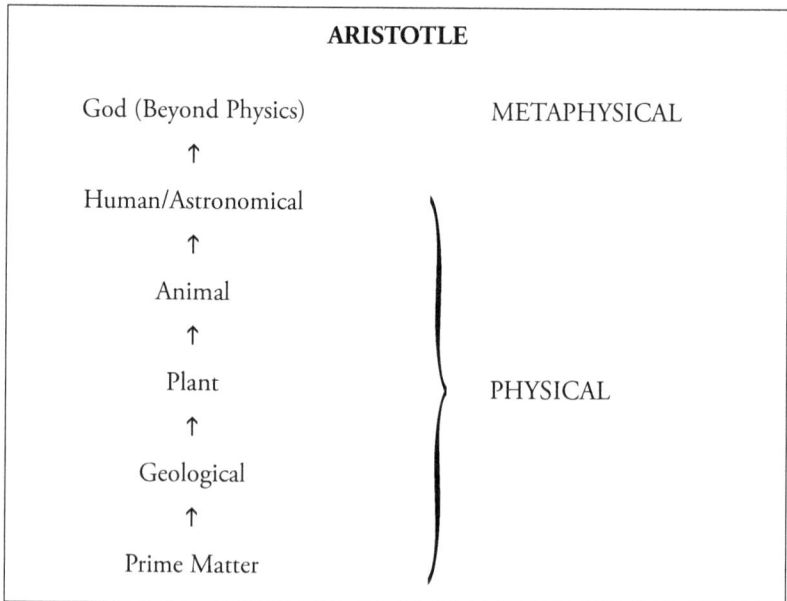

PLATO	
Idea of the Good (Beyond Being) ↓ Other Forms (Being) ↓ Soul/Energy	METAPHYSICAL
↓ Physical Things ↑ Irrational Flux (the Receptacle)	PHYSICAL

ARISTOTLE	
God (Beyond Physics)	METAPHYSICAL
↑ Human/Astronomical ↑ Animal ↑ Plant ↑ Geological ↑ Prime Matter	PHYSICAL

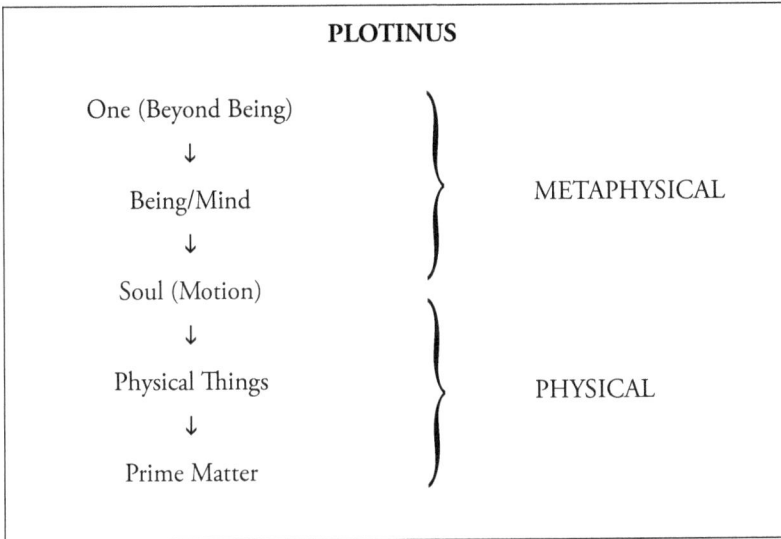

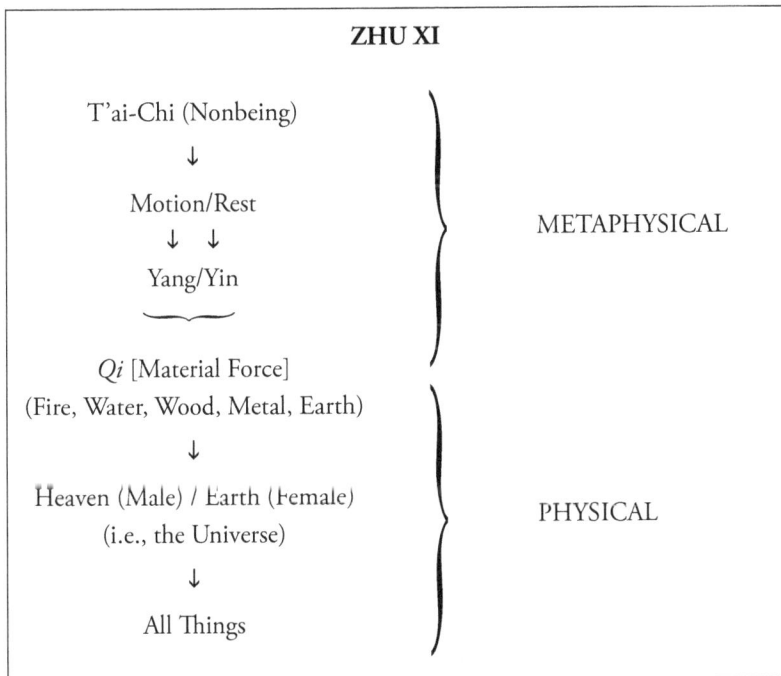

Appendix 2: Zhou Dunyi's Diagram

For a discussion of some of the controversy surrounding this diagram, see Ching (2000, 32–53 and 235–41).

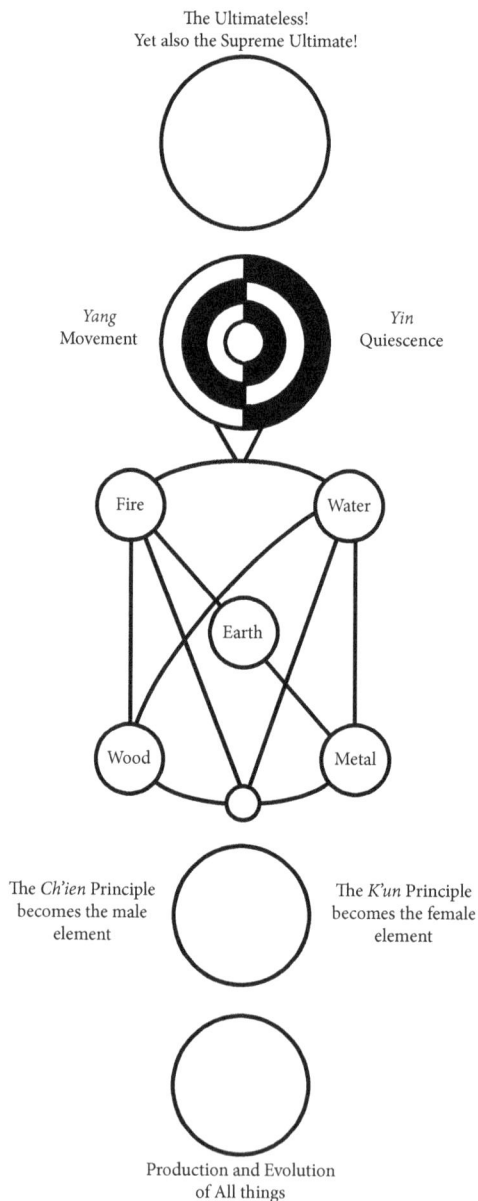

The Ultimateless!
Yet also the Supreme Ultimate!

Yang
Movement

Yin
Quiescence

Fire

Water

Earth

Wood

Metal

The *Ch'ien* Principle
becomes the male
element

The *K'un* Principle
becomes the female
element

Production and Evolution
of All things

Source: Contemporary illustration of traditional design by Liz Wilson, Hackett Publishing; from *Readings in Later Chinese Philosophy: Han Dynasty to the 20th Century*, ed. Justin Tiwald and Bryan W. Van Norden (Indianapolis: Hackett, 2014). Reprinted by permission.

Note: The middle area, beginning from top to bottom and right to left in the Chinese manner, indicates that water is transformed into wood, wood is consumed in fire, fire is quenched in earth, earth is transformed into metal, and metal dissolves in water.

CHAPTER FOUR

INDETERMINACY AND MORAL ACTION

Laozi and Heraclitus

Reversal is the action of the Dao.
—Laozi

The way up and the way down are one and the same.
—Heraclitus

The seven philosophers we looked at in the previous two chapters took a systematic approach to metaphysics, which made it easier to see the ethical implications of their views. By contrast, the kind of unsystematic metaphysics that we saw in chapter 1 presented us with indefiniteness, paradox, and contradictions that make it difficult to discover any determinate teachings in them, especially in the realm of ethics; and philosophers like Zhuangzi, Laozi, and Heraclitus are sometimes regarded as relativists. Now that we have seen how determinate metaphysics can be a basis for morality, let us consider how this can happen in indeterminate metaphysics as well.

Of all the philosophers compared in this book, Laozi and Heraclitus seem to me to be closest, temperamentally and philosophically as well as chronologically.[1] Although it might seem then that a comparative study of their thought would be especially straightforward, one of the ways they resemble each other is in the enigmatic and allusive nature of their writing, and the character of that evasiveness is different in each of them. Not only is Laozi more poetic and Heraclitus more aphoristic, but the two express themselves with very individual vocabularies. If we use a neutral language to compare their ideas we betray their mistrust of ordinary language, while if we interpret each of them entirely on their own terms there is no common vocabulary to connect them with each other. My response to this dilemma has been to interpret each of the texts as much as possible on its own terms and to draw connections and the consequences of those connections where the opportunity presents itself.

Interpretive difficulties are inevitable in any major philosopher, since no one becomes a major philosopher by stating the obvious. The difficulties are considerably magnified in philosophers who insist not only on the obscurity of their subject but even on the impossibility of finding words adequate to it, as when Heraclitus writes, "This logos holds always, but humans always prove unable to understand it both before hearing it and when they have first heard it."[2] The frequent quotation of Heraclitus by later philosophers resulted in an unusually large number of surviving fragments, but the fragments are brief—even the longest is only three sentences, while in some cases the later writers quoted only a single word. According to the Diels-Kranz edition, about 120 fragments survive, but they add up to only about one thousand words. The brevity of even the longest ones suggests that Heraclitus wrote in a terse epigrammatic style, but there is no independent evidence for it. And since we do not know the order in which they appeared in his writings we do not know how they may have been meant to reflect on and amplify one another, nor is there always agreement as to which fragments are actual quotations rather than paraphrases or misquotations. Consequently every attempt by editors or translators to put them into a coherent order results in a different mosaic.[3] Moreover, although it is sometimes obvious that Heraclitus is speaking literally, and at other times obvious that he is speaking metaphorically, he can often be interpreted either way with very different results. W. K. C. Guthrie observes: "It is discouraging, certainly, to note how many different impressions of this world-view have been put forward in the past and continue to be put forward; but one can only give one's own."[4]

Guthrie's comment applies with even greater justice to Laozi.[5] And Laozi's expression of the inadequacy of words is even more radical than

Heraclitus's: "He who knows does not speak. He who speaks does not know" (56.1–2).[6] The *Daodejing* is the most translated and commented text in any philosophical tradition, and the interpretations encompass every conceivable viewpoint. Even apart from interpretive controversies, there is no possibility of presenting anything like a comprehensive account of the multivalent riches of Laozi's book, especially in a single chapter. The point of focus that I have chosen both for Laozi and Heraclitus is the apparent tension between their denial of the adequacy of positive theoretical formulations (indeterminacy) and their concomitant endorsement of certain kinds of practical action over others (prescriptivism). If the governing principle reverts to nothingness, how can it be a guiding principle for us? How can what is formless serve as a guide to action? Laozi's words "Where they all know the good as good, / there is evil, / Therefore / Being and non-being produce each other" (2.3–6)[7] suggest that good and evil produce each other the way being and nonbeing produce each other—in which case to do good will lead to evil and to do evil will lead to good. The result threatens to become behavioral paralysis. We shall see that this is equally problematic in Heraclitus.

The chapter is divided into four sections: (1) Indeterminacy, (2) Principles, (3) Good and Evil, and (4) Impartiality. I have not tried to smooth over the differences in the two philosophers' ways of addressing and presenting these themes, or the different ways that the four themes combine and overlap in their two presentations. Some subthemes that appear in one of the four sections for one of the philosophers may appear in a different section for the other. To do otherwise would require connecting the themes in different ways than they are connected by the philosophers themselves.

Indeterminacy

Laozi

However much Laozi deprecated the power of words to express the Dao, he was not deterred from speaking and writing.[8] This tension between inexpressibility and expression is already hinted at in the opening line of the book:

> 1.1. The Dao that can be told of is not the eternal Dao.

The tension resides in Laozi's use of the character *Dao* not only for the principle that *cannot* be told of but also for the telling itself. Literally, it reads, "The Dao that we can Dao is not the eternal Dao."[9] A less literal but more structurally parallel translation might be, "The state that can be stated is not the eternal state," or, adapted to Heraclitus's terminology, "The *logos* of which there can be a *logos* is not the eternal *logos*."[10] Laozi's use of *Dao* to mean both what cannot be stated and the act of stating itself suggests that the source of all meaning, which makes meaning possible, cannot itself be encompassed by meaning. Nevertheless we must try to speak of it. The uneasy symmetry between meaning and what is meant (where what is meant is also what makes meaning possible) is repeated from the other direction in the second line:

> 1.2. The name that can be named is not the eternal name.

Instead of designating meaning by what is meant (*Dao*), here what is meant is designated by meaning. If *Dao* can be a verb for naming, *naming* can be a noun (name) for Dao. The echoing of these counterparts continues in the next pair of lines:

> 1.3. The Nameless is the origin of Heaven and Earth;
> 1.4. The Named is the mother of all things.

If we think of the Dao at the most abstract level, as the source of the *metaphysical* principles Heaven and Earth, it is nameless (1.3); but if we think of it more concretely, as the source of the *physical* world, we can name it in relation to our physical experience: it is the mother of all things (1.4). The next lines, 5 and 6, explain why both are necessary:

> 1.5a. Therefore let there always be non-being so we may see their subtlety,
> 1.6a. And let there always be being so we may see their outcome.

An alternate reading is:

> 1.5b. Therefore let there always be non-desire so we may see their subtlety,
> 1.6b. And let there always be desire so we may see their outcome.[11]

On the first of these two readings (1.5a), to give something a name is to make it a fixed being, to deprive it of its subtlety and uniqueness; so we must regard it instead as non-being (and nameless). On the other hand (1.6a), *not* to give it a name, *not* to identify it as a being with namable characteristics, prevents us from achieving any understanding of it and what follows from it, its outcome, so we must also regard it as being (and named). On the second reading (1.5b), to see the world apart from desire is to see it in its metaphysical subtlety, apart from reference to the utilitarian world, while to see it with desire (1.6b) is to see it in relation to that world. As a consequence of this unstable but inescapable interdependence (on either reading), each one taken by itself, as well as the two together, remains opaque:

> 1.7. The two are the same,
> 1.8. But after they are produced, they have different names.[12]
> 1.9. They both may be called deep and profound.

How they can be the same but have contradictory names (and concepts) is the "deep and profound" mystery that destabilizes our attempts to bring being into representation. Their identity and difference are two sides of the same principle, its inward side and outward side. But even its inwardness is not adequate to its nature—both are produced (1.8) from something more ultimate that can be thought of in these two antithetical ways but is itself conceivable only through their opposition and not in itself. Where they are deep and profound, it is

> 1.10. Deeper and more profound,
> 1.11. The door of all subtleties!

It is the source of all the disjunctions that describe the world.[13]

Heraclitus

The longest of Herclitus's fragments, which was the opening of his book according to Aristotle and Sextus Empiricus, begins: "This logos holds always but humans always prove unable to understand it, both before hearing it and when they have first heard it. For though all things come to be in accordance with this logos, humans are like the inexperienced when they experience such words and deeds as I set out" (B1).[14] That is what he means in B123 when he says that "nature loves to hide." He makes a similar point in B72, saying that people "are at odds with the logos, with which above all they are in continuous contact, and the things they meet every day appear strange to them." Why do we fail to recognize it even though it is ever present to us?

Although no one would call Heraclitus a lucid writer—his nickname was "the Obscure"—he elucidates this question, at least, more directly than did Laozi. His answer anticipates Plato's allegory of the cave: we are so used to one kind of experience that it blinds us to a more fundamental reality. This is one of the most frequent themes in the fragments, expressed in many ways. Sometimes the distinction between our ordinary view of things and their true nature is illustrated straightforwardly. When Heraclitus remarks that the sun's breadth "is the length of the human foot" (B3) he is speaking of sensible appearances, while his observation that "if there were no sun, as far as concerns the other stars it would be night" (B99) shows how inadequate our initial perception was.[15] As we saw in chapter 2, this distinction between visible appearances and their imperceptible foundation is the original insight of Western philosophy, implied by Thales's claim that all is water—that is, the true nature of reality is not what it seems.[16] Heraclitus conceives it as fire rather than water and asks not only about the underlying *material* unity of nature but also about the ultimate principle *governing* its workings: "Wisdom is one thing, to know the intelligence [*gnōmēn*] by which all things are steered through all things" (B41).[17] Moreover, for Heraclitus it is not only that we fail to perceive true reality but that even when we do perceive it its nature is so unexpected that we fail to comprehend it: "All that come upon them do not understand such things . . . but they seem to themselves to" (B17). "Divine things escape recognition because of unbelief" (B86). Therefore, "Unless he expects the unexpected [*elpētai anelpiston*], he will not find it" (B18).

What kind of truth is so unexpected that we fail to recognize it even though it is always with us? Reality is not only different from appearances but the very opposite of what we would expect: "Eternity is a child playing, playing a game of checkers; the kingdom belongs to a child" (B52), and "The most beautiful world-order is a pile of things poured out at random" (B124). This is how things normally appear to us. Throughout the world and its history we commonly believe that life is irrational and unfair, whether because it is without divine governance and therefore intrinsically absurd or because the gods themselves are unfair by our standards: either they are capricious, as in Homer, or else their justice is not our justice, as in the book of Job. A world in which bad things happen to good people and good things to bad people is, at the level of individuality, a world of random events or a game played by an arbitrary child. But if we can see it at the holistic level we will see it as a world order rather than random, and as a kingdom rather than a child's game. Where *these* fragments speak of the universe as random or irrational, B1 tells us that all things come to be in accordance with a rational logos, and B41 says that an intelligence steers all things through all things. Heraclitus expresses this double point of view unambiguously in places: "The finest harmony is composed of things at variance" (B8); "Things taken together [*sunapsies*] are . . . consonant and dissonant" (B10). The universe is beautiful or random depending on whether we look at its harmonious wholeness or its antagonistic components. "To God all things are beautiful and good and just, but humans have supposed some unjust and others just" (B102).[18] God here represents the perspective of the whole, while humans are focused on their partial point of view, but God is not *reducible* to the whole, for although "all things are one" (B50), "that which is wise is set apart from all" (B108). For Laozi too there is this double perspective: from our partial point of view life is unfair ("Heaven and Earth are not humane. / They regard all things as straw dogs," 5.1–2); but from the perspective of the Dao the way of the world is beneficial ("The Way (*Dao*) of Heaven is to benefit others," 81.10).

The double aspect means that Heraclitus is not the relativist that some of the fragments suggest. The impression of relativism derives from observations such as that sea water is palatable and safe for fish but un-drinkable and destructive to us (B61), asses prefer garbage to gold (B9), and oxen enjoy eating bitter plants (B4). By showing how our conception of what is good and bad is not necessarily shared by other species, Heraclitus shows that "good" and "bad" reflect not properties of the things themselves but only how things match up with our particular appetites and needs. In this context, "Dogs bark at everyone they do not know" (B97) suggests that the reason we think some things are better than others is merely a matter of unfamiliarity and prejudice. More generally, the famous remark "The road up and the road down are one and the same" (B60) suggests that what looks one way from one point of view looks exactly the opposite from a different point of view.[19] And the words "Hesiod considers some days good and others bad, not under-standing that the nature of every day is one and the same" (B106) imply that nothing is in itself any better than anything else.[20] Nevertheless, for Heraclitus there is also an absolute point of view: "Human nature has no insight, but divine nature has it" (B78), and "The wise is one alone; it is unwilling and willing to be called by the name of Zeus" (B32)—in the same way that, in Laozi's chapter 1, the Dao is willing and unwilling to be called Dao. The references to Zeus and the divine need not refer to an external deity but can refer to the divine within us, as when Aristotle writes: "But such a life would be too high for man; for it is not in so far as he is man that he will live so, but in so far as something divine is present in him."[21] The difference between the relative and the absolute is the difference between the perspectives of each of the individual parts and that of the whole. Since our values are normally based on particular appetites, needs, and self-interest generally, "It is not better for humans to get all they want" (B110).

The fragments indicate this double aspect in various ways, some-times literally but also through metaphor and paradox. B84a, "Changing, it is at rest," presents a paradox that challenges us to think the difference between the ever-changing parts and the unchanging nature of the whole. Heraclitus's most common metaphor is that of sleeping and waking. B89 tells us: "For the waking there is one common world, but when asleep each person turns away to a private one." Even in our waking world, however, we are asleep in a metaphorical sense: "People fail to notice [*lanthanei*] what they do when awake, just as they forget [*epila-nthanontai*] what they do while asleep" (B1). As we saw in chapter 1, there is a second sense in which we need to wake up even after we are awake in the normal sense, a second sense in which we need to go from our private worlds to a common one. In the first we go from our individual dream world to our shared waking world, in the second we go from our divisive individual interests to a recognition of what is common to us all. This idea of the common (*xunos*) is introduced in B2, where it is identified with the logos and contrasted with individuality.[22] The situation is analogous to the subordination of individuals to the law, Heraclitus says in B114: "Those who speak with understanding must rely firmly on what is common to all, as a city relies on its law, and much more firmly. For all human laws are nourished by one law, the divine law; for it has as much power as it wishes and is sufficient for all and is still left over."[23] Just as we subordinate our private wills to laws that are common to all members of our society but different from those of other societies, the diverse laws of all societies are themselves subordinate to one that is common to all, and that they all partially reflect. The two levels of law (human and divine) correspond to the two levels of waking (biological and metaphysical), as well as to the perspective of the parts and the whole.

In addition to using paradox and metaphor Heraclitus sometimes characterizes the whole-part relationship literally, as in B10's general description: "Things taken together are whole and not whole, brought together and brought apart, consonant and dissonant; out of all things comes a unity, and out of a unity all things" (B10). Other literal characterizations are more narrowly focused. B30, for example, focuses on the material aspect of the whole and parts: "The cosmos, the same for all . . . [is] an ever-living fire being kindled in measures and being extinguished in measures": individuals come and go, are kindled and extinguished, but the whole endures forever.[24] And sometimes his literal descriptions are in terms of the governing principle, the logos: "It is necessary to follow what is common to all. But although the logos is common, most people live as if they had their own private understanding" (B2)—we live as if our partial point of view were valid, instead of pursuing that of the common whole. Heraclitus's project is to lead us from our relativistic partial view to one that is universal or common. Our appetites and ambitions reflect our distinctness from each other and drive us into competition: our successes are measured against others' failures and vice versa. But rationality is different. Not only does our thinking not prevent others from enjoying the same understanding, as we saw in Spinoza, but it can even help them to do so through example and instruction. Thus "Thinking is common to all" (B113), not only in the trivial sense that all humans think, which after all is equally true of appetite and ambition, but in the distinctive sense that rational thinking abstracts from our partial viewpoint and aims at something that is impersonally true and therefore available to us all.[25] It is in this same sense that Heraclitus says the world order or cosmos is the same for all (B30). Heraclitus is a relativist at the level of the individual, the culture, and the species: what I call good, what my city calls good, and even what all human beings call good are also bad if other individuals or cities or species find them so. But he is not *ultimately* a relativist because there is a perspective other than those of the individual, city, and species, namely that of the whole, common to all, which Heraclitus calls the logos.

Principles

Laozi

Laozi's closest attempt to articulate the self-differentiation of that original source into the multiplicity of the world is in chapter 42, which begins:

42.1. Dao produced the One.
42.2. The One produced the two.
42.3. The two produced the three.
42.4. And the three produced the ten thousand things.
42.5. The ten thousand things carry the yin and embrace the yang, and through the blending of the material force (*qi*) they achieve harmony.

What is the difference between the Dao and the One, and how does the One produce the two? Both questions are resolved if we take the One to refer to what chapter 1 calls the "same" that has two names after it

has been produced (1.7–8). The Dao here is the "deeper and more profound" principle of 1.10, and the One is the subsequent double-sided
and double-named principle that is produced by it.

It is only to be expected in a book that emphasizes the inadequacy
of words, and whose starting point is the inadequacy of the word *Dao*
in particular, that in other contexts "Dao" functions more closely to the
way "the One" functions here in chapter 42. Compare the last three lines
of chapter 25 with the lines we just looked at in chapter 42 (paraphras-
ing the lines of chapter 42 and reversing the order of the lines in chapter
25 to facilitate comparison):

A (chapter 42)	B (chapter 25)
1 42.1. The One follows from the Dao.	25.19. Dao models itself after [follows from] *ziran*.[26]
2 42.2. The two follow from the One.	25.18. Heaven models itself after [follows from] Dao.
3 42.3. The three follow from the two.	25.17. Earth models itself after [follows from] Heaven.

In 1B it is *ziran* (spontaneity) that corresponds to Dao in 1A, while Dao
in 1B and 2B corresponds to the One in 1A and 2A. Thus in different
contexts *Dao* can mean either the indefinable source itself (42.1) or only
the aspect of that source that is conceptualizable by us (25.19). *Ziran*
in 25.19 corresponds not only to the Dao in chapter 42 but also to the
"deeper and more profound" source of the double-named principle in
chapter 1. As we would expect in view of Laozi's attitude toward names,
the terminology is not consistent even when the relations are the same.[27]
Because the One produced by the Dao is double-sided (1.7), it naturally
gives rise to "the two," which 42.5 identifies as yin and yang. In 1.5–6,
yin was prefigured in the nameless nonbeing and yang in the named
being. The third, *qi*, is the interrelation of yin and yang, all of which anticipates Zhou Dunyi's (Chou Tun-i's) famous diagram some 1,500 years
later (see chapter 3, Appendix 2).

Opinion is divided on whether this sequence is to be understood as
involving temporal or only ontological priority.[28] On the former view, the
universe as a whole is generated in time, so that there was a time when
the Dao existed but yin and yang did not and a subsequent time when
yin and yang existed together with the Dao but *qi* (material force) did

not yet exist. This view lends itself especially to religious and mythological conceptions of creation.[29] On the alternative view, the sequence represents ontological priority rather than temporal priority: underlying the myriad things of the universe is material force (*qi*), which presupposes the distinction between yin and yang, which in turn are a manifestation of the dialectical nature of the Dao. On this view, Laozi would agree with Zhu Xi's comment: "One can't speak of principle and material force in terms of first and later. But when we look into it, it seems as if principle exists first and material force later."[30] As Yu-lan Fung writes in reference to 40.3–4 ("All things in the world come from being. / And being comes from non-being"): "This saying of Lao Tzu does not mean that there was a time when there was only Non-being, and that then there came a time when Being came into being from Non-being. It simply means that if we analyze the existence of things, we see there must first be Being before there can be any things. . . . What is said here belongs to ontology, not to cosmology. It has nothing to do with time and actuality. For in time and actuality, there is no Being; there are only beings."[31]

There will never be a consensus on this matter because of the ambiguity of the textual evidence, depending on which chapters are taken as paradigmatic. The ontological interpretation is supported especially by chapter 21:[32]

21.1. The all-embracing quality of the great virtue (*de*) follows alone from the Dao.
21.2. The thing that is called Dao is eluding and vague.
21.3. Vague and eluding, there is in it the form.
21.4. Eluding and vague, in it are things.
21.5. Deep and obscure, in it is the life-force.[33]
21.6. The life-force is very real; in it are evidences.
21.7. From the time of old until now, its name (manifestations) ever remains.
21.8. By which we may see the beginnings of all things.
21.9. How do I know that the beginnings of all things are so?
21.10. Through this (Dao).

The Dao in its self-differentiation—its "all-embracing quality" rather than its formless simplicity—is its power or virtue (*de*) (21.1). Within its differentiation is form as opposed to the formlessness of the Dao itself (21.3). Form makes possible the further differentiation into individual things (21.4), and the existence of individual things makes life possible (21.5). Living beings have within themselves evidences of their origin (21.6), which enables our minds to return to the Dao itself (21.8–10). There is no suggestion here that the extension of the Dao through *de* is a temporal sequence. On the contrary, each level appears within its predecessor more like Chinese boxes, in a nonchronological hierarchy, a hierarchy that remains constant through all time, that "ever remains" (21.7).[34]

Here again we should not lose sight of the first chapter's caution about rigid categories. We cannot be content with a description of Laozi's "great chain of being" unambiguously in terms of ontological or logical presupposition (or, for that matter, temporal priority) as if all the levels were clearly distinct from one another like the nested boxes mentioned above. On the contrary, there is an ineluctable fluidity and ambiguity of boundaries. Spontaneity (*ziran*), Dao, the One, yin/yang, and *qi* are not discrete powers or entities but "deep" and "deeper" penetrations into the nature of reality. They are not beings or principles set over against the world; they are the being *of* the world, progressively understood: to understand the ten thousand things we must understand that they are manifestations of *qi*; that *qi* is a manifestation of yin and yang; that yin and yang are manifestations of being and non-being (1.5–6), which are ultimately different names for the same manifestation of Dao (1.7–11).[35] However naturally one may seem to follow from another at each step, conceptualization breaks down when we combine the steps in the conclusion that the being of the ten thousand things is neither namable nor non-namable, neither being nor nonbeing, and not only subtle but "the door of all subtleties." The difficulty of Laozi's writing lies in its refusal to minimize the conceptual difficulties of its message, and throughout the first forty-five chapters we are given formulations and metaphors of the inseparability of emptiness and fullness, whether as being and nonbeing or as knowledge and nescience.[36]

Centuries later in India, Nagarjuna (ca. 150–250 CE), the founder of Madhyamika Buddhism, tackled the same problem more directly and less poetically than Laozi. In considering the question of whether the elements of existence (*dharmas*) are to be conceived as being or nonbeing—in

Buddhist terms, nonempty or empty—he wrote: "Empty should not be asserted. Non-empty should not be asserted. Neither both nor neither should be asserted. They are only used nominally."[37] *Madhyamika* ("the Middle Path") refers to Nagarjuna's way of dealing with the paradoxes of namable/non-namable, and being/nonbeing by steering a middle course between both supposedly exhaustive alternatives, a deliberate contravention of the principle of excluded middle. Nagarjuna's meaning is more fully elaborated by the Chinese Madhyamika Buddhist Jizang (Chi-tsang, 549–623 CE):

> When it is said that dharmas possess being, it is ordinary people who say so. This is worldly truth, the truth of ordinary people. Saints and sages, however, truly know that dharmas are empty in nature. This is absolute truth, the truth of sages. . . . Next comes the second stage, which explains that both being and non-being belong to worldly truth, whereas non-duality (neither being nor non-being) belongs to absolute truth. It shows that being and non-being are two extremes. . . . Next comes the third stage in which both duality and non-duality are worldly truth, whereas neither-duality-nor-non-duality is the highest truth.[38]

We could similarly project a fourth stage in which the distinction between both-and and neither-nor is worldly truth, while the rejection of that distinction is the highest truth, followed by a fifth in which differentiating between the former distinction and its rejection is worldly truth, while the nondifferentiation between them is the highest truth, and so on. Like Laozi's assertion that in the case of the named and the nameless, and of being and nonbeing, "The two are the same," this deconstructive dialectic challenges our conceptualization in order to show the nondifferentiation that is the inner nature of the differentiated world. This nondifferentiation partly resembles the Aristotelian concept of prime matter, devoid of all form and therefore without actual existence even though it underlies all existence. But only partly, because Aristotle's juxtaposition of form to matter, as a distinct principle, prevents the reduction of being to nonbeing.[39] A closer analogue to the Daoist and Madhyamika reductions is Anaximander's concept of the Indefinite (*apeiron*) that is the basis of all finite beings. As Laozi puts it, "Infinite and boundless, . . . / it reverts to nothingness. / . . . / It is the Vague and Elusive" (14.7, 8, 11).

Heraclitus

Heraclitus shares Laozi's view of the oneness of the universe but conceives of that oneness not so much as a devolution from unity to multiplicity but as a harmony of opposite forces: "They do not understand how, though at variance with itself, it agrees with itself. It is a backwards-turning harmony like that of the bow and the lyre" (B51). Just as a bow and a lyre reconcile within themselves the inward pull of the string with the outward pull of the frame, the world as a whole reconciles within itself the disparate tendencies of each of its parts to go their own way in opposition to each other. That was what he meant by saying, "The most beautiful world-order is a pile of things poured out at random" (B124). At the level of individuals everything is arbitrary and random, but that same totality seen as a whole constitutes an order and a harmony. That is not apparent to us normally, but "An unapparent harmony is stronger than an apparent one" (B54). In other words, things that at the level of individuals are destructive and divisive constitute at the level of the whole a cosmic harmony. Something of the kind is also evident in Laozi's concept of the relation between yin and yang, but the harmonic tension between yin and yang is not prioritized in Laozi as fundamentally as their equivalents are in Heraclitus.

As *harmony* is the word for the way all things are related to one another at the level of the whole, the word for the way they are related to one another at the level of individuals is *strife*: "What is opposed brings together; the finest harmony is composed of things at variance, and everything comes to be in accordance with strife" (B8). Aristotle writes, "Heraclitus blames the poet who wrote, 'May strife perish from among gods and men' [Homer, *Iliad* 18.107]; for (says he) there could not be harmony without the low and the high note, nor living things without female and male, two opposites" (*Eudemian Ethics* 7.1235a25–29). Thus "War is the father of all and king of all, and some he shows as gods, others as humans; some he makes slaves, others free" (B53). The strife that carves our individuality out of the whole reveals the distinctive character that is our divinity.

Two of the terms that Heraclitus used to characterize the harmony of the whole were *justice* and *common*. Now he says, "It is necessary to know that war is common and justice is strife, and that all things happen in accordance with strife and necessity" (B80). To say that war is common is to say that what divides us also unites us, and to say that justice is strife is to say that what unites us also divides us. Finally, to say that all things happen in accordance with strife and necessity is to say that the strife that divides us is a necessary feature of the reality as a whole that we share in common. This view is not as counterintuitive as it may seem. Not only do we find it in Darwin's conception of evolution through war-like competition, but our own experience teaches that without challenge our society, and we ourselves, are likely to become complacent and stagnant, our vitality replaced with unreflective conventions and habits, and the harmonious tension of opposition replaced by the repression of one side by another. Heraclitus's metaphors remind us several times that violence is sometimes necessary to benefit us: "Every animal is driven to pasture by blows," (B11), people do not appreciate the benefit they receive from being cut and burned by doctors (B58), and "Even the barley drink separates if it is not stirred up" (B125). There would be no reason for us to rise above the simplest and most elementary modes of thinking about the world and about ourselves if we were never challenged by obstacles—whether these are obstacles to our understanding that provoke us to wonder and to reflective thought, or obstacles to our will that provoke us to rethink our values and our way of doing things. Thus "Disease makes health pleasant and good, hunger satiety, weariness rest" (B111). Without deprivations like disease we would never have become conscious of benefits like health. It is the point Heraclitus made also in B23: "They would not have known the name of justice if these things [injustices] did not exist." It is not hard for us to appreciate that without the selfish divisive behavior of Paris and Helen the greatness and beauty of the *Iliad* could not exist, or the greatness and beauty of the *Odyssey* without the enmity and challenges that continually test Odysseus.[40] It is more difficult to appreciate in life than in art that without the divisive behavior of individuals the harmoniousness of the whole could not exist, but the underlying principle is the same.

However paradoxical, there is nothing unreasonable in Heraclitus's claim that the world may at once be good in itself and distressing in its parts. To be awake in Heraclitus's sense means to hold onto this double point of view, which is our own simultaneous harmony and strife. The viewpoint of awakened thinking tells us that the whole is good and that therefore all things taken together are beautiful, just, and good. The practical viewpoint tells us that this way lies apathy and paralysis of the will. It tells us that some things are better than others and that we have the responsibility to try to bring about goodness in the world and oppose evil. Heraclitus's philosophy teaches us that we must ultimately recognize not only the harmony of the whole that unifies the strife among the parts but also the harmony that unifies the strife between these two viewpoints, that of the whole and that of the part. According to the first, we must strive to wake up to the understanding that our own place and our own set of values are one among many, all subordinated to the whole. According to the second, we must hold on to the recognition that even if our mind can rise to a godlike perspective of the whole, we are at the same time parts within that whole. We are not impersonal gods but finite persons with our own part to play within the whole. We must do what we think is right, even though others think differently, but we must at the same time recognize that those who disagree with us and oppose us have their own part to play.

We can see this at the level of the city as well as at the level of the individual. Heraclitus recognized the relativity of each city's laws when he said that "all human laws are nourished by one law, the divine law; for it has as much power as it wishes and is sufficient for all and is still left over" (B114). But he also recognized that it is the responsibility of the city to play its part in the world by championing its own laws: "The populace must fight for the law as for the city wall" (B44). What is true of the populace and its law is true of individuals and their principles: we must fight for what we believe in. But at the same time we must also keep in mind that the words of B110, "It is not better for humans to get all they want," also apply to us and that the tension of antagonism and strife is the other side of harmony. This is not a relativism. The awakened perspective that sees the limitations of any finite point of view and aims at the unification of harmony is always superior to the personal point of view that sees only its own advantage and pursues the divisiveness of competition. The personal point of view is not equally good or equally fulfilling where it does not coincide with the transpersonal view. Selfish behavior is not as good as enlightened behavior. But it is equally necessary. This teaching does not receive the same degree of focus in Laozi but is implied in passages such as the one quoted above from chapter 81: "The Way [*Dao*] of Heaven is to benefit others."

Good and Evil

Laozi

If the governing principle reverts to nothingness, how can it be a guiding principle for us—how can holding on "to the Dao of old [enable us] to master the things of the present" (14.14)? How can what is formless serve as a guide to action? The same instability that attaches ontologically to being/nonbeing attaches morally to good/evil. Chapter 2 begins: "When the people of the world all know . . . the good as good, There is evil. Therefore being and non-being produce each other." As was mentioned earlier, if the implication is that good and evil produce each other the way being and nonbeing produce each other, then to do good will lead to evil, and to do evil will lead to good. How can such a teaching enable us "to master the things of the present," rather than paralyzing our will and leaving us as indecisive as Buridan's ass?

Chapter 20 asks, "How much difference is there between good and evil? / What people dread, do not fail to dread. / But alas, how confused, and the end is not yet" (20.3–5).[41] To make a fixed distinction between good and evil, and to dread things as evil the way people usually do is confused because "the end is not yet." The meaning of these last words is illustrated in the famous story of The Lost Horse:

> [One day a farmer's] horse ran away. His neighbor commiserated only to be told, "Who knows what is good or bad?" The next day the horse returned, bringing with it a drove of wild horses it had befriended in its

wanderings. The neighbor came over again, this time to congratulate the farmer on his windfall. He was met with the same observation: "Who knows what is good or bad?" The next day the farmer's son tried to mount one of the wild horses and fell off breaking his leg. Back came the neighbor, this time with more commiserations, only to encounter for the third time the same response, "Who knows what is good or bad?" The following day soldiers came by commandeering for the army and because of his injury the son was not drafted.[42]

As long as "the end is not yet"—and it is always not yet—we cannot confidently designate something as good or evil.

A related point is suggested by chapter 32: "Dao is eternal and has no name. . . . / As soon as there are names, know that it is time to stop. / It is by knowing when to stop that one can be free from danger" (32.1, 7–8). Chan, correctly I think, takes "names" to refer to "differentiation of things," but why is it time to stop? Where would the next step have taken us? Presumably in the direction more explicitly identified by Zhuangzi:[43] "The understanding of the men of ancient times went a long way. How far did it go? [1] To the point where some of them believed that things have never existed—so far, to the end, where nothing can be added. [2] Those at the next stage thought that things exist but recognized no boundaries among them. [3] Those at the next stage thought there were boundaries but recognized no right and wrong. [4] Because right and wrong appeared, the Way was injured."[44] In chapter 40 Laozi says, "All things in the world come from being. / And being comes from non-being" (40.3–4). These two statements correspond to the first two stages in the Zhuangzi passage: "Being comes from *non-being*" corresponds to Zhuangzi's unsurpassable knowledge that (1) "things have *never existed*"; and "All things in the world come from *being*" corresponds to Zhuangzi's next stage, (2) "things *exist*" (but with no boundaries among them). If, as Chan suggests, Laozi's "names" means differentiation of things, that is, boundaries among them, then "As soon as there are names" (Laozi 32.7) corresponds to Zhuangzi's description of the third stage, (3) "Those at the next stage thought there were *boundaries* but recognized *no right and wrong*." It is reasonable to expect that the next stage in Laozi would correspond to the next stage in Zhuangzi, the recognition of right and wrong.

In that case when Laozi says, "It is time to stop. / It is by knowing when to stop that one can be free from danger" (32.8), the next step, the step from which he deters us, corresponds to Zhuangzi's final stage, (4) "Because *right and wrong appeared*, the Way was injured." In other words, for Laozi "it is time to stop" when we have differentiated individual things but have not yet distinguished them as good or evil.[45] The parallel I am imputing to Laozi and Zhuangzi can be summarized schematically:

LAOZI	*ZHUANGZI*
1 Being comes from nonbeing.	The highest knowledge is of the nonbeing of things.
2 All things in the world. . . .	There were things.
3 There are names [distinction].	Next were those who believed there was distinction.
4 It is time to stop.	There was neither right nor wrong.

If these passages were all that Laozi had to say on the subject, it would indeed seem that our basis for action—the distinction between some courses as good and others as evil—had been undermined, and the Dao would not only fail to give us a way to master the present situation but deny the very possibility of such mastery. In other chapters, however, far from dissolving the distinction between good and evil, Laozi speaks of good and evil as unambiguously distinct.[46] Moreover, although chapter 5 supports the refusal to distinguish between good and evil when it says, "Heaven and Earth are not humane. / They regard all things as straw dogs," according to chapter 81 the opposite is true: "The Way of Heaven is to benefit others" (81.10). We thus find an indeterminacy in the moral sphere comparable to that in the ontological sphere: not only that good and evil cannot ultimately be distinguished but that they both can and cannot be distinguished. Laozi explicitly connects the cognitive and practical indeterminacy: "My doctrines are very easy to understand and very easy to practice, / But none in the world can understand or practice them" (70.1–2).

As the preceding quotation shows, since our actions are motivated by the pursuit of what we perceive to be good and the avoidance of what we perceive to be bad or evil, the ambiguous relation between good and evil in Laozi carries with it a similar ambiguity in the conception of action ("practice"). If there is no clear distinction between good and evil there is no clear basis on which to take action. Consequently we are told several times that the sage takes no action, as in chapter 48:

48.1. The pursuit of learning is to increase day after day.

48.2. The pursuit of Dao is to decrease day after day.

48.3. It is to decrease and further decrease until one reaches the point of taking no action.

48.4. No action is undertaken, and yet nothing is left undone.

48.5. An empire is often brought to order by having no activity.

48.6. If one undertakes activity, he is not qualified to govern the empire.[47]

Even in the case of the Dao itself, "Dao invariably takes no action" (37.1). Not surprisingly Laozi also says the opposite, that in some sense the Dao does take action: "The great Dao . . . accomplishes its task" (34.1, 4); "Dao produces them" (51.1; cf. 51.8, 51.12). Not only does the Dao take action, but despite the statements to the contrary that we saw above, the sage too must take definite action in the world: "Withdraw as soon as your work is done" (9.9); "One who is good achieves his purpose and stops" (30.5).[48] The paradox is sharpened when both pieces of contradictory advice are juxtaposed: "Act without action" (63.1; *wei wuwei*). Similarly, since action springs from desire, we are also told that "the sage desires to have no desire [*yu bu yu*]" (64.16).

Thus action and nonaction, like good and evil, and being and nonbeing, both can and cannot be distinguished. Some chapters give clues to the possibility of a resolution of the paradox. Chapter 2 says, for example:

2.14. [The sage] produces them, but does not take possession of them.

2.15. He acts, but does not rely on his own ability.

2.16. He accomplishes his task, but does not claim credit for it.[49]

The first and third conditions seem clear—we should not act for profit ("not take possession") or glory ("not claim credit")—but how are we to understand the second condition, that we must not rely on our own ability? If relying on our own ability means taking deliberate action, then we might be said not to rely on our own ability when we act impulsively or in the throes of passion, but this cannot be what is recommended. The paradox of acting without action (*wei wuwei*) underlies an ambiguity in chapter 13:

13.1. Be apprehensive when receiving favor or disgrace.

13.2. Regard great trouble as seriously as you regard your body.

13.3. What is meant by being apprehensive when receiving favor or disgrace?

13.4. Favor is considered inferior.

13.5. Be apprehensive when you receive them and also be apprehensive when you lose them.

13.6. This is what is meant by being apprehensive when receiving favor or disgrace.

13.7. What does it mean to regard great trouble as seriously as you regard the body?

13.8. If I have no body,

13.9. What trouble could I have?

13.10. Therefore he who values the world as his body may be entrusted with the empire.

13.11. He who loves the world as his body may be entrusted with the empire.

The claim in lines 2 through 9 that our body is the source of all our troubles is not hard to understand: our body is the seat of desires, and the pursuit of desires leads to fear and frustration far more often than to even transitory contentment, so the key to happiness is to reduce our desires by overcoming our attachment to things of the body.[50] It is by the body that we distinguish ourselves from others, so the way to stop ourselves from regarding our body seriously is to see ourselves as inseparable from others rather than in competition with them: "The Way of the sage is to act but not to compete" (81.11).[51]

But if lines 13.2–9 tell us not to take our body seriously, how can lines 13.10–11 conclude that someone who values and loves the world as his body may be entrusted with the empire? If we ought not value or love our body at all, a ruler who values and loves the world as his body would neither value nor love the empire. People entrusted with the empire can hardly take the view that if ruling is giving them trouble, like their body, they should stop caring about the empire. The difficulty disappears if lines 13.10–11 represent a shift of perspective from the individual body to the body of the whole, so that "values . . . [and] loves the world as his body" does not mean "values and loves the world *as much* as he values and loves his body"—that is, as little as possible—but rather "values and loves the world *as being* his body." The goal is to recognize our inseparability from other things, and theirs from still others ad infinitum, until we see ourselves not as self-dependent individuals but as interdependent moments of the whole.[52] Thus Laozi says, "The sage, in the government of his empire, has no subjective viewpoint. / His mind forms a harmonious whole with that of his people" (49.9–10). "Become one with the dusty world," he urges. "This is called profound identification" (56.8–9).[53] To become one with the world is to regard the world as our body and therefore to value and love this inclusive body for precisely the reasons that we should not take seriously our individual body:[54] desire and competition have been left behind. When Laozi says, "The sage desires to have no desire" (64.16), the unwished-for desires are those of our individual body, those that give us pleasure independently of and even at the expense of others; and the desire to be rid of them is the desire of our inclusive body, our identification with the world as a whole, the self as what is common to all rather than what is distinctive to each. "Being all-embracing, he is impartial" (16.13).

Laozi specifies that it is a dusty world (56.8), a world not according to our personal tastes. To us dust is something to be removed, something unwanted, of no value. But the world is full of creatures that thrive on dust. To become one with the world is to leave behind the subjective distinctions between good and bad (or evil) that we talked about at the beginning of this section. In this way chapter 56 can be read as a commentary on chapter 13, and it is true in another way as well. Lines 3 through 6 of chapter 13 said paradoxically that not only disgrace but even favor is inferior. Now we are told that if someone achieves this "profound identification" with the world, "It is impossible either to benefit him or to harm him / It is impossible either to honor him or to disgrace him" (56.11–12). Favor and honor, like disgrace, place us in a competitive position, an inferior position vis-à-vis profound identification.

However, the inferiority of honor and disgrace that Laozi insisted upon in chapter 13 he seems to deny in chapter 20 where he constantly compares himself with others (emphasis added):

20.8. *I alone* am inert, showing no sign (of desires).

20.9. Like an infant that has not yet smiled.

20.10. Lost,[55] indeed I seem to be without a home.

20.11. The multitude all possess more than enough,

20.12. *I alone* seem to have lost all.

20.13. Mine is indeed the mind of an ignorant man,

20.14. Indiscriminate and dull!

20.15. Common folks are indeed brilliant;

20.16. *I alone* seem to be in the dark.

20.17. Common folks see differences and are clear-cut;

20.18. *I alone* make no distinctions.

20.19. I seem drifting as the sea;

20.20. Like the wind blowing about, seemingly without destination.

20.21. The multitude all have a purpose;

20.22. *I alone* seem to be stubborn and rustic.

20.23. *I alone* differ from others,

20.24. And value drawing sustenance from mother (Dao).

The speaker, Laozi, who has achieved experience of the Dao (20.24), seems in some places to lament his inferiority to all others: he alone seems to have lost all, he alone seems to be in the dark, and he alone seems to be stubborn and rustic (20.12, 16, 22). In other places he sounds boastful, despite all the warnings against boasting:[56] he alone has overcome desire, he alone makes no distinctions, and he alone values the Dao (20.8, 18, 23–24). Oddest of all are the words, "I alone make no distinctions" (20.18). If he makes no distinctions how can he distinguish himself from everyone else as the only one of whom this is true? "I alone" cannot, then, mean "the individual that I am as distinguished from every other individual." Apart from the difficulties just mentioned, why would Laozi suppose that he alone, and no one else, has ever valued the Dao? In fact he elsewhere acknowledges, "What others have taught, I teach also" (42.9). The apparent incoherence of these lines forces us to the same perspective switch that we needed to resolve the apparent contradiction in chapter 13 between not valuing and valuing our body. "I alone" makes sense only if it refers to someone who regards the world as being his body. To identify with the whole is to be alone: there is nothing outside of the whole. "I alone differ from others" the way the unique whole differs from its parts. Someone who thus draws sustenance from the Dao (20.24) is "inert, showing no sign (of desires)," and makes no distinctions. He "seems" to have lost all, to be in the dark, and to be stubborn and rustic, but he only seems so to others. The lines quoted above (20.8–24) were preceded by the words "The multitude are merry, as though feasting on a day of sacrifice, / Or like ascending a tower at springtime (20.5–6)." This contrast between the rewards of the multitude and those of oneself alone, is elucidated in chapter 35: "When there are music and dainties, / Passing strangers will stay. / But the words uttered by Dao, / How insipid and flavorless! / We look at Dao; it is imperceptible. / We listen to it; it is inaudible" (35.5–10).[57] The multitude are like the prisoners in Plato's cave.

Heraclitus

If all is one, and all personal values are arbitrary, and the most beautiful order is a pile of things poured out at random, what is the point of moral effort? Whatever we do, it is all one and the same, a temporal manifestation of God, so why not take the path of least resistance and do whatever we feel like? If all things happen in accordance with the logos (B1), and all things are steered through all things by an intelligence (B41), and to God all things are beautiful, good, and just (B102), and every day is as good as every other day (B106), then it seems that everything we do is equally good and our moral choices are effectively meaningless. This is not the conclusion that Heraclitus draws, but we need to understand how he can avoid it.

His description of wisdom as "to know the intelligence by which all things are steered through all things" (B41), and of the logos as that by which all things come to be (B1), suggests that there is in fact some rationale for the way things happen, and several fragments testify to the importance of achieving and living in accordance with this wisdom.

Thus "Right thinking [*sōphronein*] is the greatest virtue, and wisdom is to speak the truth and act in accordance with nature" (B112). Conversely, "Justice will convict those who fabricate falsehoods and bear witness to them" (B28). How then could Heraclitus believe that to God all things are beautiful and good and just? He seems to contradict that statement explicitly when he says that "most people are bad, and few are good" (B104). This is one of the central paradoxes of Heraclitus's thought. On one hand, from the point of view of the whole all things are good, all are constituent parts of a divine harmony. On the other, Heraclitus continually urges us to live a certain kind of life and has no patience with those who do not see things as he does. He said that "Homer deserved to be expelled from the contests and flogged, and Archilochus likewise" (B42), and elsewhere he speaks abusively not only of Homer (B56) but also of Hesiod (B40, B57), Pythagoras (B40, B129), Xenophanes (B40), and Hecataeus (B40), as well as people in general (B29, B70, B104, B121).

To see how he can say that all is good, yet that most people are bad, we have to understand his conception of our distinctive human potential, our rational mind. We saw earlier that thinking, unlike our appetites, enables us to rise above our partial point of view and discover the impartial perspective that is common to all things (B113). To the extent that our thinking succeeds in rising above partiality, we awaken to the logos that is common to all (B2) and thus within ourselves (B45, B115), and in accordance with which all things come to be (B1). To be a good person in Heraclitus's sense is to achieve this awakening. There are two aspects to our nature, then, corresponding to the difference between the divine and human natures mentioned in B78—on one hand our rational common nature that can rise above particularity and grasp the eternal, on the other our unique individuality that is wedded to ever-changing particularity. Insofar as our individual nature is part of a whole that is thoroughly good, our individuality contributes to the greater good no matter what we do, and in that sense all things and all people are good. Even the divisive actions of a selfish person contribute to an overall good, the way "the path of writing is straight and crooked" (B59)—that is, however much the individual elements may zig and zag, they contribute to the overall movement forward. Similarly, "A person's character is his divinity" (B119) means that each of us in our own way, regardless of what kind of character we have, manifests the divine nature. Thus Heraclitus says of people who are still asleep to what is common, "Sleepers are co-workers in what goes on in the world" (B75). These are people who contribute to the good of the whole despite themselves, who are good not in themselves but only because their actions have beneficial ramifications that they neither foresee nor intend. But those who live rationally, by the thinking that is common to all, contribute to goodness not only indirectly and unknowingly like the others but also directly and knowingly by embodying within themselves and within their lives the rational principle of the whole. Everyone is good in a merely natural sense, as part of the goodness of the natural world, but we are good in the moral sense, and our life is intrinsically meaningful, only to the extent that our thinking has awakened from the partial to the common, and our mind identifies itself with the whole rather than with the part that is our individual body.

Impartiality

Laozi

The process by which we may progress from our individual partial viewpoint to an impartial identification with the Dao is evoked in chapter 15:

15.1. Of old those who were the best rulers were subtly mysterious and profoundly penetrating;

15.2. Too deep to comprehend.

15.3. And because they cannot be comprehended,

15.4. I can only describe them arbitrarily.

15.5. Cautious, like crossing a frozen stream in the winter,

15.6. Being at a loss, like one fearing danger on all sides,

15.7. Reserved, like one visiting,

15.8. Supple and pliant, like ice about to melt,

15.9. Genuine, like a piece of uncarved wood,

15.10. Open and broad, like a valley,

15.11. Merged and undifferentiated, like muddy water.

15.12. Who can make muddy water gradually clear through tranquility?

15.13. Who can make the still gradually come to life through activity?

15.14. He who embraces this Dao does not want to fill himself to overflowing.

15.15. It is precisely because there is no overflowing that he is beyond wearing out and renewal.

Cautious, like crossing a frozen stream in the winter. At the beginning we can make progress only by being cautiously watchful; only if we pay careful attention will things show themselves as they are.[58] Because the Dao is hidden in plain sight, invisible and inaudible (chaps. 14 and 35), we must be alert to its "evidences" in the world (chap. 21). We must look for the nameless within the namable and for nonbeing within being (chap. 1). We must be alert to the presence of opposites within each other (chaps. 2 and 22) and to their transformations into each other (chaps. 36 and 40). And we must be alert to the danger of forcing ourselves onto the situation rather than being simply receptive to it—we must be courageous in not daring rather than in daring (73.1–2) and must seek the mean rather than risking extremes (chaps. 5, 9, 15, and 77), for "What is brittle is easy to crack" (64.3). We must proceed as if we were on brittle ice, ice that is inseparable from its opposite, the fluid water beneath the surface.

Being at a loss, like one fearing danger on all sides. Once we have embarked on this path, caution gives way to fear. We have left behind what is tangible, visible, audible, and conceivable and have turned toward emptiness. We seem to have lost all (20.12). And for that reason there is, in addition to our fear of the unknown, the fear of the known—fear of the temptation to return to familiar gratifications: "I should, in walking on a broad way [*Dao*], fear getting off the road. Broad ways [*Dao*] are extremely even [unvarying and uneventful], but people are fond of bypaths" because the terrain of the Dao seems barren compared with the splendor of the courts (53.1–8).[59]

Reserved, like one visiting. Now the emotional content of fear has been overcome. Anxious dread has been replaced by calm respect. But we are still separated from the Dao. We are visitors rather than at home in it.

Supple and pliant, like ice about to melt. Our separateness begins to dissolve. Where we originally entered into it as though crossing a

frozen stream in the winter, cautious over melting ice, now we ourselves are like ice about to melt. We are becoming assimilated to the
territory we have entered.

Genuine, like a piece of uncarved wood. At this point we have reached
our goal, although in a preliminary way. The uncarved wood (*pu*) is an
image of undifferentiated being: "When the uncarved wood is broken
up, it is turned into concrete things" (28.16). It corresponds to what is
"undifferentiated and yet complete, Which existed before heaven and
earth. . . . I do not know its name; I call it Dao. . . . Dao models itself
after *ziran* [spontaneity]" (25.1–2, 6, and 19). The present line (15.9) is
only a preliminary consummation because the Dao is understood here as
being, not yet as nonbeing or *ziran*.

Open and broad, like a valley. Beneath the frozen stream is the valley.
The stream is something positive like the uncarved wood of line 9 and
the named and Being of chapter 1, but beneath it is the unnamed and
nonbeing, like the negative space of a valley.

Merged and undifferentiated, like muddy water. The opposition between being and nonbeing was mediated by something more profound
than either and common to both (1.7–11). Here, in the same way, after
the being of the stream and the nonbeing of the valley, is the most en-
compassing image of all, the muddy water in which the water of the
stream and the earth of the valley are merged and undifferentiated.

The next two lines bring us to the essence of *wuwei*. If the muddy
water refers to the "deeper and more profound" Dao in which being
and nonbeing are originally merged (1.5–10), then line 15.12, "Who
can make muddy water gradually clear through tranquility?," is the moment of reversal.[60] Where the previous lines progressively merged distinctions, it is now time to return to the clarifying activity of distinctions in
which the earth and water that were merged in mud are once again distinguished from each other. If the previous movement of progressive de-
construction corresponded to the words "Let there always be non-being
so we may see their subtlety" (1.5), the reversal and return to the clarity
of distinctions corresponds to the words that followed, "Let there always be being so we may see their outcome" (1.6). Those who remain
in the state in which all distinctions are merged will never be able to decide on a course of action, since yes and no, good and evil, are arbitrary

distinctions (20.2–3). They will be able to take action only when they return from this "profound identification" (56.9). The first step is to once again find some way to distinguish good from bad, water from dirt, tranquility from turmoil. As we noted earlier, in other contexts Laozi has no hesitation in distinguishing good from bad.[61] The return to the world of action and distinctions is completed in the next line: "Who can make the still gradually come to life through activity?" What is involved in this gradual return from absorption in the Dao to life and activity? How does the sage now overcome the dilemma that "he who takes an action fails. . . . The sage takes no action and therefore does not fail" (64.10, 12)? In other words, how are we to understand activity without taking action, *wei wuwei*? The concept is generally agreed to mean something like natural rather than forced or arbitrary action,[62] and while there is some basis for the claim that "there are no concepts or even areas of thought in traditional Western philosophy that correspond to the ideals of naturalness and *wuwei*" (Liu 1999, 213), some themes in other traditions can help to bring the concept of *wuwei* into greater relief.

For Aristotle, virtuous people are defined by their character rather than their actions. If their character leads them to take pleasure in performing good actions and to find it painful to perform bad actions, they are virtuous. Since we naturally pursue pleasure and avoid pain, virtuous people will automatically desire what is good and be repelled by what is bad. Others may pursue the good and avoid the bad not because they have no desire to do otherwise but because, by the power of their self-control (*enkrateia*), their rational understanding of what is good is able to prevent them from following their desires that are contrary to the good. The first type, then, does the good naturally and easily, while the second can do so only through effort.[63] Even if we are not among the few who are born with a virtuous character, we can achieve it by acquiring virtuous habits as a result of performing virtuous actions (*Nicomachean Ethics* 2.1).

There is something comparable in Confucius: "At fifteen I set my heart on learning; at thirty I took my stand; at forty I came to be free from doubts; at fifty I understood the Decree of Heaven; at sixty my ear was attuned; at seventy I followed my heart's desire without overstepping the line" (*Analects* 2.4, in Confucius 1979). The difference in

Confucius before and after the age of seventy gives us something comparable to *wuwei*. To follow our heart's desires, in other words to do what we spontaneously feel like doing, and have it always correspond to what is right—as opposed to having to control our heart's desires lest we transgress what is right—is the Confucian version of *wuwei*. As with Aristotle, Confucius's way of achieving it is a combination of rationally learning what is good and firmly controlling our desires to do otherwise until we train them to coincide with the good.[64]

Laozi, on the other hand, does not regard learning as the path to *wuwei*. Most of his references to learning are negative, not only because for him learning means listening to others rather than seeing for oneself, but also because learning means a progressive accumulation of information, the pursuit of "more," whereas chapter 15 insists that the path to wisdom is the progressive reduction of distinctions, the pursuit of "less." Thus "The pursuit of learning is to increase day after day. / The pursuit of Dao is to decrease day after day. / It is to decrease and further decrease until one reaches the point of taking no action" (48.1–3). Again, "A wise man has no extensive knowledge; / He who has extensive knowledge is not a wise man" (81.5–6).[65] This leads to a different conception of the mind of a good person:[66]

> He accomplishes his task, but does not claim credit for it. (2.16, 10.8, 77.12–13)

> The sage places himself in the background, but finds himself in the foreground. He puts himself away, and yet he always remains. Is it not because he has no personal interests? (7.4–7)

> He does not show himself; therefore he is luminous. He does not justify himself; therefore he becomes prominent. He does not boast of himself; therefore he is given credit. He does not brag; therefore he can endure for long. It is precisely because he does not compete that the world cannot compete with him. (22.9–13; cf. 66.10–11)

> The best (rulers) are those whose existence is (merely) known by the people. The next best are those who are loved and praised. (17.1–2)

Nothing like this kind of self-effacement is to be found in Confucius or Aristotle. For them the pursuit of "more" in the context of learning and personal recognition is praiseworthy; the good know their own value and expect to be treated with commensurate respect. Something like Laozi's self-effacement does appear in Kant, for whom the categorical imperative is the more reliable the less it corresponds to our desires, but there is no comparable effacement of conceptualization.[67]

From these comparisons we can see that *wuwei* has two distinct components. (1) It must be spontaneous as if it happened of itself, rather than being the result of effortful self-examination and self-control—like the actions of people who can unhesitatingly trust their intuitions if they are virtuous in Aristotle's sense or are like the septuagenarian Confucius. (2) We must abstract from the consciousness of our individuality, and from the consciousness of our separateness from others and from the whole. Kant shares with Laozi this second principle but not the first; Aristotle and Confucius share the first but not the second. For Confucius love is always love with distinctions; Aristotle's god, the goal of contemplation, is individual rather than holistic; and for Kant the proper motive of action is not intuitive but duty as discerned by conceptual reason. None of them would be interested in becoming one with the dusty world.

In the way he combines the two principles of spontaneity and "profound identification" Laozi is able to find a basis for moral action within the indeterminacy of being and of conventional morality.

Heraclitus

Fragment B18 says, "Unless he expects the unexpected, he will not find it, since it is not to be hunted out and is inaccessible [*atropos*]." If it is not to be hunted out and is inaccessible, how can we pursue it? There is no direct path from empirical knowledge to the impartiality of wisdom because, in Heraclitus's metaphor, wisdom is like waking up, and the transition from empirical knowledge to wisdom, like that from sleep to wakefulness, is not merely incremental but abrupt. Heraclitus's pedagogical strategy cannot therefore merely give us information and doctrines, and in that respect it is more like that of Laozi than Confucius.

It must give us a different way of seeing the world. That is one reason for the paradoxical formulations that short-circuit our ordinary ways of thinking. It is also the reason that he says, "Listening not to me but to the logos it is wise to agree that all things are one" (B50). Listening to Heraclitus means looking for truth in words and treating what he says as one teaching among others. Listening to the logos, on the other hand, means trying to understand the truth that his words point to but can never completely embody. "Eyes are more accurate witnesses than ears" (B101a) means more than that sight is our dominant sense. It means that although the words we *hear* can give an indication of wisdom, they can never directly impart it they way they impart information; only experiencing truth with our own (doubly awake) eyes can do that.[68] Thus "The wise is one alone; it is unwilling and willing to be called by the name of Zeus" (B32). As was mentioned earlier, like Laozi's Dao, Heraclitean wisdom is unwilling to be called by any name, even the highest, because it is beyond naming; but as long as that limitation is appreciated we may name it as best we can, since only by words can it be communicated at all. Heraclitus resists dogmatism but also skepticism. Just as the oracle of Apollo "neither speaks nor conceals, but gives a sign" (B93), Heraclitus tries to communicate to us in the only way possible something that cannot adequately be put into words.

In Plato's *Cratylus* Socrates remarks, "Heraclitus says somewhere that everything flows and nothing remains still, and comparing things to the current of a river, he says that you can't step twice into the same river" (402a).[69] Heraclitus does not, however, go as far as Cratylus, who, according to Aristotle, "finally thought that nothing should be spoken but only moved his finger [pointed at things], and who criticized even Heraclitus for saying that one cannot step into the same river twice, for he himself thought that one could not do so even once."[70] If flux and individuality are all there is to the world, then speech, which uses words with fixed meanings and universal application, is always a misrepresentation. In that case, Cratylus believes, we must indicate our meaning not by speaking with our mouth but by pointing with our finger. We can imagine that a disciple of Cratylus, who similarly tried to be more rigorous than his predecessor, might criticize Cratylus for thinking one could even point at anything, since the thing pointed at would already be different by the time he raised his finger. Heraclitus is not blind to Cratylus's observation, but he recognizes that it is only half true: "We step into and we do not step into the same rivers. We are and we are not" (B49a). Heraclitus's paradoxical formulations challenge us to see beyond the words without altogether dispensing with them, much as Laozi said, "Let there always be non-being so we may see their subtlety, and let there always be being so we may see their outcome" (1.5–6).

If Heraclitus cannot give us this wisdom but can only hint at it, what *we* can do is seek it both within ourselves and in our relation to the external world. The first is suggested by his words "I searched myself out" (B101). Since "all things come to be in accordance with this logos" (B1), it is operative in each of us and discoverable within us. It is always with us whether we notice it or not, for "How can one hide from what never sets?" (B16). Thus "It belongs to all people to know themselves and to think rightly" (B116). For Heraclitus the self is a microcosm of reality as a whole, so we can discover within ourselves the nature that also encompasses us, that is, the logos.[71] "The soul has a logos that increases itself" (B115) means that the discovery within ourselves of the principle by which all things are governed is the beginning of wisdom, a beginning that is self-increasing once we become attentive to it. That is why "You would not discover the limits of the soul although you travelled every road: it has so deep a logos" (B45).[72] When Heraclitus said, "Listening not to me but to the logos it is wise to agree that all things are one" (B50), the word he chose for "agree" is *homologein*, which echoes microcosmically the reference to the *logos*.

As with Plato's subsequent doctrine of recollection, what is called for is not simply introspection but also a sensitivity to the way the empirical world points to something beyond itself, something that is accessible through our thinking rather than our senses. In B23 Heraclitus writes, "They would not have known the name of justice if these things did not exist," that is, it would never have occurred to us to conceive of justice if it were not for the kind of social interactions that make us aware of the possibilities of exploitation and redress that imply an underlying sense of rightness. Since we must examine the particulars of reality in order to become aware of what underlies them, to wake up and see what was always here, empirical investigation is indispensable to the attainment of wisdom: "Men who are lovers of wisdom must be inquirers into many things indeed" (B35).

The importance Heraclitus attaches to investigation makes him closer to Aristotle than Plotinus, but his attitude toward learning may not be incompatible with Laozi's pejorative remarks.[73] Heraclitus is under no illusion about how few of the details that such investigations require us to learn will actually be useful in our search for wisdom: "Those who seek gold dig up much earth and find little [gold]" (B22). Consequently, "Much learning does not teach insight [*nóon*]" (B40), and "Eyes and ears are bad witnesses to people if they have barbarian souls" (B107)—that is, if they do not understand the language.[74] It is not the empirical details themselves that are of interest but how they point beyond themselves. In B1 Heraclitus said that "people are like the inexperienced when they experience such words and deeds as I set out, distinguishing each in accordance with its nature [*phusin*] and saying how it is." What is important here is not the words and deeds themselves but the underlying "nature" (*phusis*)—people who regard words and deeds as sufficient in themselves are "like the inexperienced." The *nature* of a thing is a bridge between its uniqueness alongside an infinite number of other unique individuals, and the nature of the whole in which all individuals are united and reconciled. For all his emphasis on flux and uniqueness, Heraclitus has no hesitation in making generalizations about fixed species or natures such as oxen (B4), asses (B9), pigs (B13, B37), birds (B37), dogs (B97), and of course human beings (B78, passim). For Heraclitus, unlike his disciple Cratylus and others, the common natures of things count for more than their uniqueness.[75]

The tension between unique individuals and their common natures plays itself out in Heraclitus's frequent references to the way opposites are united within a common cycle. "The same thing is both living and dead, and the waking and the sleeping, and young and old; for these things transformed are those, and those transformed back again are these" (B88). They are the same because they are poles of single processes: the process of aging, the cycle of life and death,[76] and the cycle of waking and sleep. In other fragments he calls attention to similar circles or cycles of day and night (B57), up and down (B60), cold and hot, and dry and wet (B126). In one place he makes this concept of a

circle explicit and connects it with the idea of the common: "The beginning and the end are common on the circumference of a circle" (B103).
However much things are manifestations of change, they are also manifestations of constant patterns or cycles. These patterns, in turn, are
themselves manifestations of the first principle of all things: "*God* is
day and night, winter and summer, war and peace, satiety and hunger,
but changes the way <fire,> when mingled with perfumes, is named according to the scent of each" (B67).[77] Not only are day and night and
the others the same insofar as they are poles of the same cycles, but
the cycles are themselves manifestations of God. The ultimate nature of
things is in itself the unchanging unity of all oppositions, and it changes
only in its manifestations, just as a river is itself an enduring entity despite its internal flow.

The perfumes in the analogy, which, when mixed with fire, give their
name to it seem to be a metaphor for the moments of time. All finite
things exist at their appropriate time, after which they are replaced by
others.[78] Thus Heraclitus speaks of "the seasonable times [*hōras*] which
bring everything" (B100),[79] and he says, "The sun will not overstep his
measures; otherwise, the Erinyes, ministers of Justice, will find him out"
(B94). Accordingly, when Heraclitus compares God to fire that is named
according to the incense being burned in it, the point is that we name
the unnamable whole according to its present condition (day or night,
winter or summer, war or peace, satiety or hunger). God in itself is unchanging and timeless, but seen at particular times appears as one state
or another. At rest, it is changing.

What B67 said about cycles, B62 says about individuals: "Immortal mortals, mortal immortals, living the death of the others and dying
their life" (B62). Heraclitus's God is immortal because beyond change
and time; but because all things are God, God also coincides with what
is mortal, changing, and temporal. If we think away time all things disappear into God, while if we look at things temporally God disappears
into all things, as in Spinoza's distinction between *natura naturans* (God)
and *natura naturata* (the natural world). Each lives the death of the others and dies their life: "Out of all things comes a unity, and out of a unity
all things" (B10). Thus Heraclitus can say both that "all things are one"
(B50) and also that "that which is wise is set apart from all" (B108). It is

set apart not as an exception to the oneness of all things but as the atemporal oneness of all that is temporal.

While Laozi and Heraclitus are very much alike both philosophically and temperamentally, there are obvious cultural differences. Laozi addresses himself primarily to the ruler and Heraclitus to the citizen, for example, and their use of metaphor and analogy presupposes familiarity with different conventions of behavior. There are also differences in what they focus on (although in the absence of most of Heraclitus's book such judgments are only tentative). Heraclitus, for example, does not mention anything like *wuwei*, although we might expect it to be a feature of the "awakened" state that he refers to; and Laozi does not extol learning as Heraclitus does, although it is clear that Laozi has learned much about life, which may be precisely the kind of learning that Heraclitus has in mind, since Heraclitus also warns against merely intellectual learning (B40).

Whatever their differences in culture and emphasis, their fundamental vision and values are remarkably parallel. For both, language is an unpredictable instrument to provoke us to see things for ourselves, rather than a medium of explicit communication, and in crucial passages both thinkers make rich use of paradox to undermine any temptation we might feel to be satisfied with a literal interpretation of their words. Again, both are at pains to wean us from the egocentric view that interprets events as good or evil depending on their relation to ourselves, or our culture, or even our species, and to urge upon us a holistic perspective from which we see all things as contributing elements within a harmonious unity governed by something like what we understand by the good and the rational, although not in the normal senses of these words—indeed, from our *normal* perspective what is here called good and rational can well appear to be bad and irrational

CHAPTER FIVE

VIRTUE IS KNOWLEDGE

Socrates and Wang Yangming

The previous chapters showed how metaphysics can be a foundation for ethics, as well as how metaphysical thinking can be awakened in the first place. The metaphysical basis of ethics that was implicit in the second chapter became explicit in the third and fourth; however, metaphysics is not the only kind of knowledge that can ground ethics. The present chapter will look at the way a kind of knowledge that is not metaphysical can be not only a foundation for ethical virtue but identical with it.

The identity between moral virtue and knowledge has been challenged ever since Socrates first proposed it, for the equation makes no explicit allowance for *akrasia* or moral weakness, the inability to resist temptation even when we know what we are doing is wrong. If we can do wrong knowingly, then the identity between knowledge and virtue appears to be a naive oversimplification. Socrates's apparent error is often excused on the grounds that a pioneer is bound to miss things that later seem obvious. Wang Yangming, however, who maintained the identity of virtue and knowledge in much the same way as Socrates, came at the end of a two-thousand-year tradition rather than at the beginning,[1] and with the benefit of hindsight he was able to respond to criticisms similar to those aimed against Socrates. The present chapter explores the extent to which Wang's defense of his view vindicates his own claim and whether it would vindicate that of Socrates as well.

There are certain parallels between the lives of Socrates and Wang Yangming, far apart though they were in time and place. Both, for example, were successful soldiers, although Socrates's military career was more modest than Wang's, and both were prosecuted politically for their beliefs. However, these details do not contribute to the issue at hand, the view that knowledge results in virtuous behavior. People have been prosecuted for moral actions as well as immoral ones, and for our purposes it does not matter whether a soldier is more virtuous than a pacifist.

Socrates

The claim that knowledge is virtue—if we know what is good we will do what is good—remains controversial today.[2] In particular it is often maintained that belief and desire are necessarily distinct states of mind. Indeed, there is considerable debate whether knowledge is even necessary for virtue, much less both necessary and sufficient.[3] On the other hand, some support for this view can be found today in cognitive behavioral therapy, founded on the principle that by being fully conscious of our thoughts we can control our unhealthy appetites and behavior.[4]

Plato expresses himself in most dialogues through his literary recreation of Socrates, but little is known about the historical Socrates, who never committed his ideas to writing, and different pictures of him emerge from the accounts of those who knew him. Unlike Wang Yangming's, his conversations were not recorded by his students, so the difficulty of establishing his actual beliefs is daunting enough to have earned the title "The Problem of Socrates," which is dealt with extensively in the scholarship.[5] There is a general consensus on certain points, such as his claiming that virtue is knowledge and that those who know the good will necessarily do the good.[6] For example, in what is generally regarded as a dialogue faithful to the views of the historical Socrates, Plato's Socrates gets Gorgias to agree that "he who has learned what is just is just" (*Gorgias* 460b),[7] and Aristotle writes that Socrates "thought all the virtues to be kinds of knowledge, so that to know justice and to be just came simultaneously" (*Eudemian Ethics* 1.1216b6–7).[8] In chapter 3 there was no need to distinguish the historical Socrates from the "Socrates" of the

Platonic dialogues, but since the doctrine of the unity of knowledge and virtue is usually regarded as Socrates's teaching rather than Plato's (although I believe that Plato accepts a certain form of it) we should try to confine ourselves as far as possible to the beliefs attributed to the historical Socrates for the comparison with Wang Yangming.

Socrates's claim that virtue is knowledge implies that if we behave in an unvirtuous way we must be ignorant of what goodness really is. No allowance is made for the possibility that we may know what is good but act otherwise because we are too weak to resist temptation or fear—in other words that we may lack self-mastery. The claim may not have been quite as paradoxical in ancient Greek as in modern languages because *aretē*, the term we translate as virtue or excellence, was not confined to morality but also included excellence in the crafts.[9] But even artisans do not always apply their knowledge conscientiously, so the difficulty remains. As noted above, this Socratic view of virtue was regarded as naive in his own day. For example, his contemporary, Euripides, is evidently replying to Socrates when he has Phaedra say:

> We know the good, we apprehend it clearly.
> But we can't bring it to achievement. Some
> are betrayed by their own laziness, and others
> value some other pleasure above virtue.[10]

As the *Magna moralia* puts it: "The result is that in making the virtues sciences [Socrates] is doing away with the irrational part of the soul, and is thereby doing away also both with passion and character; so that he has not been successful in this respect in his treatment of the virtues. After this Plato divided the soul into the rational and the irrational part—and in this he was right—assigning appropriate virtues to each."[11] The *Magna moralia* expresses Aristotle's views but may have been written by Peripatos after Aristotle's death. In the undoubtedly authentic *Nicomachean Ethics*, written about eight decades after Euripides's *Phaedra*, Aristotle criticizes Socrates's view as a denial of *akrasia* or incontinence:

> It is problematic how someone with correct understanding can lack self-mastery [*akrateuetai*]. Some say this is not possible for someone who has

knowledge; for it would be strange, as Socrates thought, if when someone possessed knowledge something else should master it and "drag it around like a slave." Socrates in fact used to attack the account altogether, on the grounds that there is no such thing as lack of self-mastery; for no one understands himself to act against what is best, but they do so only through ignorance. Now this account clearly goes against the evidence.[12]

The evidence that Aristotle, like Euripides, has in mind is the experience we have all had of sometimes going against our better judgment because of fears or temptations. Most people agree with Aristotle, and it is hard to see how Socrates could have believed that we never go against our better judgment.[13]

Aristotle's reference to "dragging knowledge around like a slave" is from the *Protagoras* (352c).[14] In that dialogue, when Socrates disputes the view that knowledge can be overcome by pleasure and the like, he does so by analyzing these emotions as instances of mistaken opinion. When we are overcome by pleasure, pleasure means something that is good in a certain way (354b), so we are overcome by a good. But it makes no sense to say that we fail to do what is good because we are overcome by what is good (355c). Rather, it must mean that we mistakenly perceive a lesser good to be better than a greater good (355e). This can happen because immediate gratification exerts a more powerful pull than deferred gratification, just as what is near to us always looks larger than what is further away (356a–c). So what is needed is an art of measurement that enables us to weigh and compare competing goods independently of their proximity to us (356d). Since this is a kind of knowledge, it is clear that virtue depends on knowledge alone (356e–357a, c), and being overcome by pleasure means nothing other than being ignorant (357e).

Similarly Aristotle writes that some people defended moral intellectualism by claiming that although our knowledge always translates into behavior, the same is not true of our opinions, so we may act against our beliefs about goodness but not against our knowledge of goodness: "There are some who agree in one sense but not in another; for they agree that nothing is stronger than knowledge, but they do not agree that no one acts against his *opinion* about what is best; and because of this they say that someone who lacks self-mastery does not have knowledge that is overpowered by pleasures, but only has opinion."[15] This explanation appears at first to be counterintuitive. People may know that alcohol or tobacco is killing them, and not want to die, and yet be unable to break their addiction. It seems question-begging to deny that these people really know that their addiction is killing them and to insist that their acceptance of that fact is only an opinion. Nevertheless, there is a sense in which the people whom Aristotle cites are right to claim that knowledge can be overcome only when it is not knowledge in the fullest sense, and that some things that we normally call knowledge may indeed be more accurately described as only opinions.[16] In the next chapter of the *Nicomachean Ethics* Aristotle defends this view in his own way. In the case of a person who has knowledge but gives way to temptation,

> the last proposition [i.e., "This is what I should do in this situation"] both being an opinion about a perceptible object, and being what determines our actions, this a man either has not when he is in the state of passion, or has it in the sense in which having knowledge did not mean knowing but only talking, as a drunken man may utter the verses of Empedocles. And because the last term is not universal nor equally an object of knowledge with the universal term, *the position that Socrates sought to establish actually seems to result*; for it is not what is thought to be knowledge proper that the passion overcomes (nor is it this that is dragged about as a result of the passion), but perceptual knowledge.[17]

As the *Magna moralia* observed, however, even Plato seems to distance himself from Socrates's intellectualism when he formulates the concept of a tripartite soul. In the *Republic* "Socrates" says:

> Self-control[18] is surely some kind of order, the self-mastery [*enkrateia*] of certain pleasures and appetites, as they say, using the phrase "master of oneself" [*kreittō autou*]—I don't know how—and other such phrases that are like traces that it has left behind. . . . Yet isn't the expression "master of oneself" ridiculous? He who is master of himself would also be subject to himself, and he who is subject master. The same person is referred to in all these statements. . . . But the saying seems to me to want to say that in the same person there is something in the soul that is better and something

that is worse, and when the part that is better by nature is master of the worse, this is what is meant by speaking of being master of oneself. . . . But when, on the other hand, because of bad upbringing or bad company the better part which is smaller is mastered by the multitude of the larger, we blame this as something shameful, and call it being subject to oneself and licentious. (4.430e–431b)

Here it sounds as though there really is something that can overpower knowledge and drag it around like a slave and that not only knowledge is responsible for virtue but also our upbringing and the company we keep. Later in the discussion internal obstacles are added to the external examples of bad upbringing and bad company, and we learn that vice occurs when either the spirited part of us or the appetitive part of us that seeks pleasure and avoids pain and fear dominates the knowledge-loving part. The language implies that Plato is putting forward the very view that Aristotle argues for in opposition to the view of Socrates in the *Protagoras*,[19] but like much in Plato this is an initially simplified view that later becomes more nuanced. Just before the passage quoted above Socrates suggests that there is a preferable way to talk about justice that does not require reference to self-control, like the claim of the *Protagoras*: "How then might we find justice without having to bother any more about self-control?" (430d). This suggestion is strengthened when, after the discussion of self-control, Socrates says that "we will never get an accurate answer using our present methods of argument—although there is another longer and fuller road that does lead to such an answer," and he continues only at Glaucon's urging (435c–d). The longer road does not reach its destination until book 7. There we are told that the highest kind of knowledge is literally a conversion: "The instrument by which everyone understands is like an eye that cannot be turned to light from darkness except together with the whole body. Thus that instrument must be turned [literally, "converted"] from the realm of becoming together with the whole soul until it becomes able to contemplate that which is, and what is brightest of that which is; and we say that this is the good" (518c–d).

To say that the whole soul turns to it together is to say that *akrasia*, lack of self-control, is no longer possible because the emotions are no longer at odds with rationality. These people would "go through any sufferings, rather than share their opinions and live as do" those in the cave who are divided against themselves (516d). This kind of knowledge, at least, fits the Socratic equation of knowledge and goodness. Moreover, Plato would presumably agree with Aristotle's defense of Socrates quoted above (*Nicomachean Ethics* 7.3.1147b6–16), that knowledge does not have to be metaphysical knowledge in order to be infallibly moral as long as knowledge is rigorously distinguished from opinion, that is, as long as it is what Thrasymachus called "knowledge in the strict sense."[20] Neither does knowledge have to be metaphysical to result in what Plato calls "conversion." A conversion experience can also happen in quite down-to-earth ways. In the second half of the eighteenth century John Newton, the captain of a slave trader ship, suddenly saw with such clarity the evil in which he was participating that it was no longer possible for him to continue in it. The clarity of his sudden knowledge, entirely apart from any need for self-control, was sufficient to produce virtue by itself. The hymn that he wrote to commemorate that event, "Amazing Grace," contains the words "I once . . . was blind but now I see." The kind of knowledge that is sufficient for virtue is not the kind that can have teachers, because it is not like information or like craft but like the difference between sight and blindness. If we see clearly how virtue consummates our lives, and how trivial are the rewards of the activities that are counterproductive of virtue, then the latter lose their hold over us.[21]

Guthrie suggests a somewhat different defense. After surveying the reports of Plato, Aristotle, and Xenophon, he concludes that for Socrates "Knowledge, in and by itself, of the nature of virtue was sufficient to make a man virtuous; but there was little chance of his learning the truth of it if he had not subjected his body to the negative discipline of resisting sensual indulgence and his mind of the practice of dialectic, the art of discriminating and defining" (1962–81, 3:457). Guthrie's defense is a kind of complement to Aristotle's: the latter argues that a controlled state of mind is a necessary condition for access to the knowledge we have already attained; the former that a controlled state of mind is necessary for that attainment itself. Other defenses of Socrates's principle have also been suggested.[22]

Subsequent to Socrates's reference in the *Protagoras* to the need for a techne of measurement (356d), another way that the equation of knowledge with virtue has been defended is to construe "knowledge" not as the ability to formulate a definition but as a kind of skill or craft.[23] We always aim at what we perceive to be good, so if we have mastered a skill that enables us to know (1) what really is good in life and also (2) what actions to perform in order to bring about that good, then how can our knowledge not eventuate in virtue? Aristotle's original objection holds against this interpretation as well, however, for to have a skill is not necessarily to use it. What is to prevent me from leaving my skill at justice in abeyance when I prefer to use my skills at making money or at achieving power? Why should we—or Socrates—believe that reason's skillful knowledge of what is good will always and necessarily be stronger than the skillful desires of appetite and spiritedness? I may know (1) that I *ought* to return a wallet that I find and also (2) *how* to do so in the present case, and yet be too weak to resist when my appetite and spiritedness long for the pleasures and power that the money can bring. Advocates of this view sometimes reply that we need only take the identification of virtuous knowledge with skill one step further and say that the skill also includes knowing how to put the dictates of reason into effect despite the pressures of appetite and spiritedness. Thus the knowledge that is virtue would be (1) knowing what really is good, (2) knowing what actions to perform to bring it about, and now (3) knowing how to prevent ourselves from being subverted by temptation. But this would beg the question, because the whole point of Aristotle's criticism is that knowledge alone cannot prevent itself from being overwhelmed by passion and pleasure—in other words, that what is here called the third knowledge is not really knowledge. If we are to find a genuine way out of this problem, we cannot do so simply by building self-control into our definition of knowledge.[24]

The view that virtue is a kind of skill seems to be just what Socrates's exchanges with Cephalus and Polemarchus in the *Republic* aim to refute (I see no reason to doubt that this passage is faithful to the spirit of the historical Socrates). Cephalus and Polemarchus identify justice with particular skills, rules that can be put into practice, such as "Tell the truth and pay what you owe" or "Help your friends and harm your enemies." But Socrates shows that such rules are not capable of being applied with universality, as they ought to be if justice were a skill or craft. He suggests the reason for this in the second refutation of Polemarchus: if justice can be reduced to rules it is a kind of techne (332c–d), but any techne can be used for good or ill, so the most just person would also be the best thief (333e–334a), and justice a craft of stealing as well as holding in trust (334b). The *reductio* shows that justice cannot be a techne,[25] and this prepares us for the analysis in book 4 that defines justice not in terms of rules but in terms of character.

Nevertheless, many scholars believe that Plato continues to regard justice as a craft in the *Republic*.[26] The general lack of agreement on this point is due to the ambiguity of the word *techne*, "craft" or "skill." If we take it in a weak sense, to mean "knowing how to do something," then those who know how to bring order to their souls can be said to practice a craft. But if we take it in a strong sense to mean "a determinate set of teachable rules for doing something"—in accordance with Aristotle's claim that craft entails a knowledge of the universal causes within its field that we can impart by instruction (*Metaphysics* A.1.981a10–981b10)—then there is good reason for denying that justice is a craft. For it may be true that in the weak sense justice is the craft of setting one's soul in order by letting reason rule, but it is not the kind of craft that can supply precise rules for doing so, as a carpenter can provide rules for making a bed. We can tell people to rule themselves by reason, but we cannot tell them *precisely* how to go about doing so. Exhortations like "Pull yourself together!" (that is, "Rule yourself by reason") are not effective. At best, then, virtue is a craft in the weak sense of the word, but the weak sense does not really add anything to what was already implied by calling virtue knowledge in the first place.[27] We would only be replacing one imprecise term with another.

Wang Yangming

Unlike Socrates, Wang Yangming had a genius not for radical innovation but for examining or modifying some of the implications of his predecessors, which led him to work out the implications of idealistic neo-Confucianism in an unprecedentedly radical way. Again unlike Socrates, his later arrival gave him the opportunity to criticize his predecessors' views rather than only being subject to criticism by his successors. Wang's defense of the view that knowledge is virtue is formulated as "the unity of knowledge and action," but this is only a verbal rather than conceptual difference, since Wang clearly believes that actions follow from our character. Again, Wang's defense of his view does not follow the same lines as the defenses of Socrates suggested by Plato, Aristotle, and Guthrie, although it is compatible with all of them. Like Socrates, Wang is considered a moral intellectualist.[28] Wang's view is as controversial in Chinese philosophy as Socrates's is in Western philosophy. In the *Analects* Confucius several times suggests that knowledge is not sufficient for virtue,[29] and we saw in chapter 3 that for Zhu Xi knowledge of the good does not necessarily lead to good action but may be obstructed by an imbalance in our material force. Through the investigation of things we can achieve a knowledge that rebalances the elements of material force, but there is no simple equation between knowledge of the good and performance of the good. Zhu's position has its parallel in Western philosophers who propose ways that the intellect can defend itself from passion, such as Marcus Aurelius, Locke, Leibniz, and Spinoza.[30] Wang, however, goes further than claiming that knowledge can result in virtue *indirectly* by removing the obstructions to virtue. His claim is that moral knowledge *directly* produces moral action as long as one is tranquil—which can be achieved simply by sitting in meditation—or even that "knowledge and action are really two words describing the same, one effort."[31] We can see from Wang's conversations with his students how difficult it was for them to accept this equation.

How then does Wang reply to the problem we have been considering: how to account for people who know and do not doubt that a certain action is wrong but cannot resist when temptation presents itself because what their knowledge tells them is overpowered by their desires? Wang's disciple Hsü Ai raises a similar objection: "There are people who know that parents should be served with filial piety and elder brothers with respect but cannot put these things into practice. This shows that knowledge and action are clearly two different things." And in that case neither would knowledge be virtue. Wang replies: "Those who are supposed to know but do not act simply do not yet know. . . . Therefore the *Great Learning* points to true knowledge and action for people to see, saying, they are 'like loving beautiful colors and hating bad odors.'"[32] Seeing beautiful colors appertains to knowledge, while loving beautiful colors appertains to action. "However, as soon as one sees that beautiful color, he has already loved it. It is not that he sees it first and then makes up his mind to love it" (Wang 1963a, 10, 82).

When Wang says that "those who are supposed to know but do not act, simply do not yet know," he is not merely begging the question, and we saw above that the Socratic version of this principle is supported by a number of modern writers. The example of colors and odors is an effective one, as we saw in chapter 3. If someone says, "The colors of a sunset are very beautiful but I don't particularly care for them," or "Raw sewage has a bad smell but that doesn't mean I don't like it," we would feel that the consequent failed to cohere with the antecedent and even violated the normal meaning of the antecedent. It seems more reasonable to believe that people who do not dislike an odor that they say is bad, or do not like colors that they say are beautiful, are using words imprecisely and do not really think that the odor is bad and the colors beautiful, but only recognize that other people think so. By extension, people who say that they know that stealing is bad but do not hate it enough to be able to resist temptation are speaking imprecisely and do not really know, in the full sense of the word, that stealing is bad. Wang's argument supplies the middle term in the transition from knowledge to virtue: to fully know that something is good is to love it. Love motivates us to act. Therefore to fully know what is good is to be virtuous. With this in mind we can more fully appreciate the *Protagoras* passage cited above: "They think about knowledge absolutely the same thing that they think about a slave, that it is dragged around by everything else. Now then, is this the way the matter seems to you as well, or rather that knowledge is noble and capable of ruling a person, and if someone knows what is good and what is bad, that person will not be overpowered by anything so as to do anything other than what knowledge demands—but rather wisdom is a sufficient support for a person?" (352c). Socrates must mean knowledge in Wang Yangming's sense, complete knowledge that includes the full appreciation of the thing's value.[33] *This* knowledge, Socrates is saying, will be strong enough to resist the temptations of pleasure and power—appetite and spiritedness.

The distinction between knowledge and opinion that Aristotle made with reference to Socrates applies as well to the following words, in which Wang's phrase "talking about it in a vacuum" is clearly a reference to opinion: "No one really learns anything without carrying it into action. . . . Can merely talking about it in a vacuum be considered as learning?" (1963b, 100, §136). "Suppose we say that so-and-so knows filial piety and so-and-so knows brotherly respect. They must have actually practiced filial piety and brotherly respect before they can be said to know them. . . . Or take one's knowledge of pain. Only after one has experienced pain can one know pain" (1963b, 10, §5). Thus only by performing virtuous activities can we really know virtue. This is a claim that Plato maintains as well. In the *Republic* Socrates points out that the appetitive lover of profit, the spirited lover of honors, and the philosophical lover of truth would all say their own life is best, and he asks,

> Of the three men, who is most experienced in all the pleasures we mentioned? Does a lover of profit learn what truth itself is, and seem to you to be more experienced in the pleasure of knowledge than a philosopher is in that of making a profit?
>
> They differ greatly [replies Glaucon]. The one has necessarily tasted the pleasures of the other two since the beginning of childhood, but it is not necessary for the lover of profit to taste or experience the nature of learning, how sweet the pleasure of it is. Moreover even if he is eager for it it will not be easy for him.
>
> Then a philosopher differs greatly from a lover of profit in his experience of both pleasures. . . . How does he differ from a lover of honor? Is he more inexperienced in the pleasure of honor than the other is in the pleasure of thinking?
>
> No, for if they accomplish their respective aims honor follows upon all of them . . . but the pleasure of contemplating what is cannot be tasted by anyone except a philosopher. (582a–c)

For Socrates (if we can ascribe these sentiments to him), as for Wang, we know something only to the extent that we have experienced it and have been able to taste its pleasure.[34] Knowledge is virtue, then, not when it is only abstract and conceptual, or even when it is the know-how of a skill, but only when it is complete knowledge by acquaintance, the full experiencing of a certain condition.[35] To say that virtue is knowledge would then mean that once we know from experience what it is like to be virtuous our convictions will become too firmly established to be dragged around slavishly by our appetites and passions. Such an interpretation would resolve the paradox in the *Meno*, that virtue is knowledge but there are no teachers of it (89d–96b). Experience is not only the best teacher of virtue but the only one.

Achieving Knowledge

More famous than this paradox in the *Meno*—knowledge without teachers—is the earlier one called "Meno's Paradox": "In what way will you look, Socrates, for a thing [i.e., virtue] of whose nature you know nothing at all? What sort of thing, of the things you don't know, will you propose to search for? Or even if, at the most, you chance upon it, how will you know this is the thing you did not know?" (*Meno* 80d). If virtue is knowledge, and all we have at the beginning is opinion, how do we know which of our fallible and competing opinions to follow in order to achieve the validating experience? There is an apparent circularity that we must know which opinion is the right one in order to pursue the experience that confirms that it was the right opinion. Socrates's reply to Meno takes the form of eliciting from Meno's uneducated slave the demonstration of a geometrical principle, and by analogy with this demonstration we can also see the resolution of the apparent circularity with respect to virtue and knowledge. What Socrates needs to show is that it is possible to search for and arrive at virtue or anything else because we already have an implicit knowledge of these things, like recollecting a dormant memory.[36] Our own investigation here of the nature of virtue could not have been carried out unless we were guided by our latent intuitions, however imprecisely they make themselves known to us. The geometrical demonstration in the *Meno* offers mathematical learning as a paradigm of this, for in the case of mathematics we do not accept claims on the authority of others—as we do with historical knowledge, for example—since we can test them against some kind of internal intuition. We may not have been able to formulate the principle that a straight line is the shortest distance between two points, but once having heard it we can verify it from our own internal perceptions. In a similar manner, by a carefully chosen series of questions, Socrates leads the slave to see that we can produce a square that is double the area of a given square by using the diagonal of the original square as the side of the new one. Socrates concludes:

> In someone who does not know certain things, whatever they may be, can't there be true opinions about the things he does not know? And now those opinions have just been stirred up in him, like a dream; but if someone asks him the same things many times and in many ways, you know that he will finally have knowledge of them that is no less exact than anyone's. Without anyone having taught him, and only through having had questions put to him, he will have knowledge, recovering the knowledge out of himself by himself. And is not this recovery of knowledge, by himself and in himself, recollection? (85c–d, abridged)

The steps involved are: (1) the right answers are suggested to the slave; (2) the slave recognizes by his own intuitive resources that the answers are correct, though this is only a true opinion, since he has not mastered them sufficiently to reproduce the proof himself; (3) "If someone asks him the same things many times and in many ways he will finally have knowledge of them that is no less exact than anyone's."

This model of mathematical learning was introduced by Socrates to illustrate how we can achieve the knowledge that is virtue without having had that knowledge ahead of time. As with Meno's slave, we begin not with knowledge but with opinions legitimated by intuition;[37] true opinion combined with experience paves the way for full knowledge. Corresponding to the above sequence in the slave's learning of geometry—opinion, intuition, knowledge through repeated experience—the following sequence applies to our learning of virtue: (1) ideas about virtue are communicated to us throughout our lives; (2) we recognize intuitively that certain of them are correct, but this is only an opinion at first; (3) if we repeatedly put our true opinions about virtue into practice, in the end we will have full knowledge of their truth. In that way we can say that virtue is knowledge.

Practicing the right behavior does not make us virtuous if we do not have the appropriate inner intuition, however, any more than true opinion alone makes us knowledgeable. This inner intuition, which Plato calls recollection, has its Confucian parallel in Mencius's doctrine of finding the lost mind: "Humanity is man's mind and righteousness is man's path. Pity the man who abandons the path and does not follow it, and who has lost his heart and does not know how to recover it. When people's dogs and fowls are lost, they go to look for them, and yet, when they have lost their hearts, they do not go to look for them. The way of learning is none other than finding the lost mind" (6A.11).[38] This has been an influential doctrine in the history of Confucian philosophy, and Wang Yangming alludes to it in a number of places and emphasizes Mencius's doctrine of *liang chih* or "innate knowledge of the good."[39] The inborn nature of our implicit knowledge of virtue (following Mencius's claim that "humanity is man's mind") is evident when Wang says, in a passage previously quoted in a footnote to chapter 4:

That the great man can regard Heaven, Earth, and the myriad things as one body is not because he deliberately wants to do so, but because it is natural to the *humane nature of his mind* that he do so. Forming one body with Heaven, Earth, and the myriad things is not only true of the great man. Even the mind of the small man is no different. Only he himself makes it small. Therefore when he sees a child about to fall into a well, he cannot help a feeling of alarm and commiseration. This shows that his humanity [*jen*] forms one body with the child. It may be objected that the child belongs to the same species. Again, when he observes the pitiful cries and frightened appearance of birds and animals about to be slaughtered, he cannot help feeling an "inability to bear" their suffering. This shows that his humanity forms one body with birds and animals. It may be objected that birds and animals are sentient beings as he is. But when he sees plants broken and destroyed, he cannot help a feeling of pity. This shows that his humanity forms one body with plants. It may be said that plants are living things as he is. Yet even when he sees tiles and stones shattered and crushed, he cannot help a feeling of regret. This shows that his humanity forms one body with tiles and stones. This means that even the mind of the small man necessarily has the humanity that forms one body with all.[40]

The words "The mind of the small man is no different. Only he himself makes it small" express the same idea that Mencius calls "the lost mind."

We should think of this kind of innate knowledge not as directed toward isolated propositions but as expressive of the unity of thinking with being as a whole. Socrates says that since "all nature is akin," once we have recollected one thing we are led to the discovery of all (*Meno* 81c–d). Similarly, Wang says that "the knowledge of a part is the same as the knowledge of the whole, and the knowledge of the whole is the same as the knowledge of a part. All is but one original substance."[41]

The justifications for equating knowledge with virtue that we looked at in the above discussion can be reduced to three general claims: (1) If what we call knowledge does not result in virtuous action, then it is not fully knowledge but only opinion. (2) Moral knowledge cannot simply be abstract knowledge but must be a kind of knowledge by acquaintance, one that we must practice in order to know. (3) To truly know the good is to love the good with a love that leaves no room for *akrasia*, weakness of will.

(1) Although Socrates never states this principle explicitly, Aristotle echoes Plato's interpretation that what is at stake is the difference between knowledge and opinion (e.g., *Nicomachean Ethics* 7.2.1145b31–35). Wang makes the same distinction when he says, "Those who are supposed to know but do not act simply do not yet know. . . . Can merely talking about it in a vacuum be considered as learning?" (1963b, 100, §136).

(2) Wang said, "No one really learns anything without carrying it into action. . . . They must have actually practiced filial piety and brotherly respect before they can be said to know them. . . . Or take one's knowledge of pain. Only after one has experienced pain can one know pain" (1963b, 100, §136, and 10, §5). Plato interprets Socrates in this way when his Socrates says that only someone who has experienced all three kinds of lives—appetitive, spirited, and rational—knows which of them is best (*Republic* 582a–c). Socrates's words in the *Meno* pointed in this direction as well: "If someone asked him the same things many times and in many ways, you know that he will finally have knowledge of them that is no less exact than anyone's" (85c–d). Socrates is talking about a mathematical principle, but in order to make a point about knowledge of virtue, and the point here is that the slave will not have actual

knowledge until he actually experiences this truth instead of only having it pointed out to him.

(3) Wang followed *The Great Learning* in maintaining that true knowledge is "like loving beautiful colors and hating bad odors" (1963b, §5, cf. §125). In other words, to truly know something is to know its value and to love it or hate it accordingly with emotions strong enough to preclude any temptation to act against that knowledge. This is evidently what Socrates means when he says that "if someone knows what is good and what is bad, that person will not be overpowered by anything so as to do anything other than what knowledge demands" (*Protagoras* 352c, cf. *Republic* 582a–c).

These beliefs had practical consequences for both authors. To minimize the possibility that their students would have opinions rather than knowledge—only words about the subject and not the direct acquaintance of experience—both were reluctant to have their conversations preserved in writing. Plato explains this by having Socrates say: "Written words seem to talk to you as though they were intelligent, but if you ask them anything about what they say, from a desire to be instructed, they go on telling you just the same thing forever. . . . The dialectician selects a soul of the right type, and in it he plants and sows his words founded on knowledge, words which instead of remaining barren contain a seed whence new words grow up."[42] Wang Yangming's conversations, unlike those of Socrates, were preserved, but David Nivison suggests that "for Wang's reluctance to have his ideas committed to a fixed written text" the reader should consult his *Instructions for Practical Living* (Wang 1963b, 271), on the subject of his written commentary on *The Great Learning* and should also consult Hsü Ai's (1965, 1:7) preface to *The Complete Works of Wang Yangming*. In that preface, says Nivison, "Wang is represented as objecting to his disciple recording conversations with himself on the ground that what he said to a student was always adapted to that student's needs at the time he asked his questions. (Did this mean, Hsü asked himself, that Wang's *Instructions* should not be printed? Hsü rejects this suggestion on the ground that Wang's objections must themselves be regarded as teachings to suit a particular occasion)."[43]

On the issue of virtue and knowledge, at least, Socrates and Wang seem closer than do any of the figures compared in the other chapters.

Not only do they agree about the equivalence of virtue and knowledge, but each of them could accept the reasons advanced by—or in the case of Socrates attributed to—the other. Here, as much as anywhere else in this book, cultural differences appear to play little or no role in the ideas expressed, and if so in this case, it is an argument for those who believe that in cases where formulations are more obviously influenced by culture, the ideas expressed may nevertheless be the same.

THE ETHICAL MEAN

Confucius and Plato

In the previous chapter we saw how knowledge can be identical with virtue. The philosophers to be examined in what follows show the nature of the understanding engendered by that knowledge, namely the ability to discern the ethical mean. Although the philosophers considered here are not the ones considered in the preceding chapter, they are within the same traditions: Plato is a Socratic, and Confucius is the founder of the tradition that becomes neo-Confucianism and includes Wang Yangming.

Confucius and Plato are both concerned with the function and means of identifying the mean between moral deficiency and excess, but the two philosophers approach matters in an almost diametrically opposite way. Confucius applies the golden rule and asks, "What would be the right action taken toward me from the point of view of my self-interest?," then takes that action toward someone else. Plato, by contrast, asks, "What would be the right action from the standpoint of techne (craft or skill) toward its object, rather than from the standpoint of my self-interest?" The results, however, coincide, since in both cases the model consulted gives us a practical way to recognize when the principle of goodness is successfully applied in practice and the mean is achieved.

There is no clear evidence that the doctrine of the mean was formulated as such by Socrates rather than Plato, but he seems to have accepted some form of it insofar as his practices accorded with the Delphic motto, "Nothing to excess." In the previous chapter when we compared Socrates and Wang Yangming it was useful to try as far as possible to distinguish the historical Socrates from the Platonic "Socrates," but with regard to the theme of the present chapter I shall follow the conventions of identifying "Confucius" with the Confucius of the *Analects* (and the related convention of taking *The Great Learning* and *The Doctrine of the Mean* to be "Confucian"), and "Socrates" with the Socrates of the Platonic dialogues, rather than with actual but unknowable historical personages. Accordingly, when I refer to "Plato" in the title of this chapter it is a Plato who includes the Socrates of his dialogues rather than being contrasted with him historically.

Confucius and Socrates

In several ways Confucius and Socrates have much in common. Both founded the dominant intellectual traditions of their culture, both achieved their influence by teaching rather than writing, both thought the key to virtue was knowledge, both attempted to put their ideas into practice by entering political life, and both were unsuccessful because of their inability to overcome corruption within their societies. But these resemblances are merely formal, and when we turn to the content of their thought, at first glance Confucius and Socrates seem to represent opposite extremes. One was a proponent of rigorous social conventions to be obeyed without question for whom propriety and loyalty were cardinal virtues. The other was an iconoclast who devoted his life to confronting conventional values and unexamined obedience, challenging them with natural value and independence of mind, for whom courage was a cardinal virtue and loyalty was not, and who was condemned to death for his disrespect of tradition. Confucius, however, was living in a feudal monarchy and Socrates in an obstreperous democracy. Here again we see the influence of culture on thinking, but many if not all of the differences may be regarded as reflecting a difference of emphasis rather than a difference of values. Confucius may not have been a gadfly in Socrates's sense (*Apology* 30a), but for all his espousal of learning traditions rather than challenging them, his disciples were told by an official that "Heaven shall use the master as a wooden bell" (*Analects* 3.24), a metaphor not unlike that of the gadfly, since the function of such a bell was to rouse or awaken the people.[1] And for all his insistence on the conventions of propriety, he said, "If a man is not humane, what has he to do with propriety?" (3.3). On the other side Socrates, for all his iconoclasm and defiance, argues strenuously in the *Crito*, *Republic*, and *Laws* in favor of respecting and obeying the law.

It is hardly surprising that Confucius and Socrates cannot really represent opposite extremes, because each of them saw goodness as a mean,[2] rather than as something to be achieved by extreme measures. Both saw the mean as the key to successful government. Speaking of the two legendary sage-kings that he took as a model, Confucius relates that Yao told Shun, "Faithfully adhere to the mean and thy rule shall extend to the Four Seas' ends; heaven's blessings shall last throughout thy reign" (20.1). And in Plato's *Laws* the Athenian says,

> If one gives a greater degree of power to what is lesser, neglecting the mean . . . then everything is upset. . . . There does not exist, my friends, a mortal soul whose nature will ever be able to wield the greatest human ruling power when young and irresponsible, without becoming filled in its mind with the greatest disease, unreason, which makes it become hated by its closest friends. When this comes about it quickly destroys it and obliterates all its power. Guarding against this, then, by knowing the mean, is the task of great lawgivers.[3]

Socrates's conception of goodness as a mean, as distinct from that of the Eleatic visitor in the *Statesman* and the Athenian visitor in the *Laws*, is not as explicit as that of Confucius, but it is very much in evidence nevertheless. In the *Apology* and other dialogues Socrates speaks of his "divine sign," which "always turns me away from what I was about to do but never urges me forward."[4] He is guided not by positive precepts but by an awareness that to do otherwise is to go either too far or not far enough, and that is in principle the doctrine of the mean. In the *Protagoras* Socrates points out that with courageous people their boldness and fears are not disgraceful, whereas the fears of the cowardly and the boldness of the foolhardy are disgraceful because cowardly people fear too many things—not only things that they ought to fear—while the foolhardy fear too few—not even things that they ought to fear (359b–360d). So here, as later in Aristotle, courage emerges as a mean between the excessive fear of cowardice and the excessive boldness of foolhardiness. And since for Socrates throughout that dialogue all the virtues are essentially the same, they must each be a mean, even if Plato had not yet formulated the term itself.

At the beginning of the *Theaetetus-Sophist-Statesman* trilogy, Theodorus tells Socrates of his surprise at the exceptional balance of Theaetetus's character: "I would not have supposed it to exist, nor do I see it elsewhere. Rather, those who are as sharp as he is, and quick and with retentive memories, are also for the most part quick tempered, . . . manic rather than courageous. Those on the other hand who are more sedate are also somewhat sluggish when they come up against their studies, and are forgetful" (144a–b). At the end of the trilogy the statesman's task will be to produce this rare combination in the citizens generally. Normally, the Eleatic visitor says, those who tend toward moderation and those who tend toward courage have opposed natures (306a–311b). The moderate type "lacks drive and a certain sharp and active quickness" and may even be simple-minded, while the courageous type "is lacking in justice and caution" and "inclines towards brutality" (311a–b). The statesman's job will be to weave these two natures together to remove their initial incompatibility by giving them "a really true and firm opinion about the beautiful, just, good, and their opposites" (309c).

There is a comparable passage in the *Analects*:

Zilu asked: "Should I practice something as soon as I hear it?"
The Master said: "How can you practice something as soon as you hear it when your father and eldest brother are alive [and must be consulted]?"
Ran You asked: "Should I practice something as soon as I hear it?"
The Master said: "Yes, practice it as soon as you hear it."
Gongxi Hua said: "When You [Zilu] asked: 'Should I practice something as soon as I hear it?' Master said: 'Your father and eldest brother are alive.' But when Qiu [Ran You] asked: 'Should I practice something as soon as I hear it?' Master said: 'Yes, practice it as soon as you hear it.' I am puzzled. May I venture to ask why?"

The Master said: "Qui tends to hold back; therefore, I urged him on. You has the courage of two men; therefore, I held him back."[5]

Both thinkers recognize the existence of natures that are related to each other not only as extremes but as polar opposites, so that they must lead the two in opposite directions in order to arrive at a correctness of temperament. At the same time, there appears to be a crucial difference between Confucius's strategy and Plato's: whereas Plato has the statesman bring the one-sided personalities closer to the mean by giving them "a really true and firm opinion about the beautiful, just, good, and their opposites," Confucius does so by giving them conflicting one-sided opinions about the just and good. This appearance of disagreement is misleading, however, for Confucius is forever trying to teach his students the nature of the just and the good, and would no doubt have preferred Zilu and Ran You to have achieved the internal wisdom to recognize and embrace the mean on their own. Only because of their failure to do so did Confucius adjust his advice to each of their mentalities so as to bring about the mean in their actions. Similarly, although Socrates, like the Eleatic visitor's statesman, always tried to teach his students the nature of the just and the good, he understood that a teacher could never ensure the success of that endeavor. As he says in the *Protagoras*—in the presence of two of his most notable failures, Alcibiades and Critias—he does not believe that virtue is teachable, at least not completely so.[6]

When it comes to dealing with people who have not attained virtue, Socrates is just as willing to speak differently to different people as Confucius is. In the *Phaedrus* Socrates remarks that the techne of rhetoric involves "classifying the kinds of speech and soul, and the way the kinds of soul are affected, going through all the reasons, matching the kinds of speech to the kinds of soul, and teaching which kind of souls, by which kind of speeches, by causal necessity, will in one case be convinced and in another case unconvinced" (271b). The dialogues give ample evidence of Socrates's practice of this techne—tailoring his words to the character of his partner in dialogue—although to a different end than that of the rhetoricians. Rhetoricians appeal to their audience's preconceptions to persuade them of something regardless of its truth, while Socrates regards the preconceptions as obstacles to be overcome in order to gain acceptance for the truth. The reduction of his listener to a state of aporia or helplessness is one example of this and has no parallel in Confucius, but another example very much resembles the story just cited of Zilu and Ran You in *Analects* 11.20. If Gongxi Hua had read the *Apology* and *Crito* he might have asked Socrates, "At your trial when you spoke to the Athenians about one's duty to the law if the law was unjust, you said that one need not obey the law. In jail when you spoke to Crito about one's duty to the law if the law was unjust, you said that one must obey the law. I am puzzled. May I venture to ask why?" Certainly many others have been perplexed by this, if not Gongxi Hua. Numerous attempts have been made to show that the contradiction is only apparent,[7] but there is certainly an appearance of contradiction, and the most likely explanation for it is that in the *Apology* Socrates is speaking to an audience that is too conservative in its attitude toward law and traditions, so he contrasts his own position with the extreme of obedience, while in the *Crito* his audience shows too little respect for the law, so he contrasts his own position with the opposite extreme of self-indulgence.

The Mean

We know that something is an excess or deficiency because it either exceeds or falls short of the mean. We know that something is at the mean because it is neither excessive nor deficient. In the face of this circularity, which can never be completely overcome, why should we embrace the conception of virtue as a mean when conceptions of virtue as an extreme can be specified with precision?

One such conception is the puritanical or ascetic understanding of virtue. It begins from the fact that our natural inclination is to pursue pleasure and avoid pain. But the pursuit of pleasure is selfish insofar as it puts us into competition with others and is self-defeating insofar as it inevitably leads also to pain (as the hedonistic Epicureans were keenly aware). Giving in to those inclinations results in vice, and consequently opposing them by an effort of will results in virtue. Accordingly, the greater the resistance to and avoidance of pleasure, the greater the virtue. On that view what would normally be a reasonable enjoyment of pleasure becomes a corrupt and decadent self-indulgence, and a prudent avoidance of pain may be seen as a lazy and cowardly self-indulgence. In opposition to this way of thinking, the concept of virtue as a mean proposes a model on which virtue is seen as moderation, and fanaticism can be seen to be a vice, not the epitome of virtue. The concept of virtue as a mean is more in tune with our intuitions.

Another example of a conception of virtue that offers a precise formulation rather than a vague circularity is Utilitarianism, whether the modern Bentham-Mill model or its ancient counterparts in philosophers like Mozi and Protagoras. Utilitarians can define with apparent precision what they mean by the good, which is usually some form of material well-being, and would determine deficiency as the failure to achieve as much goodness as possible. Since the good is conceived as something like the greatest good for the greatest number, there can be no such thing as excess. Here again, however, the very attempt to achieve precision threatens to turn morality into something one-dimensional and therefore contrary to our intuitions. Mozi's Utilitarianism leads in the direction of puritanism, not because pleasure is an evil, as with ascetic puritans, but because arts and culture seem to have little to contribute to material well-being. Similarly English Utilitarianism has had to defend itself against the fear that it leads to an "end justifies the means" mentality in which the well-being of people who represent minorities must be sacrificed, counterintuitively, for the well-being of those in the majority.

In the *Statesman* the Eleatic visitor says, "A law would never be able, by comprehending accurately what is best and most just for everyone at once, to enjoin what is best. For the dissimilarities among human beings and actions, and the fact that nothing is ever, so to speak, at rest in human affairs, do not allow any art to declare a simple rule in any case regarding all people and for all time" (294b). For the same reason, any ethical doctrine that claims to be able to identify the right course of action with the precision of a law will be no more successful than were Cephalus and Polemarchus at the beginning of the *Republic*. Instead of precision, what the concept of the mean offers is a sensitivity to nuance and subtlety. The value of the concept of the mean is that it accords more with our intuitions about what kinds of things really are good. It does not dismiss those intuitions either as unpurified apparitions of our natural hedonism or as symptoms of a sentimentality undisciplined by rational calculus. Its lack of precision is exculpated by its implicit denial that precision in such matters is possible. No inflexible formulation can capture the fluid and infinitely variable nature of events and circumstances. We know that something is good, not positively, because we can compare it with a pregiven definition of the good, but only privatively, because within the context of the present situation it seems improper either to do less or to do more.

Nevertheless, if all that the doctrine of the mean can offer us is our own intuitions, mutually supporting each other by circular arguments, its content not only is vague but disintegrates into the relativism of individual perceptions. We do not need moral teachers like Confucius and Socrates to tell us what our intuitions are: no one knows that better than we do ourselves. Accordingly, those who propound the conception of goodness as a mean must offer us something against which to measure our intuitions, some way to perceive more clearly what the mean truly is, or what is truly a departure from the mean. Confucian learning and Socratic education can contribute to our moral abilities by expanding our knowledge and sharpening our critical faculties so that we become more aware of what strategies are most likely to achieve our goals. But if our goals are determined in accordance with our intuitions, these will be left untouched unless our teachers can also give us a way to increase our intuitive powers. This is the function of the Confucian golden rule and of the Socratic conception of virtue in terms of techne.

Confucius

The golden rule appears repeatedly in Confucian literature, stated in both positive and negative forms. Positively, for example, "A man of humanity is one who, wishing to establish himself, helps others to establish themselves and who, wishing to gain perception, helps others to gain perception" (6.30). An example of the negative form occurs when Zigong asks, "Is there one single word that one can practice throughout one's life?" and Confucius replies, "It is perhaps *shu*, like-hearted considerateness. What you do not wish for yourself do not impose on others."[8]

Confucius may not have been the first to formulate the golden rule, but its importance for him can hardly be overestimated if he considers it to be an encapsulation of morality in general, a "single word that one can practice throughout one's life." In this he is followed by *The Great Learning*, which says of the golden rule:

> The ruler has a principle with which, as with a measuring square, he may regulate his conduct. What a man dislikes in his superiors, let him not show it in dealing with his inferiors; what he dislikes in those in front of him, let him not show it in preceding those who are behind; what he dislikes in those behind him, let him not show it in following those in front of him; what he dislikes in those on the right, let him not apply it to those on the left; what he dislikes in those on the left, let him not apply it to those on the right. This is the principle of the measuring square.[9]

The image of the golden rule as a measuring square implies a connection between the golden rule and the mean, since the mean refers to the correct degree of measure, which is what a measuring square would determine. How can the golden rule lead to a conception of goodness as a mean? The golden rule directs us toward certain actions and away from others, but it employs a two-valued model rather than a three-valued one. It sees actions simply as right or wrong, not as either deficient, correct, or excessive. The explanation lies in the fact that the golden rule is designed as a check on our selfish impulses. In opposing them it presupposes them, and the two together result in a model of right action that is flanked by two opposed possibilities of error. The golden rule works on the assumption that we want good things for ourselves and therefore when we apply the rule we will do good to others. But once we seek to apply the rule there is the danger of complete self-sacrifice. Perhaps I would like it if my superiors resigned their jobs to make way for my promotion. Perhaps I would like it if everyone I knew gave me all their possessions except what they would need in order not to have to borrow from me. According to the golden rule, taken in the abstract, I might feel that it was morally incumbent on me to resign my job and give away my possessions. What prevents the golden rule from deteriorating into that kind of extremism is the understanding that our basic self-interest can be taken for granted and relied upon to protect us from such excesses. Our native self-interest pushes us toward an extreme of selfishness and exploitation of others. The purpose of the golden rule is to teach us empathy with our potential victims so that we do not treat them worse than ourselves. It does not explicitly tell us not to treat them better than ourselves only because that much is understood: not only should we treat others the way we ourselves would like to be treated, but we should also treat ourselves the way we would like to be treated. This self-evident point provides the transition from the golden rule's two-valued model to the doctrine of the mean's three-valued model. The golden rule warns us away from excessively selfish behavior, but it takes for granted that our native self-interest will warn us away from behavior that is not self-interested enough.

Since the golden rule must be employed in the context of a certain level of self-interest and other variables that cannot be precisely specified, such as those that attend to the uniqueness of every set of circumstances, it cannot be applied mechanically like the rules for employing an actual measuring square. People frequently act with good intentions and yet unwisely. They fail to make allowances for the differences between themselves and others, and so apply the principle too literally and inflexibly. If talented musicians believe that their parents should have forced them to practice, and they apply this to their children whose talents and interests may be very different, they may be doing their children not good but harm. It is no easy matter to decide when it is appropriate to employ the principle and when it is not. Or even if we apply the principle in the right kinds of situations, and to people who are similar to ourselves in the relevant ways, our self-knowledge may be deficient or compromised by self-deception, so that we are mistaken about the way we would really like to be treated, and once again we would behave improperly. The effectiveness with which the golden rule is employed depends on the person who is employing it, and the difficulty of its application does not escape Confucius. When Zigong says, "What I do not wish others to impose on me, I also do not wish to impose on others," Confucius replies, "Ci, this is beyond your reach" (5.12).

The Great Learning proposes a sequence of steps by which the kind of character and state of mind may be achieved that are necessary to the proper application of the golden rule:

When things are investigated, knowledge is extended; when knowledge is extended, the will becomes sincere; when the will is sincere, the mind is rectified; when the mind is rectified, the personal life is cultivated; when the personal life is cultivated, the family will be regulated; when the family is regulated, the state will be in order; and when the state is in order, there will be peace throughout the world. From the Son of Heaven down to the common people, all must regard cultivation of the personal life as the root or foundation. (86–87)

The actual reference to the golden mean (quoted earlier) is in the context of the final inference—"Peace of the world depends on the order of the state"—but since "cultivation of the personal life [is] the root or foundation," this cultivation must describe the proper character and state of mind in which the golden rule can be employed effectively. Cultivation of the personal life is necessary for the regulation of the family because our impartiality would be compromised by feelings of love, hate, fear, reverence, pity, and disrespect. Therefore, unless we can overcome these prejudices we will not be able to regulate our family (chap. 8, p. 90). Cultivation of our personal life is achieved by rectification of the mind because the mind will be correct only if it is not affected by wrath, fear, fondness, or anxiety (chap. 7, p. 90). It follows that if we can make our minds correct, our judgment will not be affected by passions and will not be compromised by prejudice. How then can we can make our minds correct in the face of the importunities of our passions?

At this point the Confucian and Socratic positions are very close, because the answer of *The Great Learning* lies in terms of self-knowledge, the extension of knowledge, and the investigation of things, just as in Socratic philosophy virtue is knowledge, and especially self-knowledge. If *The Great Learning* originally contained explanations of "the extension of knowledge" and "the investigation of things," they are now lost. All that remains is the explanation of "making the will sincere," which leads to rectification of the mind. The passage that Wang Yangming cited in the previous chapter says: "What is meant by 'making the will sincere' is allowing no self-deception, as when we hate a bad smell or love a beautiful color. This is called satisfying oneself. Therefore the superior man will always be watchful over himself when alone. When the inferior man is alone and leisurely, there is no limit to which he does not go in his evil deeds. Only when he sees a superior man does he then try to disguise himself, concealing the evil and showing off the good in him."[10] As we saw, the examples of the bad smell and beautiful color are chosen because they are especially resistant to self-deception. If something smells repulsive it is virtually impossible to convince ourselves that we really like the smell, just as if we find colors beautiful it is virtually impossible to convince ourselves that we do not really like them. But if the issue is self-deception, what is the relevance of the inferior man's attempt to disguise himself before the superior man but not when he is alone? There it seems that the issue is not self-deception but the deception of others. The connection is that self-deception arises because of our concern for how we are perceived by others. In attempting to appear a certain way we may begin to believe that we really are that way, and if we come to believe it we have fallen into self-deception. Since the golden rule cannot operate if we do not know what we ourselves would like and what we would not like, self-deception must be eliminated. We may wish to be treated well by others, but if we have put on a false humility to impress others, and to impress our own self-regard, we may fail to treat others well because we have deceived ourselves into thinking that we ourselves do not wish to be treated that way.

Suppose, however, that we are honest with ourselves and know that what we want is riches and power. In that case we might refuse to apply the golden rule at all. But from what has been said so far can we not still be said to have attained sincerity of the will, since we are not guilty of self-deception? If we look at the examples in that context, an additional element becomes clear. The examples that the passage gives of not deceiving ourselves are not simply "when we hate a certain smell or love a certain color," but rather when we hate a "bad" smell or love a "beautiful" color." It is not sufficient not to be deceived about what we love or hate; we also have to love what deserves to be loved and hate what deserves to be hated.[11] If people genuinely hated the color of a sunset or loved the smell of sewage, there would be something faulty in their perceptual faculties or their power of judgment. In the same way, if people love money and power more than they love their fellow human beings, and more than they love the virtue of humanity or humaneness, then something is wrong with their intellectual perceptions or their judgment. They are ignorant or confused. Socrates too, and even Epicurus, argued that if those who pursue corporeal pleasure or political power as the good truly understood the price that they pay for their pursuits, they could not have continued in their pursuit. Here as well, sincerity of the will is not only authenticity or honesty about our emotions but also a matter of seeing things as they really are and for what they are really worth. That is why the key to sincerity is not merely honesty but the extension of knowledge. For *The Great Learning*, as for Socrates, virtue is knowledge.

The way to extend our knowledge, the text tells us, is by the investigation of things. Does this refer to investigating the nature of all things, or only of the things that pertain to the self and the will? The former alternative is advanced by Zhu Xi and corresponds to the Plato of the *Timaeus*, who believed that in order to understand the presence of the good in the cosmos—and therefore contribute to our own goodness—we must understand the nature of things in detail. The latter alternative is advocated by Wang Yangming and corresponds to the Socrates of the *Phaedrus*, who has no interest in investigating things that are not directly relevant to his self-understanding (229e–230a).[12] Regardless of whether we interpret "the investigation of things" in the broadest sense or only in the sense of moral matters, what is important is that the foundation of sincerity—the root of the golden rule—lies in knowledge as well as candor. We must make every effort to achieve not only self-understanding but also understanding of what is good and bad. These two, knowledge and candor, are the key to our ability to effectively employ the golden rule and, using it as a measuring square, to discern the mean in concrete situations.

When we turn to the last of the Confucian texts under discussion, *The Doctrine of the Mean*, we find that although the tone is often more poetic and Daoist than the *Analects* and *The Great Learning*, the themes and general point of view are continuous with them. One of the opening sentences repeats the words of chapter 6 of *The Great Learning*: "Therefore the superior man is watchful over himself when alone" (chap. 1, p. 98). Whether we translate *zhong* in the title *Zhongyong* as "mean" or (as is sometimes proposed) "equilibrium," it too indicates that the Confucian "Way of the superior man" lies between extremes. Once again the golden rule is central, and once again the difficulty of applying it can hardly be more strongly emphasized:

> Confucius said . . . "What you do not wish others to do to you, do not do to them. There are four things in the Way of the superior man, none of which I have been able to do. To serve my father as I would expect my son to serve me: that I have not been able to do. To serve my ruler as I would expect my ministers to serve me: that I have not been able to do. To serve my elder brothers as I would expect my younger brothers to serve me: that I have not been able to do. To be the first to treat friends as I would expect them to treat me: that I have not been able to do." (chap. 13, pp. 100–101)

If Confucius himself—at least the Confucius of *The Doctrine of the Mean*—cannot apply the golden rule, what chance is there for the rest of us? And if we are doomed to fail, how can this be the right path to morality? The answer is given in that work's previous chapter, where Confucius says of the Way of the superior man, "Men and women of simple intelligence can put it into practice; and yet in its utmost reaches there is something which even the sage is not able to put into practice" (chap. 12, p. 100). The fact that we (and Confucius himself) are unable to succeed completely does not mean we are unable to put it into practice at all. Nor does it mean that we should be satisfied with our partial success: "There are superior men who act in accordance with the Way, but give up when they have gone half way. But I can never give up" (chap. 11, p. 100).

Here too sincerity is the key to achieving the Way, and sincerity applies not only to lack of deception about what things we value but also to an understanding of what is valuable in itself, namely the good—or at least to our constant effort to achieve such an understanding: "If one does not understand what is good, he will not be sincere with himself. Sincerity is the Way of Heaven. To think how to be sincere is the Way of man" (chap. 20, p. 107). How are we to achieve it? Some people may be capable of achieving a state of simplicity and purity comparable to Daoism's "uncarved block of wood," but *The Doctrine of the Mean* differs from Daoism in insisting that for some the goal may need to be achieved by accretion rather than simplification. "Before the feelings of pleasure, anger, sorrow, and joy are aroused [the Way] is called mean. When these feelings are aroused and each and all attain due measure and degree, it is called harmony."[13] The "mean" here is similar to the Daoist state of simplicity, while "harmony" refers to the attainment of the same wisdom by the ordering of complexity. Later we are told: "Some are born with the knowledge [of wisdom, humanity, and courage]. Some learn it through study. Some learn it through hard work. But when the knowledge is acquired, it comes to the same thing. Some practice them naturally and easily. Some practice them for their advantage. Some practice them with effort and difficulty. But when the achievement is made, it comes to the same thing" (chap. 20, p. 105). They come to the same thing because if we are born with sincerity our nature itself will give us knowledge, but if we must acquire knowledge then that knowledge will in turn lead to sincerity: "It is due to our nature that enlightenment results from sincerity. It is due to education that sincerity results from enlightenment" (chap. 21, p. 107). Since each leads to the other, both must be present in the outcome, and "the superior man [both] honors the moral nature and follows the path of inquiry and study" (chap. 27, p. 110). The difficulty of this path is emphasized by the importance placed on a refusal to give up, echoing the passage from chapter 11 cited above:

> Study it extensively, inquire into it accurately, think over it carefully, sift it clearly, and practice it earnestly. When there is anything not yet studied, or studied but not yet understood, do not give up. When there is any question not yet asked, or asked but its answer not yet known, do not give up. When there is anything not yet thought over, or thought over but not yet apprehended, do not give up. When there is anything not yet sifted, or sifted but not yet clear, do not give up. When there is anything not yet practiced, or practiced but not yet earnestly, do not give up. If another man succeed by one effort, you will use a hundred efforts. If another man succeed by ten efforts, you will use a thousand efforts (chap. 20, p. 107)

In all three works, then, the good is conceived as a mean; the measuring square by which the mean can be determined is the golden rule; and the state of mind that can employ the golden rule is called sincerity, and is constituted by self-knowledge and knowledge of the good. The importance of both kinds of knowledge figures prominently in the

Platonic dialogues as well, as does the conception of goodness as a mean. Nowhere in the dialogues, however, does Plato propose the golden rule as a measure of the mean.

Plato

In Plato's philosophy the role of the golden rule, as the measuring square of the mean, is filled instead by techne, although not techne in the narrow sense of a precise set of rules, as is sometimes supposed. The concept of virtue as a mean makes its first appearance near the end of the *Protagoras* (359b–360d—the term used is *equality* rather than *mean*), in a passage previously cited in the first section of this chapter. Earlier Socrates had said, "Since the salvation of our life has shown itself to consist in the right choice of pleasure and pain—of the more and less, the greater and smaller, and the further and nearer—then first of all does it not show itself to be a measuring, a consideration of their excess, deficiency, and equality in relation to one another? And since it is measurement, is it not clear that, of necessity, it is a techne and episteme? What techne and episteme it is we will consider at a later time" (357a–b, interjections omitted). This passage has led some readers to believe that Plato was aiming at a precise hedonistic calculus of the type that Utilitarians would later devise, but nowhere do the dialogues propose anything of the kind.

The *Republic* repeats the need for a principle of measurement like the one called for in the *Protagoras*. At the end of the myth of Er, Socrates speaks of the importance of studying the good life and says we must "seek out and learn this study . . . [that provides] the ability [*dunaton*] and episteme of distinguishing the good from the bad life" (618c). One must know how to combine things with one another or separate them: for example,

> Knowing how beauty, combined with poverty or wealth and with what kind of character of the soul, produces good or evil, good birth and bad birth, private life and governing, strength and weakness, ease of learning and difficulty of learning, and all such things regarding the soul, both natural and acquired, so that from all these things—and looking at the nature

of the soul—he will be able to choose rationally between the better and worse life, calling a life worse which leads him to become more unjust, better if it leads him to become more just, and disregarding all other considerations. . . . He would know how to always choose the mean among such lives, and avoid each of the extremes.[14]

Since what is sought is conceived as a mean rather than a maximum, a rigorous formal calculus of the Utilitarian sort could not be what is envisioned. The same conclusion holds for the *Protagoras*. In the absence of any evidence to the contrary, the most reasonable assumption is that the *Republic* provides us with the best indication of where Plato's thought was leading when he spoke of a techne and episteme of measurement for our actions in the *Protagoras*, even if he was not ready to formulate the position of the *Republic* when he wrote the *Protagoras*.

The views put forward in the *Statesman* are a further development of what is said in the *Republic* passage, and in the *Statesman* Plato explicitly distances himself from the application of precise measurement to the moral mean. The Eleatic visitor maintains that the techne of measurement has two species:

One is with respect to the shared largeness or smallness of things toward one another. The other is with respect to the necessary essence of coming into being. Doesn't it seem to you that, in the nature of it, we must say that the greater is greater than nothing other than the less, and, again, the less is less than the greater and nothing else? But what about this? With regard to what exceeds or what is exceeded by the nature of the mean, whether in words or actions, must we not also say that it really exists? And that in this lies the chief difference between those of us who are bad and those who are good? . . . If someone does not allow that the nature of the greater stands in relation to anything other than the less, it will never stand in relation to the mean. Isn't that so? Would we not destroy the kinds of techne themselves and all their works with this doctrine, including indeed the techne of statesmanship that we have been seeking? . . . For all these presumably are on guard against anything that is in excess of or deficient to the mean, which they regard, not as nonexistent, but as something difficult that exists in relation to their activity. And when they preserve the mean in this way, all of their works are good and beautiful. . . . For if this [mean] exists those [technes] exist, and if those exist this exists also; but neither one of them can ever exist if the other doesn't. (283d–284d)[15]

A precise calculus of relative pleasures belongs to the first kind of measurement, "the shared largeness or smallness of things toward one another." There is no question of the "right degree," but only of relative size. One number is large or small relative to another, but no number is, in itself, any more correct than any other; the entire range of numbers is nothing but a series of quantitative relationships. The precision of numerical measurement must be combined with a way of measuring the right degree, a mean between too little and too much, which is discovered not by precise numerical calculation but in some other way. As in the *Protagoras* it is connected with techne—the *Republic* passage used the more general term *ability* (*dunaton*)—and in particular "the techne of statesmanship that we have been seeking." Precisely what is the nature of the connection between techne and the mean? How does the nature of techne enable us to discern and apply the mean?

Since techne differs from unconceptualized experience by the formulation of precise rules and measures, we might expect it to be associated with relative measure (arbitrarily chosen units of precise measurement) rather than the mean. The reason that it is not can be seen from the Eleatic visitor's description of the second kind of measure as comprising "whatever measures things in relation to the mean, the fitting, the timely (*kairos*), the needful, and anything else that dwells in the middle away from the extremes" (284e). In book 2 of the *Republic* Socrates says that if someone who is working at a techne "lets the right moment [*kairos*] go by, the work is ruined" (370b). What is remarkable about techne is that it bridges the two kinds of measure: it formulates and relies on precise rules, but the rules function properly only if the practitioner also has the sensitivity to discern what the moment calls for, the kairos. Thus, for example, Socrates says in the *Phaedrus* that those who are naturally suited to it will attain the techne of rhetoric to a notable degree if they supplement their natural ability with "both episteme and practice" (269d). For the rhetorician must both have "adequate knowledge [of the various kinds of speeches and souls, and how they are related] and in addition must be able to discern these things in practical affairs and follow them clearly with his senses" (271d–e). Accordingly, to perfect his techne he must acquire not only knowledge about these matters but also "the understanding of when it is timely [*kairos*] to speak and when to stop, when to speak briefly, or piteously, or hyperbolically, and all the other kinds of speech he has learned—when they are well-timed [*eukairian*] and when they are untimely [*akairian*]" (272a). For Plato this dual aspect of techne, rather than the golden rule, is the measuring square. How then do we attain it?

The answer is most visible in the education of the *Republic*'s guardians who are to govern the just city by means of the techne of ruling.[16] They will not be able to achieve infallibility, any more than Confucius was able to apply the golden rule infallibly, and the city will ultimately fail because at some point the rulers will apply the calculation governing procreation, contrary to kairos (*para kairon*, 546d). Even if their techne is not infallible, however, it is our model for the best we can hope to achieve in the application of justice.[17]

The education of the guardians comprises two stages that correspond to the two aspects of techne: knowledge of principles and sensitivity to kairos. The road from the cave to a vision of the good results in an understanding of first principles, and the road from enlightenment back into the cave results in the ability to apply those principles in whatever way the moment calls for. The upward road is characterized by progressive education in the mathematical technes of arithmetic, plane geometry, solid geometry, astronomy, and harmony, until the student is ready for dialectics. The mathematical character of these studies achieves two things. First, it turns us away from the potentially corrupting world of appetite: "All other kinds of techne are directed to human opinion and appetites, or generation and composition, or to serving things that grow and things that are put together" (533b). Mathematical studies, by contrast, aim at what is incomposite and eternal, and the eternal and unchanging cannot be objects of appetite. Second, mathematical thinking leads us to a greater understanding of the nature of reality, for "This thing in common that is employed by every techne, dianoia, and episteme . . . [is] the humble matter of distinguishing the one and the two and the three. I mean, in short, number and calculation" (522c). This is the *Statesman*'s first kind of measure, where relative sizes and quantities are calculated, but not the "just right" of the mean.

When the guardians return to the cave something new must be added to counteract the impetus of mathematics and dialectics away from the composite world of generated things. In terms of motivation this is an appeal to their sense of duty: "We will say, 'You have received a better and more complete education than the others, and are more able to participate in both realms. You must take your turn at going down then to the common dwelling place of the others and habituate yourselves to see the things in the dark'" (520b–c). The guardians' appetites will be held in check during their reentry into the world of corporeal concerns by a prohibition against possessing any private property beyond what is absolutely necessary (416d), touching gold or silver, or even being under the same roof with it (416e–417a).[18] Those steps are only a preparation for their efforts at habituating themselves to seeing things in the dark of the cave. The habituation itself begins when they are thirty-five and are required to "hold command in war and other offices suitable for youth" (539e). For the next fifteen years they gain experience (habituation) in various kinds of techne related to ruling. It is their habituation and experience that enables them to recognize in the moment how to apply the knowledge and understanding that their education produced in them.

The two aspects of techne—knowledge of principles and sensitivity to kairos—correspond respectively to the extension of knowledge and the golden rule in Confucian philosophy.[19] Both philosophies recognize two components to moral goodness: the formation of what we might call a good will—good intentions informed by an understanding of the nature of goodness—and an ability to effectively translate our good intentions into actions. In Confucius the former is sincerity of the will and the latter the measuring square of the golden rule; in Plato the former is the conversion of the soul though a vision of the good (*Republic* 518c–519b, 516d) and the latter the ability to apply it in the way that the moment requires, as a techne applies its principles through a sensitivity born of experience. Nevertheless there are important differences in both components.

For Plato the kind of knowledge characteristic of techne is eventually superseded by a more abstract knowledge, episteme, which culminates, not in the practical knowledge of techne, but in the pure intelligibility of the forms. When *The Doctrine of the Mean* says that "there is nothing more visible than what is hidden and nothing more manifest than what is subtle" (chap. 1, p. 98), it agrees up to a point with the allegory of the cave, that the reality to which we are initially blind is ultimately more manifest than the one we first can see. But it would not develop the contrast between the visible and the hidden into the conception of a realm of incomposite and unchanging being accessible only to thought, in opposition to the composite realm of becoming that is accessible only to the senses. Nor would it take knowledge of the good to mean a kind of contemplation that turns us away from the world of action. Not until some 1,500 years later in neo-Confucianism, especially that of Zhu Xi, will something like Platonic dualism enter the Confucian tradition. Even there, as we saw in chapter 3, it is more like Neoplatonic emanationism, which makes dualism derivative from monism. Yet even Zhu Xi would not approve of something that takes our attention away from the material world.[20]

When it comes to the downward moment, when we seek to apply in concrete situations our knowledge of and commitment to the good, there is another important difference. Confucianism locates the measuring square of action—the golden rule—in the subjectivity of the agent. If I want to know what is right I must look within myself. Plato locates it in the object: the moral agent recognizes what is appropriate to behaving toward someone, the way the practitioner of techne recognizes what is appropriate to making or doing something. What makes this an effective strategy is that the nature of techne is to seek the advantage of its object—to make or do something as well as possible—rather than the advantage of its practitioner (*Republic* 341c–342e). Accordingly, the Confucian and the Socratic approach these matters in an almost dialectically opposite way. The Confucian asks, "What would be the right action taken toward me from the point of view of my self-interest?" and then takes that action toward someone else. The Socratic, by contrast, asks, "What would be the right action from the standpoint of techne toward its object, rather than from the standpoint of my self-interest?" The results, however, will coincide, since in both cases the model consulted gives us a practical way to recognize when the principle of goodness is successfully applied in practice and the mean is achieved.

CHAPTER SEVEN

NONVIOLENT WARRIORS

The Bhagavad Gita and Marcus Aurelius

With this final chapter we turn from ethical theory to an issue in applied ethics, the perennial question of nonviolence. The two texts considered here consistently uphold the ideal of nonviolent action, and yet both do so within the context of violence: the Bhagavad Gita is the story of Krishna's persuasion of Arjuna to do battle against his relatives; the *Meditations* were written while Marcus was on military maneuvers. In both cases violence turns out to mean, in accordance with the virtue ethics that we explored in the previous two chapters, not only injurious action but such action done with the wrong state of mind. For actions to be forceful without counting as violent they must be done out of a sense of duty rather than personal advantage, and therefore without any emotional attachment to the outcome. Thus far it sounds compatible with Kant's categorical imperative, but here, as with virtue ethics generally and unlike the categorical imperative, there is no way to calculate what our duty is: it can be discerned only by eliminating the obstacles to our moral vision.

The Gita appears at first to be a series of explanations of various kinds of yoga, strung together in no obvious order. Although the traditional thematic identifications in the colophons at the end of each chapter were not part of the original text, they give a good sense of the thematic arrangement of the chapters and the apparent absence of any linear ordering principle.[1] The chapters are even less orderly than the colophons suggest. Chapter 6, for example, described by its colophon as "The Yoga of Meditation" (*dhyanayogo*), begins with an explanation of *karma* yoga (selfless action), followed by an explanation of *bhakti* yoga (religious devotion), returns to *karma* yoga, and turns next to renunciation, then to *jñanavijñana* yoga (the yoga of knowledge), before arriving at *dhyana* yoga (meditation) in the tenth stanza. This appearance of repetition and cyclical arrangement is not because the Gita is poorly organized but because its principle of organization is recursive rather than linear. However, beyond repetition and discursiveness the book sometimes gives a more worrying impression of inconsistency. A number of its claims and arguments seem directly contradicted by one another,[2] but these apparent contradictions disappear if we see the arguments as related to one another dialectically rather than analytically. The dialectic embedded in this recursive structure is recursive as well, as hierarchal strata within the conversation rather than a linear progression. Its individual moments are related in terms of conceptual rather than narrative priority.

What I mean by *dialectical* can be seen by contrast with *analytic*. From an analytic perspective contradictions either are merely verbal or else render the statement meaningless. If verbal they can be immediately disambiguated by making an appropriate distinction. "Arjuna is fighting and not fighting" would be meaningless if "fighting" were used in precisely the same respect both times, but if it is understood that he is "fighting" insofar as he is struggling to arrive at the right decision and "not fighting" because he has not entered the physical battlefield, the appearance of contradiction is gone; it was only a rhetorical trope. But it is more than a trope when Krishna says that Brahman is "neither existent [*sat*] nor non-existent [*asat*]" (13.12). The entities that we perceive with our senses, which are our primary referents for the meaning of words, either exist or do not, either are present in space and time or are not. As long as we include becoming as a species of being, there is no middle ground between "is" and "is not." By that standard, Krishna's statement is analytically false, self-contradictory and therefore meaningless; there is no simple adjectival distinction to resolve the tension by speaking of Brahman as existing in one familiar sense but not in another. The statement becomes meaningful only if we come to recognize, perhaps as a result of the paradox itself, a reality to which concepts derived from the world of sensory experience are not adequate, including the concepts of existence and nonexistence. If we understand existence in terms of presence in space and time, and nonexistence as absence from space and time, the source of space and time itself cannot be said either to exist or not to exist.[3] Unlike an analytic resolution, which requires a simple terminological clarification, a dialectical resolution requires a change of perspective. That is what happens in the Bhagavad Gita.

The following discussion is divided into three main sections: (1) the arguments for Arjuna's entry into the war; (2) the status of the principal varieties of yoga; and (3) the concept of nonviolence. In each case the discussion of the Gita will be followed by a comparison with Marcus Aurelius.

The Arguments

Bhagavad Gita

I suggested that the Bhagavad Gita is dialectical not only in the obvious sense of being a dialogue between two speakers who begin with opposing points of view and progressively come into agreement but also in the way its arguments are related to one another. It has been widely noted that the arguments Krishna employs to persuade Arjuna to enter into battle sometimes conflict with one another, as for example, when he appeals to Arjuna's pride, warning that people will lose respect for him if he does not fight (2.34–36), but two stanzas later tells Arjuna not to be concerned about such things at all but rather to fight only out of a sense of duty. Such reversals may give the impression that Krishna is being manipulative, telling Arjuna anything that might produce the desired result; but that would go against the central teaching, that we should be concerned only with the action and not with its fruits, the means rather than the ends. That sentiment is expressed only a few verses later: "To action alone hast thou a right and never at all to its fruits; let not the fruits of action be thy motive" (2.47).[4] So how can Krishna urge upon Arjuna the rewards of being honored by others?

Personal Feeling

The initial antitheses begin sequentially—the order of narration here mirrors the order of dialectical priority—starting when Arjuna recoils from the battle not for reasons of pacifism but because of personal attachments and their attendant pleasures and pains. He sees in the enemy lines "my own people arrayed and eager for fight. . . . Those for whose sake we desire kingdom, enjoyments and pleasures—they stand here in battle, renouncing their lives and riches: teachers, fathers, sons, and also grandfathers; uncles and fathers-in-law, grandsons and brothers-in-law, and other kinsmen. These I would not consent to kill, though killed myself. . . . What pleasure can be ours, O Krishna, after we have slain the sons of Dhritarashtra?" (1.28–36). Arjuna himself provides the other side of the dilemma in the next lines when he characterizes these same people as criminals (*atatayina*)[5] overpowered by greed (*lobhopahata*) who see nothing wrong in the destruction of the family and treachery to friends (1.36–38). How should greedy, destructive, treacherous criminals go unpunished and even unopposed?

The reply to this was already present in the previous passage immediately after the words just quoted—"Only sin will accrue to us if we kill these criminals" (1.36)—and continues in what follows: "In the ruin of a family its ancient laws [*dharmah*] are destroyed: and when the laws [*dharme*] perish the whole family yields to lawlessness [*adharmo*]. . . . And to hell does this confusion bring the family itself as well as those who have destroyed it. . . . The men of the families whose laws are destroyed needs must live in hell" (1.40–44). This initial antithesis is at the level of passion—familial affection on one hand, revulsion at their behavior on the other—and is followed by a resolution at the level of dharma: to violate the duty (*dharma*) to his family would be to bring upon himself and everyone he cares about a suffering far greater than they would incur at the hands of Duryodhana and his followers. "Far better would it be for me if the sons of Dhritarashtra, with weapons in hand, should slay me in the battle, while I remain unresisting and unarmed" (1.46). But it is not a happy resolution, with "his spirit overwhelmed by sorrow" (1.47).

Dharma

The unhappy resolution at the level of dharma, of the antithesis between Arjuna's family feeling and his disapproval of their behavior, will soon be given its own antithesis by Krishna. After listening to two preliminary arguments, Arjuna appeals to Krishna for clarification and instruction, "with my mind bewildered about my duty [*dharmasammudhacetah*]" (2.7).[6] Krishna responds at length, saying at one point: "Further, having regard for thine own duty [*dharmam*], thou shouldst not falter, there exists no greater good for a Kshatriya[7] than a war enjoined by duty [*dharmyad*]. . . . But if thou doest not this lawful [*dharmyam*] battle, then thou wilt fail thy duty [*dharmam*] and glory and incur sin" (2.31, 33). Here the antithesis returns, this time at the level of dharma rather than that of feeling. The dharma of the family requires Arjuna not to fight (1.40–46), but the dharma of his caste requires him to fight (2.31, 33). For Arjuna, as for the hero of Aeschylus's *Oresteia*, or Sartre's student who must choose between his patriotic and filial duties, whichever duty he follows will cause him to violate an antithetical duty. Accordingly Arjuna reproaches Krishna for the ambiguity of his explanation: "With an apparently confused utterance thou seemest to bewilder my intelligence" (3.2).

If Arjuna resolved the conflict among his personal feelings by an appeal to dharma, how can a conflict between two dharmas be resolved? A few stanzas later Krishna says, "When thine intelligence, which is bewildered by the Vedic texts, shall stand unshaken and stable in spirit [*samadhi*], then shalt thou attain to *yoga*" (2.53).[8] Arjuna is indeed bewildered by the Vedic texts, some of which emphasize family dharma while others emphasize caste dharma. The resolution then is to be found in yoga. The guide to moral behavior is not a deontological obedience to formulaic rules but a version of virtue ethics. We cannot identify a set of rules that will always result in virtuous behavior regardless of the circumstances, but we can identify what kind of person will always be able to recognize the appropriate way to behave. This way of being can be clarified by contrast with its opposite, the demonic: "There are two types of beings created in the world—the divine [*daiva*] and the demonic [*asura*]. The divine have been described at length. Hear from me, O Partha, about the demonic. . . . They say that the world is unreal [*asatyam*], without a basis, without a Lord, not brought about in regular sequence [*aparasparasambhutam*],[9] caused by desire, in short" (16.6, 8). In other words, "the demonic" refers to those who do not believe there is an inherent meaning or purposeful direction in the world and who believe that the only thing that gives our experience value is pleasure and absence of pain, so that reality is constructed out of perceptions colored by our desires ("caused by desire"). Although the demonic is the most extreme case, the same thing applies to all of us: "All beings are born deluded [*sammoham*], O Bharata, overcome by the dualities which arise from wish and hate" (7.27). It is in fact delusion (*mohat*) that makes Arjuna reluctant to fight (18.60). We must overcome this, Krishna says, by casting away both good and evil and striving for yoga instead (2.50).

Verse 37 of chapter 2 marks the point of transition from delusion to yoga. Prior to that, Krishna warned Arjuna that if he refrained from battle, "men will ever recount thy ill-fame, and for one who has been honored ill-fame is worse than death. The great warriors will think that thou hast abstained from battle through fear, and they by whom thou wast highly esteemed will make light of thee. Many unseemly words will be uttered by thine enemies, slandering thy strength. Could anything be sadder than that?" (2.34–6). But two verses later Krishna says, "Treating alike pleasure and pain, gain and loss, victory and defeat, then get ready for battle" (2.38). The earlier passage appealed to these very things—the pain of being thought a coward and the loss of the respect of others— while this one tells Arjuna to be indifferent to such matters and treat them all alike. The earlier appeals to personal pleasure and pain are here replaced by appeals to a standard that is indifferent to pleasure and pain. The turning point was verse 37: "Either slain thou shalt go to heaven; or victorious thou shalt enjoy earth; therefore arise, O Son of Kunti, resolve on battle." Right and wrong are no longer measured by pleasure and pain, victory and defeat, or praise and blame. As long as what we do is right, the consequences will be acceptable, either heaven or earthly enjoyment in this case. There is still some vestigial appeal here to self-interest in the references to heaven and to enjoyment, but such references eventually disappear altogether: "He who holds equal blame and praise, . . . content with anything that comes . . . is dear to Me" (12.19).

Nonattachment

If Arjuna is supposed to be "content with anything that comes" why should he take up arms against what comes from his cousins? If he aims at a condition with "desires stilled" (15.5), why does this not lead to quietism rather than activism? "'Action should be given up as an evil,' say some learned men" (18.3). Here the dialectic returns to the negative pole—abstention from battle—and a new tension arises between Krishna's explanation and his exhortation. But for Krishna giving up attachment does not imply giving up activity: "Not by abstention from action [*karmanam*] does a man attain freedom from action [*maiskarmyam*]. . . . For no one can remain even for a moment without action [*karma*]. . . . Do thy allotted activity [*karma*], for action [*karma*] is better than inaction [*akarmanah*]" (3.4–5, 3.8; cf. 18.11). The test of whether our action is allotted or deluded is whether it is the means or the end that we care about. We are unattached only if we are concerned purely with the performance of the action and not with its success; it is "the abandonment of the fruits of all actions [*karmanam*]. . . . But even these actions [*karmani*] ought to be performed, giving up attachment and desire for fruits" (18.2, 18.6), a view shared by Marcus Aurelius, who says that the function of our will is only to make the effort; success is out of our hands (6.50).

At the previous stage yoga was to resolve the confusion created by different Vedic dharmas. Now yoga must resolve the tension within itself between quietism and activism, in terms of the rival conceptions of good/evil and desire/nondesire. The desires contrary to absolute dharma are attachments from which we are liberated by yoga: "Listen now to the *Yoga*. If your intelligence accepts it, thou shalt cast away the bondage of actions. . . . When one does not get attached to the objects of sense or to actions, and has renounced all purposes, then he is said to have attained to *yoga*" (2.39, 6.4). We become attached because of immediate gratification, so we must learn to think beyond the short term and realize that immediate gratification leads to long-term suffering. We must become motivated not by passion (*rajas*), "which is like nectar at first but like poison at the end" (18.38), but by "goodness" (*sattvikam*), "which is like poison at first and like nectar at the end" (18–37). The problem is that we can be sure of the presence of what *rajas* aims at far more easily than we can be sure of the reality of what *sattva* aims at. Most of us lack the experiential evidence to resist the demonic belief that "the world is unreal [*asatyam*], without a basis, without a Lord" (16.8). The objects of *rajas* are known before they are loved, but the object of *sattva* must be loved before it can be known, a far more difficult path.

Predestination

If this concept of action without attachment resolves the tension between the directive that we make an effort to do our appropriate activity, including military activity, and the directive that we accept whatever comes, a new difficulty now appears at this level. On one hand, "No one can remain even for a moment without action [*akarma*]" (3.5),[10] but on the other, "The man whose delight is in Atman alone, . . . for him there exists no action [*karyam*] that needs to be done" (3.17). The paradox is succinctly stated in the next chapter: "He who in action sees non-action [*karmani akarma*] and in non-action sees action [*akarmani ca karma*]— he is wise among men, he is a *yogin*, and he has accomplished all action [*karma*]" (4.18).[11] More than nonattachment is involved here. The reason no action exists for someone whose delight is in Atman alone is that it is not we who act but Atman. "The man who is united with the Divine and knows the truth thinks, 'I do [*karomiti*] nothing at all'" (5.8, cf. 3.27). There are two reasons for this. One is that divine providence (*daivam*) is a cause of all things (18.13–14): "*Karma* is the name given to the creative force that brings beings into existence" (8.3). The other is that it is through our body alone that we are the cause of or affected by anything:[12] "But he who knows the true character of the distinction (of the soul) from the modes of nature and their actions [*gunakarma*], . . . understanding that it is the modes which are acting on the modes (themselves), does not get attached" (3.28). Again, "Having abandoned attachment to the fruit of actions [*karma*] . . . he does [*karoti*] nothing though he is ever engaged in action [*karmani*] . . . performing action [*karma*] by the body alone" (4.20–21).

In what sense is divine providence a cause of all things, in what sense is it with our body alone that we are the cause of things, and how are the two related? The answer to the first question is hardly straightforward. Krishna says, "There is not for me, O Partha, any action [*kartavyam*] in the three worlds which has to be done . . . yet I am engaged in action [*karmani*]" (3.22), and again, "The fourfold order was created by Me. . . . Though it is my action [*kartaram*], know me to be incapable of action [*akartaram*] or change" (4.13).[13] The key here is the word *change* (*avyayam*). Krishna once again exhorts Arjuna to attack his cousins, saying, "By Me alone are they slain already. Be thou merely the occasion" (11.33). The reason they are already slain even though Arjuna has yet to slay them is that in the creation of the world the causes of all things have already been set in motion, everything is fated. As the *Iśa Upaniṣad* puts it, Atman "distributed objects through the eternal years" (8.4).[14] Thus, "If indulging in self-conceit, thou thinkest 'I will not fight,' vain is this, thy resolve. Nature [*prakrtis*] will compel thee. That which, though delusion, thou wishest not to do, that thou shalt do even against thy will, fettered by thy own acts born of thy nature [*svabhava-jena*]. The Lord abides in the hearts of all beings, O Arjuna, causing them to turn round by His power as if they were mounted on a machine" (18.59–61).

If this is determinism, it is compatibilistic determinism. Arjuna fights only because he is finally and freely persuaded by Krishna's teachings. "Do as thou choosest," says Krishna (18.63), and Arjuna concludes, "Destroyed is my delusion and recognition has been gained by me through Thy grace, O Acyuta. I stand firm with my doubts dispelled. I shall act according to Thy word" (18.73).[15] Arjuna fights because he decides to, not because he is coerced to, but it was always going to happen that Arjuna would resist the fight because of his scruples and that his charioteer would finally enlighten him to see that his scruples were misguided. With all our decisions, whatever we decide, our decision was inevitable from the beginning of time; nevertheless, the decision is ours alone to make. As with Western compatibilists like Spinoza, what is incompatible with freedom is not determinism but passion, when our choices are reactive rather than active. When Arjuna asks, "By what is a man impelled to commit sin, as if by force, even against his will?" Krishna says, "This is craving [*kama*], this is wrath [*krodha*], born of the mode of passion [*rajoguna*]" (3.36–37).

If Arjuna reached his decision "by recognition . . . gained by me through Thy grace" (18.73), how is this grace compatible with freedom? If God gives Arjuna (and Samjaya: 18.75) knowledge that makes one choice obvious, and withholds knowledge from Duryodhana that would have shown him the folly of his own choices, and so with all of us, then our "free" choices can be predicted from what God (or else chance) allows us to understand and we are puppets moved by hidden strings.[16] Thus "The Lord abides in the hearts of all beings, O Arjuna, causing them to turn round by His power as if they were mounted on a machine" (18.61) This problem of freedom and providence has a long and vexed history in theology, and attempts have been made to resolve it in various ways.[17] The issue brings us to the connection between the two causalities mentioned earlier, the divine causality of all things (18.13–14) and the fact that what we do is done "by the body alone" (4.20–21).[18] As the source of time (11.32), God in himself is timeless, incapable of change (4.13) and eternally aware of the whole of time (7.26).[19] Nature, not God, *prakriti*, not *puruṣa*, is the locus of change and time: "All action is done only by nature [*prakrtyai*] and the self [*atmanam*] is not the actor" (13.29). *Prakriti* is the moving image of *puruṣa*, as for Plato time is the moving image of eternity.[20] The modes following their own internal laws, like the machine referred to in 18.61, unfold the events that were timelessly present from eternity.[21] Thus despite "causing [people] to turn round by His power as if they were mounted on a machine" (18.61), God is "seated as if indifferent, unattached in those actions" (9.9). The latter passage describes God's timeless, unchanging nature; the former describes God's nature in its temporal dimension.

We can understand the concept of grace as an image of this. It does not mean that God intervenes to give knowledge to one person but not to another. It means that as all of us arise sequentially in the temporal manifestation of the timeless divine, some of us will attain to insight and make wise choices because of the local conditions that produce our nature and circumstances, while others will not. "Grace" is a metaphor for those who happen to be of the first kind. This is the ultimate resolution of the dialectical movement implicit in the Bhagavad Gita. We can summarize that movement in the following table:

Level	Criterion	Reason Not to Fight	Reason to Fight	Resolution
i	Personal feeling	Family feeling	Their criminal greed	Family dharma
ii	Dharma	Family dharma	Caste dharma	Yoga
iii	Activity	Yoga stills desire	Act without desire	Nonattachment
iv	Predestination	No action need be done	Body alone is active	*Prakriti* manifests *puruṣa*

What appear to be contradictions are different levels of the argument that are not identified as such.

Marcus Aurelius

It hardly needs saying that Marcus Aurelius renounces the claims of pleasure and pain in favor of duty in exactly the way the Gita's dialectic does. He writes, for example, "With respect to pain, then, and pleasure, or death and life, or honor and dishonor, which the universal nature employs equally, whoever is not equally affected is manifestly acting impiously" (9.1).[22] And just as yoga is characterized in the Gita by the understanding that the immediate gratification of emotions (*rajas*) is like nectar at first but like poison at the end, and the delayed gratification of truth or goodness (*sattva*) is like poison at first and like nectar at the end (18.37–38), a comparable understanding appears in the *Meditations* in terms of the competition variously described as between the soul (*psuchē*) and pleasure-pain (2.16), the mind (*dianoia*) and the passions (*pathōn*) (8.48), or our diviner parts (*theioterou*) and our more dishonorable parts (*atimotera*): the body and its gross pleasures (11.19).[23]

Marcus also shares the Gita's notion of duty: "Let it make no difference to you whether you are cold or warm, if you are doing your duty; and whether you are drowsy or satisfied with sleep; and whether ill-spoken of or praised; and whether dying or doing something else" (6.2).[24] But Marcus does not quite mean by duty what Arjuna meant by dharma. For Arjuna there can be conflicting dharmas, as when the dharma that condemns damaging the family conflicts with Arjuna's warrior caste dharma to take up arms against his cousins. But for Marcus Aurelius duties are defined, not by scriptures that may conflict with one another, but by reason, which is internally consistent.

The Gita resolved the warrior mentality with the principle of accepting whatever comes, by means of nonattachment. Marcus Aurelius has no term exactly equivalent to "nonattachment" but makes the same point in other ways:[25]

> Take care that you do not through being so pleased with them accustom yourself to overvalue them, so as to be disturbed if ever you should not have them. (7.27)

> Why do you not pray for the gods to give you the faculty of not fearing any of the things which you fear, or of not desiring any of the things which you desire, or not being pained at anything, rather than pray that any of these things should not happen or happen? (9.40)

> As to avoidance (aversion) he should not show it with respect to any of the things which are not in our power. (11.37)[26]

Since duty, for Marcus, is based on reason, how close is his conception of reason to Krishna's concept of yoga? The Gita recognizes four basic yogas: *jñana* (knowledge), *bhakti* (devotion to God), *karma* (selfless action), and *dhyana* (meditation).[27] It goes without saying that Marcus's life of reason parallels the yoga of knowledge, and, given the philosopher-king that he was, it is not difficult to find a commitment to selfless action in him as well, for example: "Am I doing anything? I do it with reference to the good of mankind" (8.23).[28] There is no expectation in yoga that everyone will pursue all four equally, but Marcus does also occasionally show a regard for *bhakti*, the celebration of God, as when he writes, "Why then do you not wait in tranquility for your end, whether it is extinction or removal to another state? And until that time comes, what is sufficient? Why, what else than to venerate the gods and bless them, and to do good to men, and to practice tolerance and self-restraint" (5.33, cf. 6.30). Only the fourth of the yogas, *dhyana* or meditation, is altogether missing from the *Meditations*. Here are no Platonic Isles of the Blessed or Aristotelian *theoria* (contemplation). This means more than that one of the four yogas is absent: it means that the other three are present only in an incomplete sense. The Gita's yogas are connected with one another, so the absence of any one of them points to a limitation in the rest—for example, Marcus's selfless action is not offered as a sacrifice to the gods, as in *karma* yoga. In other words, the mystical union with the divine that is at the very heart of the Bhagavad Gita is not part of Marcus Aurelius's world.

In the Bhagavad Gita it is clear that even *sattva*—translated here as "reason" to facilitate comparison with Marcus Aurelius's "reason" (*logos*)—is attached to *prakriti* (nature) and does not reach *puruṣa* (God): "*Sattva* binds the Self [*atman*] by attachment to knowledge" (14.6). We can experience *puruṣa* only by abandoning knowledge.[29] In Marcus Aurelius, however, there is no going beyond reason the way Samkhya goes beyond *sattva*. The status of reason in the *Meditations* is never fully clarified, but it appears to be a principle to which even gods are subject, because "Reason . . . is common to gods and men" (7.53),[30] and "All things are made and perfected according to this reason" (6.1). It further appears to be endowed with self-consciousness because "the reason which governs knows what its own disposition is" (6.5).[31] Thus it appears to be a monotheistic god, as distinct from the polytheistic ones mentioned in 7:53: "Every man's intelligence is a god, and is an efflux of the deity" (12.26).[32] There is nothing beyond reason, and reason, as in the Gita, is identified with nature,[33] while nature is clearly the whole of physical existence for Marcus, rather than the reality of which physical existence is an illusion.[34] Thus, just as nothing in the *Meditations* corresponds to the yoga of meditation in which consciousness is united with the source of all being, so too there is no equivalent to the concept of *puruṣa*, the singularity underlying the illusion of multiplicity.

Where does Marcus Aurelius stand in relation to the views that it is not we that act but Atman or *puruṣa* that acts through us, and that we act freely yet everything is predetermined? In the first case Marcus is explicit about our role as manifestations of a single soul: "There is one soul, though it is distributed among infinite natures and individual circumscriptions (or individuals). There is one intelligent soul, though it seems to be divided" (12.30).[35] He also shares the second view, that of compatibilistic determinism. He repeats, for example, Epictetus's remark that "no man can rob us of our free will" (11.36),[36] and he affirms that "so long as nothing [compels me] I remain, am free" (5.29), but he also recognizes that this freedom from compulsion does not imply freedom from causation: if someone has "such and such opinions, it will seem nothing wonderful or strange to me, if he does such and such things; and I shall bear in mind that he is compelled to do so" (8.14, cf. 6.27). Marcus Aurelius further agrees with the Gita that this determinism is not blind causality but providence:[37]

> That which happens to every man is fixed in a manner for him suitably to his destiny. . . . For there is altogether one fitness, harmony. (5.8)

> The universal nature employs [pleasure and pain] equally . . . by virtue of a certain original movement of Providence [*pronoias*], according to which it moved from a certain beginning to this ordering of things. (9.1)

> Whatever may happen to you, it was prepared for you from all eternity; and the implication of causes was from eternity spinning the thread of your being, and of that which is incident to it. (10.5, cf. 4.26)

> Trust the future to Providence [*tē pronoia*]. (12.1)

Yoga

Bhagavad Gita

The principal yogas of the Bhagavad Gita are generally considered to be *karma*, *jñana*, and *bhakti* (selfless action, knowledge, devotion), but although *dhyana* (meditation) is not normally accorded the same status, in the passages I discuss below it appears to be on an equal footing with the other three (also see above, note 26). Indeed, the whole of the Gita can be looked at as an exercise in meditation: "O Partha, has this been heard by thee with thy thought fixed to one point?" (18.72).[38] Within the discussions of these four yogas, as with the arguments discussed previously, there are contradictory statements.[39] But unlike the tensions between the grounds for fighting and grounds for not fighting, the discussion of the four yogas does not even implicitly contain a dialectical hierarchy from lowest to highest. Nor are the tensions eventually resolved at an ultimate level, as were the previous ones in the conception of predestination. Nevertheless, these tensions too call for some kind of resolution, although of a different kind. They revolve around the question of whether one kind of yoga is being recommended more highly than the others. Commentators have pointed out that *karma* yoga has a prima facie claim to this honor because the goal of Krishna's arguments is to spur Arjuna into action.[40] Nevertheless Krishna's words sometimes point in a very different direction.

First Krishna suggests that *jñana* yoga is superior to *karma* yoga: "Knowledge [*yajñaj, jñana*] as a sacrifice is greater than any material sacrifice . . . for all actions [*karma*] culminate in knowledge [*jñane*]. . . . There is nothing on earth equal in purity to knowledge [*jñanena*]" (4.33, 4.38).[41] Thus knowledge is the goal that makes karmic sacrifice desirable, in which case knowledge is intrinsically good, and karmic sacrifice appears to be good only instrumentally in the service of knowledge. Later the superiority of *jñana* yoga appears to extend over *dhyana* and *bhakti* yoga as well: "To those who are in constant union with me and worship me with love, I grant the power of understanding [*buddhiyogam*] by which they come unto me. Out of compassion for those same ones . . . I destroy the darkness born of ignorance by the shining lamp of knowledge [*jñana*]" (10.10–11). If "those who are in constant union with me" is a reference to *dhyana* yoga, then Krishna is apparently saying that the reward for meditation and for worship is knowledge; knowledge is good in itself, while meditation and worship are good only as means to attain it. However in chapter 6, "The Yoga of Meditation," *dhyana* yoga is said to be superior to both *jñana* and *karma* yoga: "The [*dhyana*] *yogin* . . . is considered to be greater than the man of knowledge [*jñanibhyo*], greater than the man of ritual actions [*karmibhyas*]."

Krishna appears to resolve at least some of the tensions by suggesting that *dhyana, jñana,* and *karma* yoga are equally valid paths, each in its own way, while *bhakti* yoga is inferior to them because it depends on things heard (*sruti,* scripture) rather than direct experience.[42] *Bhakti* yoga is recommended only for those who are ignorant of the other three: "By meditation [*dhyanena*] some perceive the self in the self by the self; others by the path of knowledge [*samkhyena*] and still others by the path of actions [*karmayogena*]. Yet others, ignorant of these paths [*ajanantah*] hearing from others [*srutva*] worship; and they too cross beyond death by their devotion to what they have heard [*sruti*]" (13.24–25). This apparent resolution too turns out to be premature, for other passages suggest that *bhakti* may be in first rather than last place. Krishna says, "Neither by the Vedas, nor by sacrifices nor by study [*adhyayanaih*] . . . can I be seen in the world of men by any one else but thee. . . . But by unswerving devotion [*bhaktya*] to me, O Arjuna, I can be thus known, truly seen and entered into" (11.48, 54). Arjuna asks him which seekers have the greater knowledge of yoga, "those devotees [*bhaktas*] who, thus ever harmonized, worship Thee, [or] those, again, who worship the Imperishable and the Unmanifested" (12.1)—in other words, those who practice *bhakti* yoga or those who practice *dhyana* or *jñana* yoga. Krishna replies, "Those who fixing their minds [*manah*] on me worship me, ever harmonized and possessed of supreme faith [*sraddhaya*]—them do I consider most perfect in yoga [*yuktatama*]. But those who worship the Imperishable, the Undefinable, the Unchanging and the Immobile, the Constant . . . they come to me indeed" (12.2–4). This passage is the exact opposite of 13.24–25. Where the former seemed to say that *bhakti* yoga is the least perfect and should be employed only by those ignorant of the others, the latter says it is "most perfect" and that it is the others that are less perfect avenues to the goal.

The succeeding stanzas of chapter 12 provide a microcosm of these tensions. First it seems that all four yogas are of equal value: "But those, who, laying all their actions [*karmani*] on me, intent on me, worship, meditating [*dhyayanta*] on me, with unswerving devotion [*yogena*], whose intellect [*cetasam*] is set on me, I straightway deliver from the ocean of death-bound existence" (12.6–7). But this is followed by a new assertion of hierarchy. "On Me alone fix thy mind [*mana*], let thy understanding [*buddhim*] dwell in me. . . . If, however, thou art not able to fix thy thought steadily on me, then seek to reach me by the practice of concentration [*abhyasa-yogena*]," that is, meditation (12.8–9).[43] Here *dhyana* is recommended only for those unable to achieve *jñana*, while in the next stanza *bhakti* is recommended only for those unable to practice *jñana* or *dhyana*: "If thou art unable even to seek by the practice of concentration [*abhyase*], then be as one whose supreme aim is my service; even performing actions for my sake, thou shalt attain perfection" (12.10). Last of all is *karma* yoga: "If thou art not able to do even this, then taking refuge in my disciplined activity [*kartum*] renounce the fruit of all action [*karma*], with the self subdued" (12.11). The hierarchy descends, then, from *jñana* to *dhyana* to *bhakti* to *karma*. In what at first appears to be a summation of the preceding stanzas Krishna says: "[a] Better indeed is knowledge [*jñanam*] than practice [*abhyasat*]. [b] Better than knowledge [*jñanat*] is meditation [*dhyanam*]. [c] Better than meditation [*dhyanat*] is the renunciation of the fruit of action [*karma*]" (12.12). Why is there no mention of *bhakti* yoga? According to the commentary by Sankara's disciple Anandagiri, "*Abhyasa* (practice)—occur[r]ing in the text and the commentary—may mean either (1) the act of listening to the teaching of the srutis with a view to obtain knowledge, or, (2) the practice of *dhyana* with a firm resolve."[44] In the previous paragraph *abhyasat* was interpreted in the second sense, but if we take it here in the first sense, since Krishna connects *sruti* with *bhakti* (13.25),[45] it can be construed as a reference to *bhakti* "devotional practice." In that case all four yogas would be present in this summation, and Krishna's three statements would amount to the assertions that (a) *jñana* is better than *bhakti*, (b) *dhyana* is better than *jñana*, and (c) *karma* is better than *dhyana*. The resultant hierarchy—*karma, dhyana, jñana, bhakti* —would be consistent with the Gita's stated purpose of spurring Arjuna into action, but it flatly contradicts the verses immediately preceding, where the hierarchy was *jñana, dhyana, bhakti, karma*.

Suppose, then, that we take *abhyasat* in the second sense, "the practice of *dhyana* with a firm resolve." That is what *abhyasa* seemed to mean in 12.9–10, and it is what is implied by Radhakrishnan's amplification of *abhyasaj* in 12.12 as "the practice of concentration." In that case "a" would be saying, "Better indeed is *jñana* than *dhyana*," which is now perfectly consistent with what we were told in 12.9. However, it is directly contradicted by the very next line: "Better than knowledge [*jñanat*] is meditation [*dhyanam*]." However we interpret *abhyasa*, then, problems arise, as a conflict either within 12.12 itself or between 12.12 and 12.8–11.

Why is all this so confusing and even incoherent? Just before 12.8–11, where Krishna said that if we cannot practice *dhyana* or *jñana* we should practice *bhakti*, and if not *bhakti* then *karma* yoga, he explained, "The difficulty of those whose thoughts are set on the Unmanifested is greater, for the goal of the Unmanifested is hard to reach by the embodied beings" (12.5). In other words, not everyone is capable of the concentration required by *dhyana* or the abstraction required by *jñana*, but for them there are other alternatives. We could also say, however, that not everyone is temperamentally suited for devotional worship or a life of practicing selfless service, and that the important thing is to be concerned not about hierarchies but about which path is appropriate for us individually: "Beings follow their nature. What can repression accomplish? . . . Better is one's own law though imperfectly carried out than the law of another carried out perfectly" (3.33, 35). Even if we think of *jñana* as the ideal to strive for, it is an imperfect ideal: "Because of his subtlety he is unknowable [*avijñeyam*]."[46] Ultimately all four are mutually reinforcing. Meditation (*dhyana*) gives a kind of knowledge (*jñana*), and knowledge gives something to meditate on, while both teach us to act unselfishly (*karma*) and to respect rituals (*bhakti*) as a symbol of truth. As Krishna says, "He who, undeluded, thus knows [*janati*] Me, the Highest Person, is the knower of all and worships [*bhajati*] Me in all his being" (15.19). The different yogas work on us simultaneously in different ways, *bhakti* on our emotions, *karma* on our will, *jñana* on our intellect, and *dhyana* on our spirit.[47] Again, unselfish action and pure-hearted worship promote each other and also promote meditation and knowledge. In essence there is no difference between theory and practice: "The ignorant speak of *Samkhya* and *Yoga* as different, not the wise" (5.4). In chapter 18 all four converge. The way one "attains to the Brahman, that supreme consummation of knowledge [*jñanasya*]" (18.50) is composed of not only understanding (*buddhya*, 18.51) but also meditation (*dhyanayogopara*, 18.52), devotion (*madbhaktim*, 18.54), and selfless action (*sarvakarmany*, 18.56–57).[48]

If each path of yoga is equally valid in its own way and leads to the same goal, why not simply say so instead of proclaiming mutually exclusive hierarchies?[49] Perhaps in recognition of the inexperience of its audience the Gita speaks to us at our own individual level. The more deeply we go into yoga the more we realize that the paths converge and are mutually reinforcing, but at the beginning the tendency is for people to want simple answers rather than qualified and complicated ones. Plato and Aristotle distinguish between what is most clear to us and what is most clear by nature. In this case what is most clear to us—before we have begun to rid ourselves of delusion—is that these four paths are obviously very different. *To us*, at this stage, one is always superior, and to tell us that we reach the same place by participating in the group ceremonies in devotion to a personal deity and by sitting silently in solitary meditation of an impersonal oneness is incomprehensible at first. By telling us that our own particular path is the best of all, Krishna protects us from feeling overwhelmed by the different choices available, and from feeling confused by claims that such apparently incompatible ways of life are essentially the same. If we recognize our path as the most highly praised in one of Krishna's formulations we will be more inclined to pursue it with full confidence (and can easily ignore the other passages). Each of the four yogas is presented in one passage or other from its own point of view, from which the other three look to be inferior. This ultimate dialectic is the same as the tension within religious tolerance, which stands ambiguously between dogmatism and inclusiveness. Whereas inclusiveness means accepting that different religions may be equally valid alternative expressions of truth, tolerance, as I am using it here, means tolerating views that we think are misguided—unlike dogmatists who want to root out whatever they perceive as error.

In the *Phaedrus*, as we saw in the previous chapter, Plato's Socrates helps us understand why the historical Socrates left no writings. He tells Phaedrus that for our rhetoric to be effective we must know what type of person responds to what type of speech, and we must be able to identify to which type the person we are speaking to corresponds, and we also must be sensitive to the circumstances of the moment, since we cannot say exactly the same words to the same person under all circumstances and at all times with equal effectiveness. We saw examples of this where Confucius gives different answers to different disciples as to whether to practice something as soon as it is heard, and where Socrates gives different answers to his jurors and to Crito about the inviolability of the law. The author of the Bhagavad Gita may be employing a similar strategy. Krishna's words are addressed in the first instance to Arjuna, but in the second instance to other auditors like Samjaya (18.74), then at one remove to Samjaya's immediate audience (1.2) and to the audience of the Bhagavad Gita. In addition to suggesting that all four approaches are equally true, although from different points of view, the paradoxes that result from juxtaposing these incompatible recommendations also reflect that all are equally false. God is indefinable (*anirdesyam*), unmanifest (*avyaktam*), and unthinkable (*acintyam*) (12.3), so no path can do full justice to what it aims at. The impossibility of reconciling the paradoxes may lead us to recognize the impossibility of any account that is not paradoxical. It prevents us from resting in the words and forces us to look beyond them.

Marcus Aurelius

We saw that Marcus Aurelius recognizes the equivalent of three kinds of yoga—knowledge, selfless action, and devotion—but not meditation, and that for Marcus, as for the Gita, these three pursuits are mutually reinforcing. But there is no hint in Marcus of the challenging way that the Gita presented the relationships among them. Since he was writing for himself—the title of the journal that has come to be known as *Meditations* is *To Myself*—there was no reason for him to use the kind of rhetorical techniques and paradoxes by which the Gita seeks to stimulate its readers to see things for themselves, and no need for him to appeal in different ways to those who are temperamentally more suited to the different yogas. Consequently, just as his writing was not dialectical in the way the Gita is, neither does it contain the Gita's incoherencies on the relation of different ways of achieving wisdom.

Nonviolence

The Bhagavad Gita

Does a dialectical reading resolve the apparent contradiction within the question of whether all things are identical with God, even ungodly ones like violence? Franklin Edgerton writes:

> Since *all* comes from God, it seems impossible to deny that origin to anything. "Whatever states of being there are, be they of the nature of goodness, passion, or darkness, . . . know that all of them come from Me alone"

[7.12]. In another passage, God is declared the course of all "psychic" states and experiences, *good and bad alike*, tho [*sic*] the good predominate in the list. "Enlightenment, knowledge, freedom from delusion, patience, truth, self-control, peace, pleasure, *pain*, coming-into-being, passing away, *fear*, and fearlessness too; harmlessness, indifference (equanimity), content, austerity, generosity, fame, and *disrepute*—the states of creatures, of all various sorts, come from Me alone" [10.4–5]. More definite recognition of the origin even of evil in God is found in this: "I am the gambling of rogues, the majesty of the majestic; I am conquest, I am adventure (of conquerors and adventurers); I am the courage of the courageous. . . . I am the violence of conquerors, I am the statecraft of ambitious princes; I too am the taciturnity of things that are secret, I am the knowledge of the learned" [10.36 and 10.38]. If even in these passages we seem to find a tendency to slur over the evil of the world and its necessary relation to a quasi-pantheistic God, in other places the Gita feels it necessary to qualify its semipantheism by definitely ruling out evil from God's nature. Thus to a passage in the seventh chapter which is strongly suggestive of pantheism . . .—"I am the taste in water, etc.; I am the intelligence of the intelligent, the majesty of the majestic"—there is added this significant verse [7.11]: "I am the strength of the strong, *free from lust and passion*; I am desire in (all) beings (but) *not* (such desire as is) *opposed to righteousness*." Thus the Gita strengthens its appeal to the natural man, or to "common sense," at the expense of logic and consistency.[50]

Are logic and consistency dispensed with here, or can these contradictions be resolved by distinguishing different levels of the argument?

That there are contradictory statements is undeniable. Throughout the Gita Krishna regularly tells Arjuna what he ought to do and what he ought not to do. Even the pivotal verse 2.38 concludes by saying, "Thus shalt thou not incur sin." How then can he soon afterwards tell Arjuna to cast aside the distinction between good and evil (2.50) or wish and hate (8.27)? On the contrary, the message seems to be that we ought to hate sin as evil and wish to do good in accordance with dharma. Krishna even uses the promise of approval to motivate Arjuna not to care about approval: "He who holds equal blame and praise . . . is dear to Me" (12.19). To urge Arjuna to renounce dualities already implies a distinction between the good renunciation of duality and the evil hateful demonic making of dualities. Krishna is evidently aware of the tension, since he says in the same verse both that he is devoid of desire and that he *is* a desire: "I am the strength of the strong, devoid of desire [*kama*] and passion [*raga*]. In beings am I the desire [*kama*] which is not contrary to law [*dharma*]" (7.11).

Rather than resulting from a sacrifice of logic and consistency, here, as with the inconsistent ranking of the different yogas, the tension pushes us to a deeper level of understanding. It pushes us to distinguish two senses of good and evil, and two senses of desire, one of which is relative to our individual pleasures and pains and is prohibited by dharma, while the other is absolute and is required by dharma.[51] The tension is resolved by moving from the human perspective of relative dualities to the divine perspective of an absolute duality between enlightenment and delusion. Insofar as everything that happens follows from the nature of the divine, in accordance with the determinism discussed earlier, then everything that happens is in accordance with goodness and is good. But as we saw in chapter 4, there are two ways that an action can be good. An action done in accordance with an enlightened state of mind, without attachment and with its fruits relinquished, is good both intrinsically and instrumentally, good in itself and good because it is part of divine predestination, or the goodness of the whole. However an action done for *rajasic* or *tamasic* reasons, done because of an attachment to its fruits, is good not in itself but only instrumentally, as an intrinsic element in the *overall* good. Duryodhana's actions are part of the divine design, and so far good, but in themselves evil because their goal is to achieve a personal advantage rather than to manifest dharma. The desire to manifest dharma, to do what is impersonally right, is "the desire which is not contrary to *dharma*," as opposed to the combination of "desire [*kama*] and passion [*raga*]," that is, attached desire. The *Katha Upaniṣad* says: "Whatever is here, that is there. What is there, that again is here. He obtains death after death who seems to see a difference here" (4.10). Actions that are good only instrumentally and not intrinsically follow from the belief in a difference, a belief that our "self" is that by which we differ from all others rather than that which we have in common with all others. By contrast, those actions are good intrinsically that follow from a belief that "whatever is here, that is there. What is there, that again is here." It is the

golden rule taken to its ultimate justification: there is no ultimate difference between myself and others.

It is in this same spirit that Krishna can urge Arjuna to fight while at
the same time praising nonviolence. So when Krishna several times tells
Arjuna to reject dualistic thinking and says that (among other things)
pain is as good as pleasure, death as good as birth, and blame as good as
praise, we might have expected him to add that violence is as good as nonviolence. But he does not: he supports *this* kind of dualistic thinking and
praises only *non*violence.[52] The difference is that in the first group of dualities both sides are characterized by attachment and difference, whereas
in the latter pair only violence is attached and nonviolence unattached.
Precisely because Arjuna does not want to fight, his fighting would not
be an act of violence, that is, attached. To act from dharma rather than
desire exempts the action from being violent. Acts of violence have often
been committed in the name of duty, but what Krishna means by duty is
very specific. Not only must we "expect no reward and believe firmly that
it is [our] duty to offer the sacrifice" (17.11), but we must make sure we
are free of "the dualities which arise from wish and hate" (8.27). As with
Kant, we can most be sure we are acting from duty when our course of
action does not coincide with our self-interest.[53] We must be "able to resist the rush of desire and anger" (5.23) and be impartial (*samabuddhir*)
among those we love and those we hate (6.9). Krishna does not simply
urge Arjuna to fight but to "fight, delivered from thy fever" (3.30). What
Arjuna must do, what any of us must do if we want to be certain of acting
from duty rather than inclination, is make sure that our decision is made
in a state of tranquility (*prasadah*, 17.16), free from wish and hate, desire
and anger, favoritism of any kind. The presence of any of these emotions
undermines our sense of duty, and it is unlikely that violent acts performed in the name of duty are free of such influences.[54]

In saying that pleasure and pain both proceed from the divine, but
not both nonviolence and violence (10.4–5), Krishna distances himself from the ordinary understanding of violence as inflicting pain. Not
the fruit of the action but the source of the action is what determines
whether it is intrinsically good and free from violence (every action is instrumentally good as contributing to the predestined course of events).
What Laozi expresses starkly—

Heaven and Earth are not humane.
They treat all things as straw dogs.
The sage is not humane.
He regards all people as straw dogs.
          (Chan 1963b, chap. 5)

—Krishna puts more discursively: "Wise men do not grieve for the dead or for the living. . . . Just as a person casts off worn-out garments and puts on others that are new, even so does the embodied soul cast off worn-out bodies and take on others that are new" (2.11, 22). For Krishna as for Laozi, individuality is inessential. Reality lies only in the undifferentiated and eternal.

From an analytic point of view Edgerton is right to say that some of Krishna's teachings are "at the expense of logic and consistency." No linguistic distinction alone can justify the statement that to be divine is to be free of desire and yet also to manifest the ultimate desire, or that we must "cast away both good and evil" in order to pursue the good and escape evil, or that it is permissible to go to war and kill people as long as we do not do so violently. Until the paradox or its equivalent pushes us to conceive a perspective that we were blind to when the contradiction brought us to a halt, merely verbal distinctions will seem arbitrary. The paradox is dialectical because it can be resolved only when we are able to *see* a difference that we were not able to see before.

Marcus Aurelius

Although there is no explicit concept of nonviolence in Marcus, the literal meaning of *ahimsa*, "nonharming," is something he unequivocally aspires to:

I have never intentionally given pain even to another. (8.42)

A spider is proud when it has caught a fly, and another when he has caught a poor hare, and another when he has taken a little fish in a net, and another when he has taken wild boars, and another when he has taken bears, and another when he has taken Sarmatians. Are not these robbers, if you examine their opinions? (10.10)[55]

How can he reconcile his engagement in military slaughter with these two statements, the insistence that he has never intentionally inflicted pain, and the condemnation of predators both animalistic and militaristic—especially since he himself took Sarmatian prisoners of war? Here, as with the Gita, it is the state of mind of the actor rather than the action itself that determines whether it is violent—hence the words "if you examine their opinions."

Again, like the Gita, it is the freedom from passion, being in a state of tranquility, and being a transparent instrument of God that renders our actions nonviolent:

> For the man who is such and no longer delays being among the number of the best, is like a priest and minister of the gods, using too the deity which is planted within him [reason], which makes the man uncontaminated by pleasure, unharmed by any pain, untouched by any insult, feeling no wrong, a fighter in the noblest fight, one who cannot be overpowered by any passion, dyed deep with justice, accepting with all his soul everything which happens and is assigned to him as his portion. . . . And he remembers also that every rational animal is his kinsman, and that to care for all men is according to man's nature; and a man should hold on to the opinion not of all, but of those only who confessedly live according to nature. (3.4; cf. 6.44)

> Suppose that men kill you, cut you in pieces, curse you. What then can these things do to prevent your mind from remaining pure, wise, sober, just? . . . Form yourself hourly to freedom conjoined with contentment, simplicity and modesty. (8.51; cf. 8.57)

*   *   *

The Bhagavad Gita and Marcus Aurelius agree that we should never intentionally harm others, but that "harm" is meant in a very specific sense, namely when we are acting through personal attachment rather than in an impersonal release from all attachments. In the latter case, when our sense of duty is validated by a lack of emotional involvement in the outcome, our forceful actions are not considered violent; they are not a deliberate infliction of harm but an unattached attempt to create goodness in the world. But the level of impersonal detachment is not as radical in Marcus as it is for the Gita. For Marcus Aurelius the rationalist there is no ultimate state of union with the divine in which we leave nature, *prakriti*, behind altogether and attain to God, *puruṣa*. It is only to be expected, then, that the concept of human perfectibility that Arjuna seems to have attained by the end is not expected by Marcus. He writes:

> Drama, war, astonishment, torpor, slavery, will daily wipe out those holy principles of yours. . . . For when will you enjoy simplicity? (10.9)

> The art of life is more like the wrestler's art than the dancer's, in respect of this, that it should stand ready and firm to meet onsets which are sudden and unexpected. (7.61)

Although in the philosophy of life there are significant parallels between the *Meditations* and the Gita, and although both see God as working through human beings, only the Gita sees human beings as potentially gods themselves. Even if a Stoic should attain to the perfection of a sage, becoming the equal of God, the Stoic God is not the *puruṣa* of the Bhagavad Gita but the god of *prakriti* (nature), at the level of *sattva* (reason).[56] For Marcus Aurelius the world is never anything but real.

CONCLUSION

Metaphysics and Ethics

One aim of this book has been to explore fundamental issues in metaphysics and ethics, and the relation between the two, tracing how the practical thinking of ethics arises out of knowledge, whether metaphysical or experiential, and how it is a matter of enabling ourselves to discern what is called for in the moment. Since we have examined these issues through the works of thinkers in three traditions, different voices are heard in the different chapters, so it may be helpful to review the trajectory of the book as a whole.

We began with the question of how metaphysics can arise from ordinary thinking. Most philosophers in the West have employed rational argument and demonstration to achieve this goal. That is also true for many Asian philosophers, but the latter are more likely than Western philosophers to use nonargumentative techniques. Paradox brings our logical thinking to a standstill and pushes us to look beyond simple logic to something more elusive. Humor presents us with a contravention not so much of logic but of our expectations, thereby leading us to see things differently than before, sometimes innocuously but sometimes significantly. Allegorical or evocative stories do this more directly by using the ordinary to signify the extraordinary. The attention to bodily comportment recognizes the connection between mind and body and the importance of disciplining the latter to provide more scope to the former. The importance of mentoring derives from the limitation of written words that Plato calls our attention to in the *Phaedrus* (276a–277a).[1]

Chapter 2 turned to what is usually considered the most fundamental issue in metaphysics, the difference between the world as it appears to the senses and as it is for thought—that is, the world as appearance and reality. At the origin of Western philosophy, our perception of the world as a multiplicity of individuals was conceived as a misperception of what is in reality a unity, described metaphorically as one of the elements ("water" for Thales, "air" for Anaximenes) or nonmetaphorically as Anaximander's "indefinite" and Parmenides's "it is." At the origin of Indian philosophy reality was similarly conceived as Atman (self), whose unity is hidden from us by maya; and we have seen that for Laozi and Zhuangzi there is also a conception of original oneness that is misperceived by the senses. In examining this model we saw how its metaphysical point of view leads to ethics, with all three philosophers identifying the whole with goodness. For Spinoza, whose metaphysics is elaborated in a book entitled *Ethics*, the goal is to live according to reason, and we can best accomplish this if others live by reason as well, so "we necessarily strive to bring it about that men live according to the guidance of reason," which is the true meaning of morality, and "We know nothing to be certainly good or evil, except what really leads to understanding or what can prevent us from understanding."[2] For Shankara as well, "The ignorance characterised by the notions 'I' and 'Mine' is destroyed by the knowledge produced by the realisation of the true nature of the Self."[3] When we cease to compete with others there is no incentive to behave immorally. So metaphysics in this basic form naturally leads to morality.

Chapter 3 examined more explicitly the relationship between metaphysics and morality that was a subsidiary theme in the first two chapters. Zhu Xi, Plato, Aristotle, and Plotinus all saw metaphysics not only as a powerful instrument of morality but as the only way we can appreciate the relationship between existence and goodness. Through metaphysical thinking we may become aware of a pure rationality within the imperfectly rational material world, which gives that world its meaning, and we may become aware, by extension, that our own lives become more meaningful as well as more moral by means of rational thought and behavior. Metaphysical thinking shows us the inadequacy of corporeal reality to intelligible reality, and by combating the belief that happiness can be found in corporeal pleasure, power, or wealth it undermines the temptations of immorality.

The philosophers of chapter 4 were also metaphysical but not in the systematic way characteristic of those in the preceding chapter. Consequently the interpretation of their views is much less straightforward, as is also true of the moral implications of their writings. Nevertheless, here too the metaphysical thinking gives rise to moral principles, especially the principle of impartiality. Everyone is good in a merely natural sense, as a contributor to the mosaic goodness of the natural world, but to be *morally* good we must awaken to our identity with the principle of the whole rather than with the part that is our individual body. That is the meaning of impartiality.

Not only metaphysical thinking but a more ordinary thinking can not only lead to virtue but be identical with virtue, as we saw in chapter 5. The view that virtue is knowledge has sometimes been dismissed not only as false but as obviously false. We have all had the experience of thinking, "I know I shouldn't do this but I'm going to do it anyway" or, more dramatically, "I know I'll hate myself in the morning but I just can't resist." Socrates's early date made it easy to dismiss his identification of virtue with knowledge as the result of a lack of prior discussion of the issue that would have shown him its limitations. Wang Yangming, however, who had a long tradition of such discussion behind him, made the same identification that Socrates did in full awareness of the objections. The weakness of the objections is that they establish a lower threshold for what counts as knowledge: what they take as knowledge Socrates and Wang take to be a species of opinion. Knowledge as they define it has a strong claim to be identical with virtue.

In the Socratic and Confucian traditions the knowledge that is identical with virtue enables us to discern in every situation the mean between going too far and not far enough. That is the theme of chapter 6. The ethical mean cannot be calculated like a mathematical mean by splitting the difference between the extremes; rather, it is discerned immediately as the correct action, and the extremes are known by their departure from the mean. It is a kind of knowledge that has no specific name in

Plato and Confucius but that Aristotle calls *phronesis*, usually translated as "practical wisdom" or "prudence," a kind of "seeing" that perceives the nonformulaic right course of action in each unique situation, and to which we can train ourselves by an earnest attempt to envision what a good person would choose to do in the circumstances. Thus it is not uncommon for people who are undecided what to do to try to imagine what someone they admire would do in that situation.

In the final chapter we looked at a particular problem in ethics that illustrates the importance of the mean, the problem of nonviolence. It is a common theme in all three cultures that we should love our neighbor as we love ourselves, and not do to others what we would not want done to ourselves, which leads to the belief that it is wrong to inflict harm on others (the Sanskrit word *ahimsa* literally means "not harming," but the concept is more often referred to as "nonviolence"). There are some, such as the Jains and other fruitarians, for whom nonviolence is not a mean but an absolute, while for those at the opposite extreme, like the Aztecs, the Nazis, and terrorists of whatever persuasion, nonviolence is not a virtue at all. This is a special case of what we saw at the beginning of chapter 6, that some conceptions of ethics rely on absolutes rather than the mean. Here, as elsewhere, I am claiming, not that there is a universal philosophy, but only that particular philosophies cross cultural boundaries. For those who do seek nonviolence and who believe that there are some situations in which forceful action is required, the problem is to find the mean between violence and passivity. When is "violence" not violence? The short answer is "When it is necessary," but this answer quickly breaks down into incompatible subjective understandings of what necessity means. The resolution provided in chapter 7 is that necessity means when calm rationality, unagitated by passions and attachments, perceives the duty to act forcefully. Many philosophers from Nietzsche to Foucault among others would dispute that an impartial standpoint is conceivable, let alone possible, but neither view is uncontroversial. There is also the practical problem of freedom from self-deception: it is easy to convince ourselves that we see our duty when we see only our advantage. There is no certain technique for immunizing ourselves to such deception; the best we can do is to be aware of the danger and to work toward the kind of knowledge discussed in chapters 5 and 6.

Comparative Philosophy

A further aim of the book has been to assess to what extent philosophers from different cultures can be considered to have comparable thoughts. No one doubts that there are both similarities and differences among philosophers from different traditions, but going back at least to Hegel it has often been asserted that the similarities are only superficial and the differences decisive. This issue has been discussed at length in the Introduction, but I would like to add some further remarks arising from the subsequent comparisons. In the preceding chapters we have seen varying degrees of similarity and difference. The two philosophers who appear closest, and least tied to a particular culture, are Socrates and Wang Yangming on the identity of virtue and knowledge. In other chapters the influence of culture is more evident, especially in the case of Indian philosophy, such as the Upaniṣads, the Bhagavad Gita, and Shankara. In the first chapter we saw that the Upaniṣads use religious language far more than does Zhuangzi or, for that matter, any of the other Chinese or Western philosophers discussed above. The same can be said of Shankara and the Bhagavad Gita. In chapter 2, for Shankara our tendency toward superimposition is a karmic consequence of our past lives, while for Spinoza it is a consequence of the fact that our individual mind is the idea of our body and thus looks first to the body and the faculty of imagination. There is no concept of reincarnation in Parmenides or Spinoza, nor can there be in Spinoza since there is no concept of the soul—something that might be said of Parmenides too except that much of his book has not survived. As we saw in the final chapter, Marcus Aurelius does not share the Bhagavad Gita's view of human beings as potentially gods themselves. Even if a Stoic should attain to the perfection of a sage and become the equal of God, the Stoics' God is not the *puruṣa* of the Bhagavad Gita but the god of *prakriti* (nature), at the level of *sattva* (reason). For Stoics like Marcus Aurelius the world of our senses is less important than the world of reason, but it is no less real.

This book claims, then, not that thinkers in different cultures think identical thoughts but only that they think comparable and often compatible thoughts. It is even questionable whether two thinkers in the *same* culture can think identical thoughts. The tactics by which Zhuangzi and the Upaniṣads seek to raise us from our ordinary view of reality to an extraordinary one are basically the same, despite differences in emphasis and in cultural expression. Again, Parmenides, Shankara, and Spinoza all see the multiplicity of the world of ordinary experience as dependent on the inadequacy of our perceptual powers—which they may diagnose in different terms—while *in itself* reality is one and undivided by time and place. In Heraclitus and Laozi the influence of their culture is relatively small; both writers have unique voices that set them apart from other writers of their generation. There is enough stylistic difference between them that there is no doubt to which culture each belongs, but the vision they articulate is very much alike. The greatest differences in the book are found in chapter 4, where Zhu Xi, Plato, Aristotle, and Plotinus agree and disagree with one another in various ways, but these are not necessarily cultural differences, as we can see in the case of Plato and Aristotle and perhaps Plotinus. It turns out that the one whom Plotinus is closest to is not one of the other Greeks but the Chinese philosopher Zhu Xi. In chapter 5, as in chapter 3, the cultural differences between Socrates and Wang Yangming play a relatively small part. One is recognizably Greek and the other Chinese, but this has little or no effect on their beliefs. Chapter 6 acknowledges the cultural and theoretical differences between Confucius and Plato, yet their views of morality as the ability to discern and act on the mean are virtually identical in practical terms. Again in chapter 7 there is no lack of cultural difference between the Stoic philosophy of Marcus Aurelius and the Samkhya philosophy of the Bhagavad Gita, differences as fundamental as whether we have souls that are reincarnated and whether there is a higher kind of reality than even reason (*logos, sattva*) can apprehend. Yet these differences, significant as they are in themselves, do not prevent the authors from arriving at similar conclusions for similar reasons. I conclude that although culture makes a significant difference in some of our beliefs, and provides the conceptual scheme within which we must express our beliefs, it does not prevent us from having shared experiences. Philosophers differ in many ways, but we have seen that philosophers can have more in common with thinkers from a different culture than they do with some thinkers from their own culture.

NOTES

Introduction

1. Comparative philosophy has been influential in the West at least since Schopenhauer and has been "vital in America at least since Ralph Waldo Emerson" (Neville 2016, 503).

2. Cf. McLeod: "What some Western traditions take as sufficiently basic and general may turn out not to be so at all, when we look at Chinese traditions" (2016, x).

3. The concept of "tradition," while convenient, is not unproblematic. See McLeod (2016, 180–84).

4. Cf. Scharfstein (1998, 45).

5. "Lao Tzu" and "*Tao Te Ch'ing*" are the older Wades-Giles transliterations, "Laozi" and "*Daodejing*" the more recent *pinyin* versions. I use the *pinyin* transliterations because they are increasingly predominant, but I supply the Wade-Giles equivalent when the name is first mentioned because it is more likely to be familiar to Western readers.

6. For detailed comparisons among the three traditions, see Scharfstein (1998, 16–54) and "The Three Philosophical Traditions" in Scharfstein (2014, 132–37); also Blocker (1999, 34–41). According to Joel Kupperman, "The central issues (by and large) in classical Indian philosophy and also classical Chinese philosophy concern ways in which one can modify and develop one's self, and create a path of life that reflects this development. In much Western philosophy after Hume, in contrast, decisions in problematic circumstances have been regarded as central, and there has been especial attention to the development of decision procedures" (2010, 187); for a fuller version of his claims, he refers the reader to his *Learning from Asian Philosophy* (1999) and his *Classic Asian Philosophy* (2007). Zong (2010) argues that one difference between Chinese philosophy and Western philosophy is that the latter is predominantly sentential and the former primarily nonsentential.

7. See McLeod's (2016, 11–12) discussion of the contentious case of *Analects* 12.11.

8. Cf. Ma and van Brakel (2016, 28–29, 36–37).

9. Unless otherwise stated, all references to the *Analects* are to Huang's translation and numbering (Confucius 1997).

10. *Shu.* Huang has "like-hearted considerateness."

11. See Huxley ([1944] 1970): 1. That Art Thou; 2. The Nature of the Ground; 3. Personality, Sanctity, Divine Incarnation; 4. God in the World; 5. Charity; 6. Mortification, Non-attachment, Right Livelihood; 7. Truth; 8. Religion and Temperament; 9. Self-Knowledge; 10. Grace and Free Will; 11. Good and Evil; 12. Time and Eternity; 13. Salvation, Deliverance, Enlightenment; 14. Immortality and Survival; 15. Silence; 16. Prayer; 17. Suffering; 18. Faith; 19. God Is Not Mocked; 20. *Tantam religio potuit suadere malorum*; 21. Idolatry; 22. Emotionalism; 23. The Miraculous; 24. Ritual, Symbol, Sacrament; 25. Spiritual Exercises; 26. Perseverance and Regularity; 27. Contemplation, Action and Social Utility.

12. Two other authors who have done this are Burik (2009) and Smid (2009).

13. Hegel, at least, does not extend to art the cultural-historical relativism that he applies to philosophy: "In art, that of the Greeks sets the highest standard just as it is" (1988, 50).

14. I use *linguistic* here in its most general sense, including the "language" of art.

15. The relevance of Davidson's argument for comparative philosophy has been discussed in some detail by Chinn (2007) and by Ma and van Brakel (2013; 2016, esp. 152–54, 298). Scharfstein writes: "It is possible to take an extreme position and claim that each of the traditions is incommensurable with the others, that is, that no tradition can be grasped at all by means of the categories and habits of thought of the others. This extreme is empirically implausible and the attempt to argue in its favor entails its own denial: Whoever goes beyond the mere assertion and undertakes to explain how and why traditional Indians, Chinese, and Europeans were—and, to later interpreters, remain—impenetrable worlds apart, is most probably assuming the ability to enter into each of the worlds far enough to show that they are closed to one another. The explanation explains what, it is claimed, is impossible to explain" (1998, 34).

16. Cf. Blocker: "A crosscultural comparison is unavoidable in any crosscultural description; the concepts must be ours while the beliefs are theirs. But how can that possibly be fair? Only if the concepts by which we describe their beliefs and the concepts by which they describe the same beliefs in their society are synonymous or at least similar in meaning" (1999, 7). Blocker goes on to defend

this assumption while acknowledging the differences of vocabulary among the three traditions (7–15). Cf. Scharfstein (1998, 16–21).

17. Ma and van Brakel "argue for a pragmatic Wittgenstein-inspired understanding of language and of family resemblance of the referents of general terms both within and across traditions. . . . Something like the principle of charity and something like the principle of humanity [or "soul"—human beings share the same basic nature] both play a role in subsequent stages of linguistic interpretation" (2016, 4, 13; cf. 107–19, 135–39, 265, 265n7, 275–81). Also see their discussion of the *geyi* method of matching concepts between different traditions (201–7). Cf. Roger Ames's response to Eske Møllgaard: "Cross-cultural understanding must proceed analogically with each tradition having to find within its own resources a vocabulary that enables it to restate in some always imperfect way the philosophy and cultural assets of the [other] tradition that it would understand better" (Ames 2005, 349); also quoted in Ma and van Brakel (2016, 217). Wittgenstein's concept of "family resemblance" is also used by McLeod (2016, 177).

18. Walter Kaufmann and R. J. Hollingdale's translation (*On the Genealogy of Morals* 3.2, in Nietzsche 1969), emphasis in original, substituting "that" for "one" as a translation of *dieselbe*. The original German is "Es gibt *nur* ein perspektivisches Sehen, *nur* ein perspektivisches 'Erkennen'; und *je mehr* Affekte wir über eine Sache zu Worte kommen lassen, *je mehr* Augen, verschiedne Augen wir uns für dieselbe Sache einzusetzen wissen, um so vollständiger wird unser 'Begriff' dieser Sache, unsre 'Objektivität' sein" (*Zur Genealogie der Moral* 3.12, in Nietzsche 1963b). I leave aside the question of whether Nietzsche's conception of perspectivism is intended to be distinct from relativism.

19. That is the point of the Indian parable of the blind men and the elephant. According to one version of the story, one man touches the elephant's leg and says that an elephant is like a tree, another touches its side and says an elephant is like a wall, a third touches the tail and says an elephant is like a rope, a fourth touches an ear and says an elephant is like a fan, a fifth touches a tusk and says an elephant is like a spear, while a sixth, touching the trunk, says an elephant is like a snake.

20. Cf. Blocker (1999, 6–7). Scharfstein writes: "As the person within a certain tradition sees it, to try to compare its philosophy with that of another tradition is like trying to play two discordant games at the same time. However, the comparatist is not the practitioner of any philosophy but a theme-and-variation philosopher, whose interest is in the variety of philosophies. . . . The philosophical traditions are either unique or alike depending on one's position in relation to them—inside or outside—and the standard of judgment one adopts, that is, the kind and degree of abstraction one allows oneself in order to deny or justify

comparison. Both sides are quite right, if one wishes, or neither, if one insists" (1998, 38).

21. See Gadamer (1972, 289); English translation, Gadamer (1975, 273). Ma and van Brakel write, "Insofar as we can speak of a fusion of horizons at all, it should be understood as pragmatic consensus in concrete situations for the purpose of continuing the exchange" (2013, 299). They prefer what they call mutual attunement (307–9). Their primary concern, however, is with intercultural dialogue rather than with the interpretation of fixed texts. When, as in this book, we interpret a philosophy from the past, there is no possibility of *mutually* continuing the exchange or *mutual* attunement. We may try to fuse our horizon of understanding with that of the text, but we cannot expect the text to do the same for us.

22. "His familiarity with the *Zhuangzi* is witnessed during the period 1930 to 1972" (Ma and van Brakel 2016, 181).

23. Page numbers refer to the German edition that the translators insert in the margins.

24. For Heidegger's lack of sympathy with Indian philosophy, see Ma and van Brakel (2016, 184).

25. Translated as *Discourse on Thinking* (Heidegger 1966). Heidegger writes: "This discourse was taken from a conversation written down in 1944–45 between a scientist, a scholar, and a teacher" (58n).

26. For additional discussion of Heidegger's evolving attitude toward Asian philosophy, see Ma and van Brakel (2016, 180–87).

27. In fact, the Buddhist concept of *anatta*, a Pali word equivalent to the Sanskrit *anatman*, i.e., "no self," was bitterly opposed by Shankara. What lay behind maya for Shankara was Atman, the divine self; while what lay behind maya for the Buddhists, given their doctrines of *anicca* and *anatta*, was "emptiness," a "middle way" between existence and nonexistence. For Shankara's attitude toward Buddhism, see Scharfstein (1998, 378–81). Also cf. Blocker: "By coopting a large part of Buddhism, Shankara was able to halt the spread of Buddhism, that is, the conversion by Hindus to Buddhism" (1999, 33).

28. Quotations from Marcus Aurelius, *Meditations*, are modernized from the translation of George Long (Marcus Aurelius 1862).

Chapter 1

1. E.g., *Meno* 80a, *Republic* 487b–c.

2. Stephanus numbers for Plato's works correspond to the Burnet edition of the Oxford Classical Texts (Burnet 1900–1907). Bekker numbers for

Aristotle correspond to the Oxford Classical Texts series (Oxford: Clarendon Press, various dates) except where otherwise noted.

3. Translations from Zhuangzi are by Burton Watson (Zhuangzi 2013) unless otherwise stated. I confine myself to the first seven "inner" chapters, which are generally regarded as Zhuangzi's own work. Like Plato, Zhuangzi often attributes what appear to be his views to other speakers. For the purposes of this study I abstract from those distinctions.

4. *Kun* can also mean "whale," but most translators prefer "roe" because the paradox between the smallest and the largest is characteristic of Zhuangzi. Cf. Izutsu (2004, 9).

5. North is the "Yin pole of the universe" (Wu 1990, 56; cf. 71–72).

6. Scott Cook points out that in a later passage the northern darkness too is called "Heaven's Pool," so Kun will "end up in the same place from which it began its journey" (2003, 69). If this is the same pool or lake of heaven, the north and south become inseparable and the yin/yang interpretation becomes more plausible (although that is not Cook's point). The passage in question says: "In the bald and barren north, there is a dark sea, the Lake of Heaven. In it is a fish that is several thousand *li* across, and no one knows how long. His name is Kun. There is also a bird there, named Peng, with a back like Mount Tai and wings like clouds filling the sky. He beats the whirlwind, leaps into the air, and rises up ninety thousand *li*, cutting through the clouds and mist, shouldering the blue sky, and then he turns his eyes south and prepares to journey to the southern darkness" (chap. 1, p. 2). Here too nothing is said about Peng turning (back) into Kun; in fact, in this passage, unlike the earlier one, Kun and Peng seem to exist side by side rather than as transformations of one another. If Kun/Peng do end up where they begin, it may be a reference to the view that after awakening we are still in the same world although everything is transformed, as when Plato's liberated prisoners, after experiencing true reality, return to the cave with a different perspective.

7. So too the quail, half a page later: "The little quail laughs at him, saying, 'Where does he think *he's* going? I give a great leap and fly up, but I never get more than ten or twelve yards before I come down fluttering among the weeds and brambles. And that's the best kind of flying, anyway!' . . . Such is the difference between big and little."

8. Cf. Wu: "Southern darkness means the bright-separate realm which we yet do not know" (1990, 333). In Plato's cave only the highest level, looking directly at the sun (the Idea of the Good)—the consummation of dialectic—corresponds to the ineffable (533a).

9. Cf. the *Katha Upaniṣad*: "Arise! Awake! . . . He who is awake in those that sleep . . . That indeed is the Pure. That is Brahman" (3.14, 5.8). All translations

from the Upaniṣads are by Robert Hume (1877), modernized. Parentheses are in the orginal, bracketed words are added.

10. Cf. *Mundaka Upaniṣad* 3.2–3.

11. Cf. Graham: "The Taoist does not permanently deem himself a man or a butterfly but moves spontaneously from fitting one name to fitting another" (1981, 61n); see also Girardot (1983, 79–80); Roth (2003, 29); and Kohn (2011, xv, 74). For a different view, see Allinson (1989, 81–84), and Scharfstein (1998, 124–25).

12. A reference to the statement of the logician Gongsun Long, "A white horse is not a horse" (Zhuangzi 2013, 10n7). The reference is clearer in context. Graham takes the passage to refer to "arbitrary acts of naming"—the universe could be called "horse" (1981, 53). I think it has more to do with the presence of the whole in every part. Cf. Izutsu (2004, 2).

13. Cf. Wu (1982, 134). Because of passages like these I do not share Graham's view that Zhuangzi never says all is one "except as one side of a paradox" (1981, 56).

14. Similarly, in the *Republic* Socrates says he cannot put the highest truth into words because words are only an image of truth, not truth itself (533a). I've discussed Plato's response to this challenge in Dorter (1996) and Dorter (2010).

15. For an account and refutation of the relativistic interpretation, see Allinson (1989, 14–22, 111–42). Also see Merton ([1965] 1997, 16, 20, 24, 30); Scharfstein (1998, 120–21, 21n).

16. Eske Møllgaard writes: "Zhuangzi shuns propositional truth. . . . The main function of Zhuangzi's double-questions [about language and the peeping of birds]—is it so? or is it not so?—is to suspend propositional discourse and open up a space between affirmation and negation in which saying [*yan*] is able to speak the world" (2007, 71–72).

17. This reciprocal relationship prefigures the relation between principle (*li*) and material force (*qi*) in Zhu Xi: "Without the material force and concrete stuff of the universe, principle would have nothing in which to inhere" (*Chu Tzu yü-lei* 10a–b, in Zhu Xi 1967, 73), and "If the nature of heaven's endowment is lacking in material substance, then there is no place where it can be. It is like a spoonful of water: if there is nothing to hold it, then there is nowhere for the water to be" (*Further Reflections* 1.13, 1991, 60). Cf. the relation between the forms and the receptacle in Plato's *Timaeus* (49a). These parallels are not exact, but a lengthy digression would be needed to discuss their relationship.

18. Cook, citing Guo Xiang, suggests that the pipes of the Earth, like pan-pipes, each produce a different pitch and thus "represent well the idea of equality through diversification, each producing a different pitch through a similar standard" (2003, 72).

19. Plato's Eleatic visitor notes that "it is difficult . . . to show without models [παραδείγματα] any of the greater things. For each of us knows everything almost as if in a dream, and then is ignorant as if he has awakened" (*Statesman* 277d). (All translations from Plato are my own unless otherwise specified.) As Møllgaard points out, "The theoretical discourse of Plato may be very different from that of Zhuangzi (Plato talks about the Forms, Zhuangzi about the Way), but the practical goal of their philosophies may be the same, namely to attain the universal (cosmic) perspective" (2007, 8).

20. Merton ([1965] 1997, 32) gives a different interpretation.

21. "Jie Yu, the madman of Chu, . . . [said,] 'All men know the use of the useful, but nobody knows the use of the useless!'" (chap. 4, pp. 32–33).

22. Nevertheless, Bergson denies that the comic reveals hidden reality the way art does (1911, 150–71); rather, "It relieves us from the strain of thinking" (196). Both points fail when applied to Zhuangzi.

23. Also see Swabey (1961, 163). In other places Swabey compares the deepest source to the metaphysical (11, 240), to penetration into the noumena (170), and to religious experience (89, 241).

24. Cf. Kupperman: "A brief prose statement of the meaning of the passage would not say nearly all that the passage says. Shades of irony, doubt, and self-mocking are difficult to capture in such a summary; but also the passage is a key to a dialectical series of responses, and it is by no means clear that any formula for the series could be contained in a prosaic summary" (1989, 313). Froese suggests that "if we are to live well with our language, we must learn to also continuously undo it through humour. If language is to remain robust, it needs humour as its playful sidekick. By revealing the meaninglessness of language, it also unveils the 'meaning' of the 'meaning-less,' taking us beyond language" (2013, 138). Wu writes that "we need a playful setting for basic themes . . . because delightful fantasy is the force of creation" (1990, 88). But why should that be more true of humorous fantasy than serious fantasy?

25. *Chandogya Upaniṣad* 8.7–9, emphasis added. In the *advaita* (nondual) tradition of the Upaniṣads there is no distinction between Atman and Brahman.

26. Barnes edition (Aristotle 1984). Unless otherwise stated, all translations from Aristotle are from this edition.

27. In Watson's translation, Zhuangzi seems dismissive of complete emotional acceptance: When "the True Man of old . . . [was] reluctant, he could not help doing certain things; annoyed, he let it show in his face" (chap. 6, p. 43); cf. Martin Palmer's translation (Zhuangzi 1996, 49). But reluctance and annoyance are incompatible with the acceptance of fate characteristic of Zhuangzi's teaching. Only five pages later we're told: "Be content with this time and dwell in this order, and then neither sorrow nor joy can touch you" (chap. 6, p. 48).

Yu-lan Fung translates the first passage more persuasively: "He responded spon-taneously, as if there were no choice. His accumulated attractiveness appeared in his expression" (Zhuangzi [1933] 1964, 114); cf. Brook Ziporyn's translation (Zhuangzi 2009, 42).

28. Cf. Girardot (1983, 100); Roth (2003, 15–16); and Møllgaard (2007, 126). "Breathing with the heels" is hyperbole for breathing deeply, even if it re-fers to the Daoist practice of sitting on one's heels while meditating.

29. *Nicomachean Ethics* 4.1125a13–16. Replacing Ross's translation of μεγαλόψυχος as "proud man" with the more literal "great-souled man."

Chapter 2

1. Western scholars have traditionally accepted the dates 788–820 for Shankara's life, but the evidence is uncertain. See Isayeva (1993, 83–87); Scharf-stein (1998, 368).

2. References to the pre-Socratics are to the Diels-Kranz fragment num-bers (Diels and Kranz 1966), and, unless otherwise specified, translations from the pre-Socratics are by Richard McKirahan (1994), occasionally modified. For a more detailed discussion of Parmenides, which discusses textual problems that cannot be dealt with here, see Dorter (2012a).

3. My translation.

4. See, e.g., Burnet ([1930] 1957, 178–79) and Finkelberg (1986). But cf. Cornford (1939, 45); Palmer (2008, 3.5). Unless otherwise specified, trans-lations from the pre-Socratics follow those of McKirahan (1994), occasionally modified.

5. Thus Karl Reinhardt writes that for Parmenides, "Muß diese ganze Welt notwendig falsche sein, das heißt subjektiv sein, griechisch ausgedrückt, sie kann nur νόμῳ und nicht φύσει existieren" ([1916] 1977, 30; If this entire world is necessarily false, that is, subjective, in Greek terms it can exist only by conven-tion and not by nature) and "Über die Schwierigkeit hinwegzuhelfen hat er sich freilich nur durch einen ungeheuren Sprung gewußt; aber wo gibt es einen Ide-alisten, der über dieselbe Frage glatt hinübergekommen ware?" ([1916] 1977, 81; The only way he knew to help get past the difficulty was, of course, by means of a gigantic leap; but where is there an Idealist who could get beyond this question smoothly?). For the phenomenology-influenced interpretation of Heidegger, see Heidegger (1954c; 1957, 73–133 passim). For discussion of the materialist and idealist interpretations, see Tarán (1965, 195–201).

6. Cf. Cornford: "Parmenides is the prophet of a logic which will toler-ate no semblance of contradiction" (1939, 28); "He will set all common sense

at defiance, and follow reason" (29). For a more recent variant of this view, see Lewis (2009), which argues that Parmenides's rejection of the ordinary view of reality derives from an illicit modal inference.

7. See, e.g., Mourelatos (1970); Nehamas (2002); Curd (2004).

8. See Bowra (1937); Verdenius (1949); Lagan (1982); Kingsley (1999, esp. 49–149); Kingsley (2003, esp. 17–294); Geldard (2007); Gemelli Marciano (2008); Granger (2010, 35–36); also see the discussion in Guthrie (1962–81, 5:7–13).

9. Cf. Owen (1975, 60–61).

10. Cornford does not put it strongly enough when he writes that Parmenides "seems to suggest that mortals are responsible for the apparent (though unreal) existence of sensible qualities. . . . Why the senses delude us, how false appearances can be given, he cannot tell" (1939, 50). The problem with this view is not merely how mortals are deluded but how the multitude of changing human beings can be said to be deluded if they do not exist. Cf. A. A. Long: "More serious is the denial of reality to Parmenides himself and all men if the sensible world is entirely false. Yet it is not clear that this troubled Parmenides himself or later Eleatics" (1975, 97). Although the most widely held twentieth-century view of Parmenides, it has had numerous dissenters. Heidegger, for example, connects appearance with being rather than with nonbeing: "Sein und Schein zusammengehören stets beieinander sind und im Beieinander immer auch den Wechsel von einem zum anderen und damit die ständige Verwirrung und aus dieser die Möglichkeit der Verirrung und Verwechslung anbieten" (1957, 83; Being and appearance always belong together side by side, and this side-by-side always invites the possibility of a switch from one to the other and thereby constant confusion, and from this arises the possibility of going astray and interchanging them). Previously Reinhardt reconciled the ways of truth and appearance in terms of the oppositions out of which the physical world is constructed: Parmenides's opposites, like Empedocles's elements, are themselves eternal and unchanging; only the things formed by their combination are transitory ([1916] 1977, esp. 70–81); also see Miller (1978) and Finkelberg (1999). More recently Curd reconciles them by what she calls predicational monism: "Each thing that is can be only one thing; and must be that in a particularly strong way" (2004, 3, 80n38).

11. "What Parmenides has not succeeded in establishing is any logical relationship between the truth and its counterfeit, or any logical status for the world of seeming. . . . It is hardly a criticism of Parmenides to say that in the very moment of a discovery which changed the whole face of philosophy there was not also revealed to him a means of accounting for the false semblance of reality exhibited to mortals by the world of appearances, nor of bringing the two worlds

into any logical relationship again without contravening the new and austere canons of thought which he himself had just laid down" (Guthrie 1962–81, 3:75–76). Cf. Verdenius ([1942] 1964, 58); Kahn (1969, 705); Stokes (1971, 142). Nevertheless, if Parmenides failed to notice a difficulty so devastating, or if he saw the problem but was not bothered by it, and even if he was bothered by it but saw no way to resolve it, then Guthrie is too generous, for it should be very much a criticism of Parmenides that he was oblivious to such a fundamental objection, or that he continued to promote in the most uncompromising terms a philosophy that he saw no way to reconcile with our experience of reality.

12. Palmer defends what he calls the modal interpretation, which is based on the principle that "Parmenides was the first philosopher rigorously to distinguish what must be, what must not be, and what is but need not be" (2008, 3.5). Unlike the aspectual interpretation, according to which the same reality can be seen as necessary and unitary in one aspect but contingent and multiple in another aspect (like Spinoza's *natura naturans* and *natura naturata*), Palmer's interpretation is that Parmenides is referring to two kinds of reality, the world of contingent beings and a necessary being that permeates it the way Anaxagoras's *Nous* permeates all things. B4 constitutes "an apparently insurmountable difficulty" for the aspectual view, Palmer believes. I shall show later why I do not believe that to be the case.

13. Words in angle brackets added. This difficult fragment is extensively discussed in Mourelatos (1970, 253–59).

14. Cf. Mourelatos: "Thought is the whole (cf. οὖλον), the all-together-one (cf. ὁμοῦ πᾶν ἕν), the cohesive (cf. συνεχές), the fullness of what-is (cf. ἔμπλεον ἐόντος), the consorting of what-is with what-is (cf. B8.25)" (1970, 258).

15. "Permeating all things completely" is Gallop's (1984) translation of διὰ παντὸς πάντα περῶντα. McKirahan (1994), following Owen's text, has "being always, indeed, all things."

16. Like most assertions about Parmenides, the spatiality of reality is debated on both sides. See, for example, Granger (2010, 29n34).

17. This is a difficult passage. In B1 Parmenides says:

8. the daughters of the Sun
9. were hastening to escort <me> after leaving the house of Night
10. for the light, having pushed back the veils from their heads with their hands.
11. There are the gates of the roads of Night and Day,
12. and a lintel and a stone threshold contain them.
13. High in the sky they are filled by huge doors
14. of which avenging Justice holds the keys that fit them.

15. The maidens beguiled her with soft words
16. and skillfully persuaded her to push back the bar for them
17. quickly from the gates.

The translation (by McKirahan) accepts Diels's punctuation of lines 9–10, instead of alternatives on which the journey is from light to Night. At first it may seem that "leaving the house of Night for the light" means the road leads from the mortals' realm of Night to the goddess's realm of light (9–10). In that case the gates of the roads of Night and Day, referred to in line 11, could be understood to separate night from day, rather than separating the timeless realm of the goddess from the temporal world of night and day. But in line 9 the travelers have already left the house of Night and they do not arrive at the gates of the roads of Night and Day until two lines later. In that case the gates cannot be what separate night from day. Night and day must both be on our side of the gates, and the gates must lead to a realm beyond the alternation of the two. There are thus two boundaries: the door of the house of Night, which separates night from day; and the gates of the roads of Night and Day, which separate the timeless realm of the goddess from both sides of the duality of night and day. For further discussion of the interpretive problems in the proem, see Owens (1979, 15–29); Granger (2008; 2010, 17n7); and Gemelli Marciano (2008).

18. The noun modified by "all" is a matter of conjecture. "Cities" is the most common conjecture, but see Gallop (1984, 48n1), and Cordero (2004, 26–27). Since the path of Parmenides's journey is "far from the beaten path of humans," I agree with Tarán that "Parmenides did not intend his journey to be taken as a reality in any sense" (1965, 22–23, 30)—against those who interpret "through all cities" literally to mean he was an itinerant philosopher, or that it was an actual journey whose route may be discoverable.

19. In favor of the authenticity of the *Vivekachudamani*, see George Victor (2002, 49, 97). Against, see Hirst (2005, 23). I have not hesitated to cite the *Vivekachudamani* where its doctrines clearly accord with Shankara's undisputed works because, as George Victor (2002, 100) puts it, it "contains the cardinal truths of Advaita Vedanta in simple terms without ambiguous disputations."

20. Regarding Spinoza, see, for example, the beginning of the appendix to Part I. This aspect of Spinoza's project is especially emphasized by Steven Smith (2003). Melamed argues that the traditional beliefs of Judaism play no part in Spinoza's philosophy, in opposition to the "many commentators, critics, and historians [who] have cried that Spinoza's excommunication was not justified since his doctrine was traceable to Jewish sources" (1933, 136). He argues that there is a "line extending from the Upanishads to Buddha, St. Paul, St. Augustine, and Spinoza" (5, cf. 299–363) and that mysticism was no part of traditional

Judaism. For all his erudition, however, Melamed never mentions the Zohar. He does mention Hassidism, but after acknowledging that it arose independently of Spinoza, he circumvents this counterexample to his thesis by means of a non sequitur: "Chasidism—although it is not a consequence of, is a parallel to, Spinozism . . . [There is a] deep-rooted pantheistic tendency in Chassidism. In view of these facts, the assertion is justified that Spinoza's influence on the cultural process of his own race in modern times was almost as powerful as was his influence upon the general cultural process in the West" (146–47). Melamed's antipathy to Spinoza is continually in evidence (even apart from the book's subtitle): Spinoza not only was "the patron saint of Lenin's state" (30) and "the official philosopher of Red Russia" (31) but was "actually responsible for the cultural anti-Semitism of modern Europe" (147).

21. Although George Victor writes, "Sankaracarya asserts that scripture (*sastra*) is the only source of knowledge to decide what is good and what is bad. Consequently, he is of the opinion that an individual cannot rely upon himself for the knowledge of good and bad" (2002, 114, cf. 149), later he says, "When Sankara says that the scriptures or the Veda are eternal and infallible, he means that the rituals are intended for the lower state and the study of Upaniṣads for the higher state" (2002, 127). Both statements are true if we distinguish between beginners and advanced students: until we have overcome our attachments our own judgments are unreliable, and following religious teachings can help us rise above our self-centeredness in much the same way that the "sure maxims of life" do for Spinoza (part V, proposition 10, scholium; hereafter in citations to Spinoza's works *proposition* is abbreviated as "p" and *scholium* as "s," so Vp10s; also, *definition* is abbreviated as "d," *axiom* as "a," and *corollary* as "c"), and the requirements of "propriety" (*li*) for Confucius. But ultimately we must be able to go beyond the limitations of words.

22. The former is from his *Taittiriya Upaniṣad* commentary (hereafter TC) 1.11.4 in Shankara (1957–58, 1:275); "to the contrary" is the translator's amplification; throughout, bracketed insertions within quotations are mine while those in parentheses are the translator's; the latter from his *Mundaka Upaniṣad* commentary (hereafter MC) 1.2.10 in Shankara (1957–58, 2:99). However, Scharfstein believes that "Shankara was conventionally and devoutly religious . . . but only a Vedantic exegete of his, Shankara's persuasion knows how to test its passages" (1998, 367, 371).

23. The influences on Spinoza are documented extensively in Wolfson (1934).

24. Some writers have argued that the geometrical method is irrelevant to Spinoza's philosophy, others that it is indispensible to it. After reviewing the arguments on both sides, Nadler concludes that Spinoza's philosophy "finds its

most adequate (but not necessary only) expression in that mode of presentation" (43). Della Rocca makes the stronger claim that for Spinoza there is "no other way of doing philosophy than in geometrical fashion" (2008, 11).

25. Indeed, he must have recognized that the geometrical method, however valuable it might be to clarity of exposition, had limitations as a science of investigation, since he had already used the same method to present the philosophy of Descartes, with which Spinoza substantially disagreed. Spinoza understood that from different preliminary definitions arise different models of reality. Thus in the *Principles of Descartes' Philosophy* Spinoza defines *substance* this way: "Every object to which belongs as a subject, some property, or quality, or attribute, or through which some things which we perceive exist, or of which we have some real idea is called *substance*" (Id5). Quotations from this work are taken from the translation by Halbert Hains Britan (Spinoza 1905). But in the *Ethics* he writes: "By substance I understand what is in itself and is conceived through itself, that is, that whose concept does not require the concept of another thing, from which it must be formed" (Id3). Quotations from the *Ethics* are taken, occasionally with minor modifications, from the translation by Edwin Curley (Spinoza 1994). In the first case *substance* is understood in the traditional way as the subject of an attribute, which is compatible with Descartes's claim that mind and body are distinct substances, but in the later work *substance* is understood as that whose concept is entirely independent of anything else. This more restrictive understanding allows Spinoza to conclude that there cannot be more than a single substance, since only an all-encompassing substance can be entirely independent of anything else. In view of the presuppositions inherent in definitions, the conclusions can never be arrived at with mathematical inevitability, however rigorous the deductions may be. While the conclusions derive logically from the definitions, the definitions derive anticipatorily from the conclusions to be reached. This is not to say that Spinoza begs the question but that, as with all philosophy, our intuitions of the nature of the whole and the nature of the parts mutually inform each other.

26. This conception is so far from what is usually meant by theism that Spinoza is sometimes regarded as an atheist in disguise. Even in the Lurianic Kabbalah, God as the Infinite (*En Sof*) creates the world by contracting himself to make room for it. If, by contrast, God is defined so broadly as to be indistinguishable from the sum total of all things, an affirmation of the existence of Spinoza's God would be equivalent to a denial of the traditional God. When Spinoza asserts in Ip11 that God exists, this amounts to no more than the assertion that an all-inclusive substance exists. For a discussion of alternative views, see Nadler (2006, 73–83).

27. *Vedânta-Sûtras* commentary (hereafter VSC) 1.1.4 in Shankara (1904, 23). Cf. *Vivekachudamani* (hereafter VC) §469 in Shankara (n.d.-c); all further

citations are to this translation, occasionally slightly modified. Although the *Vivekachudamani* may, as some scholars have argued, be the product of Shankara's disciples, it is largely consistent with better-attested works and has the advantage of bringing the full range of his doctrines together in a uniquely concise way.

28. Error occurs when the mind happens "to lack an idea which excludes the existence of those things which it imagines" (IIp17&s). For example, we may think people are still nearby because we did not notice them leave. "Falsity consists in the privation of knowledge which inadequate, or mutilated and confused, ideas involve" (IIp35).

29. Examples of common notions would be the attributes of thought and extension but not transcendentals like "being," "thing," and "something," or universals like "man," "horse," and "dog," which are only indefinite extensions of the products of our imagination (IIp40s1). On the question of whether individuals can be known by the second kind of knowledge, see Nadler (2006, 178–85).

30. Nevertheless, while we are still at the first stage we can progress in virtue if we rely on "sure maxims of life . . . [and] apply them constantly to the particular cases frequently encountered," for example, that "hate should be repaid by love" (Vp10s).

31. VSC, intro. and passim; VC §§189–338 passim. His frequent example of mistaking a rope for a snake originates with the founder of Advaita, Gaudapada, whose student Govinda was Shankara's teacher. See George Victor (2002, 13, 15). I am not claiming that Spinoza lacked an ontology or Shankara an epistemology, but only that their explanatory approaches have different emphases.

32. VSC 1.1.4 in Shankara (1904, 43). Cf. VC §189: "Though immutable, [Atman] becomes the agent and experiencer owing to Its superimposition. . . . This contradiction between them is created by superimposition, and is not something real. . . . The idea of "me and mine" in the body, organs, etc., which are the non-Self—this superimposition the wise man must put a stop to, by identifying himself with the Atman."

33. The metaphor is often used by Shankara, e.g., in VSC 1.3.7 in Shankara (1904, 151): "It is denied that the individual soul which, owing to its imagined connexion with the internal organ and other limiting adjuncts, has a separate existence in separate bodies—its division being analogous to the division of universal space into limited spaces such as the spaces within jars and the like—is that which is called the abode of heaven and earth. That same soul, on the other hand, which exists in all bodies, if considered apart from the limiting adjuncts, is nothing else but the highest Self. Just as the spaces within jars, if considered apart from their limiting conditions, are merged in universal space, so the individual soul also is incontestably that which is denoted as the abode of heaven

and earth, since it (the soul) cannot really be separate from the highest Self." For additional discussion, see George Victor (2002, 139–42).

34. Also see Verdenius (1942, 57–58; 1949, 131).

35. The problem of universals in Aristotle arises because in his view a being (οὐσία) is an individual (τόδε τι) but individuals cannot be known rationally by definition (*Metaphysics* Z.15.1039b27–1040a8), so the relation between what is (individuals) and what can be known (universals) becomes problematic.

36. For the meaning of "reason" (νόος) in Parmenides's day, see Guthrie (1962–81, 3:17–19); also Verdenius (1942, 9–10).

37. *Metaphysics* A.5.986b29–34, emphasis added, Barnes edition (Aristotle 1984). Unless otherwise stated, all translations from Aristotle are from this edition.

38. Diels-Kranz A34, from Simplicius's Commentary on Aristotle's *Physics* (*Comm. Arist. Gr.* IX, 39), Gallop translation (1984, 115), modified. But what of Plato's *Sophist*? Plato too had the whole text available to him, and does not the Eleatic visitor say it is necessary to refute Parmenides in order to accept the existence of a multiplicity of things that are different from one another (see, for example, Cordero 2004, 133–34; this view is pervasive in the literature on the *Sophist*), and does he not go so far as to confess that he is a kind of parricide for having to overthrow the philosophy of his intellectual father Parmenides? And what about Parmenides's disciple, Zeno of Elea? (Cordero questions whether Zeno was a disciple of Parmenides [Cordero 2004, 182].) Did he not defend Parmenides by arguing that motion is impossible even in the sensible world? In the case of Plato's *Sophist*, although the Eleatic visitor's remark is often recalled as a confession of parricide, in fact what he says is the opposite: "Do *not* suppose that I am becoming a kind of parricide," he tells Theaetetus (241d). (Stephanus numbers for Plato's works correspond to the Burnet edition of the Oxford Classical Texts [Burnet 1900–1907]. All translations from Plato are my own unless otherwise specified.) He does speak of attacking (ἐπιτίθεσθαι) and even refuting (ἐλέγχειν) Parmenides's words (241d–242b); however, the attack and refutation are directed not against Parmenides's ontology itself but only against his statement (λόγος) quoted at 237a, "For in no way may this prevail, that things that are not, are" (B7.1). If Plato thought that this was not merely a semantic correction, as I believe it is, but a refutation of Parmenides's whole ontology, then the Eleatic visitor would indeed be a parricide in the figurative sense used. The visitor's assurance that he is not a parricide, as well as the subsequent discussion, shows that it is only Parmenides's stark formulation, and not his ontology, that is under attack (also see Bormann 1979, 30–42, 38). As for Zeno's paradoxes, in the absence of their original context it is possible to interpret him to be arguing that all activity is impossible, but it seems unlikely that he would have been

nonplussed by a pre-Socratic Samuel Johnson who walked across the room and said, "Thus I refute Zeno," or by someone who pointed out that Zeno himself is engaging in the activity of *bringing into existence* new arguments, attempting to *change* people's minds, and going about the ordinary activities of life. The usual reply is that he would say it is all an illusion, but what exactly would that mean and who exactly is deluded? It is less problematic to read him as denying not that change exists but that it is rational. Whatever we may think of their validity, the implication of his arguments is not that motion does not exist but that it exists only for the senses and not for reason. When we superimpose the logically contradictory categories "is" and "is not" onto the sensible world of change, in which "is" and "is not" converge in "becoming," the lack of fit will always leave space for paradoxes (including the problem of universals in Aristotle and the Buddhist paradox of *anicca*: i.e., from moment to moment an individual is neither the same nor not the same). So if we wish to understand the nature of reality in a logically coherent way we must look beyond the world of our senses and be guided by abstract rationality.

39. This freedom is the opposite of the usual sense: "Most people apparently believe that they are free to the extent that they are permitted to yield to their lust" (Vp41s). On compatibilist determinism, see Ip29–33 and Appendix, IIp48. Since mental and physical events are parallel noninteracting chains of causality (IIp6, IIp7), mind and body cannot influence each other, so the traditional view of free will must be false that regards the mind as determining the body's action. Rather, all our actions are products of physical causes, and all our thoughts are products of ideal causes: "The decision of the mind and the appetite and the determination of the body . . . are one and the same thing" conceived under different attributes (IIIp2&s).

40. "If we could have adequate knowledge of the duration of things, and determine by reason their times of existing, we would regard future things with the same affect as present ones, and the mind would want the good it conceived as future just as it wants the good it conceives as present. Hence it would necessarily neglect a lesser present good for a greater future one, and what would be good in the present, but the cause of some future ill, it would not want at all. . . . But we can have only a quite inadequate knowledge of the duration of things" (IVp62s).

41. Bhagavad Gita commentary (hereafter BGC) 13.19–21 in Shankara (1977, 355–60); VSC 1.4.3 in Shankara (1904, 243); MC 2.1.1 in Shankara (1957–58, 2:107); VC §§131–35.

42. VSC 1.1.1–12 in Shankara (1904, 3–34); VC §§72–96.

43. *Atma Bodha* (hereafter AB) §14 in Shankara (n.d.-a); all further citations are to this translation. See also VC §120. By comparison with Plato's tripartite soul, *rajas* is the common genus of the two irrational factors that Plato

distinguishes (appetite and spiritedness), while *tamas* corresponds not to anything in the soul but to the corporeal element that impedes the soul. For Shankara as for Plato (and Spinoza), *sattva* is the faculty that pursues knowledge dispassionately, although there is a kind of knowledge that is higher still because it replaces conceptual description with immediate acquaintance: with Spinoza's "intuition" and Shankara's *puruṣa*, cf. Plato, *Republic* 533a.

44. The connection between virtue and power is obscured by the Christian conception of virtue as humility (which is not a virtue for Spinoza: IVp53) but survives in expressions like "by virtue of" ("by the power of"). Insofar as it is related only to the mind, *conatus* appears as will; as appetite when related to the mind and body together; and as desire in the consciousness of appetite. Passions that fulfill our will are types of joy and insofar as they also fulfill our appetite are types of pleasure, while those that frustrate our will or appetite are called sadness or pain respectively (IIIp11s). These distinctions provide Spinoza with the basis for his exhaustive classification of our affects. Love, for example, is "joy with the accompanying idea of an external cause," and hate is "sadness with the accompanying idea of an external cause" (IIIp13s).

45. BGC 14.6 in Shankara (1977, 382–83).

46. VC §174. Cf. BGC 14.7–8 in Shankara (1977, 383–84).

47. VSC 1.4.8 in Shankara (1904, 253); cf. VC §47.

48. VSC 1.1.12 and 1.4.19, both in Shankara (1904, 65, 274).

49. Cf. Bowra (1937, 107–8). McKirahan's "not incomplete" appears to be an erratum.

50. Since the world of appearance in space and time, too, is presided over by a goddess (B12), it has its own kind of value, just as it has its own kind of existence.

51. VSC 1.1.4 in Shankara (1904, 31); TC 2.1.1, in Shankara (1957–58, 1:288); VC §512. For Shankara, as an *advaitist* or nondualist, Atman or the universal soul is identical with Brahman or God.

52. Some readers regard this as a breakdown in Spinoza's reasoning: for example, see Bennett (1984, 357–63, 372–75); S. Smith (2003, 174); Curley (1988, 83–86). For sympathetic accounts of Spinoza's position, see Donagan (1989); Genevieve Lloyd (1994, chap. 4); Nadler (2006, 261–72); Della Rocca (2008, 236–72).

53. Cf. Vp29. Cf. Shankara's argument that in our awareness of the reality of a pot, although insofar as the object of that awareness is the pot it is something transient, insofar as the object of that awareness is the *reality* of the pot it is something intransient, i.e., eternal (BGC 2.16 in Shankara 1977, 35–36).

54. This puts into perspective Spinoza's previous claim that we cannot strive that God return our love (Vp19). There love was conceived as a passion (Vp17),

here it is conceived as a perfection. The distinction is missed by those who, like Lewis Feuer, believe that Spinoza advocates an unrequited love for God (1958, 215–18).

55. This implies more than some readers ascribe to Spinoza's goal. S. Smith, for example, describes it as only "a worldly or secular redemption based on the moderation of the passions and leading the one true way of life" (2003, 158).

56. *Nicomachean Ethics* 10.7.1177b31–1178a5.

57. As Hoy points out, this timeless unity must be more than a fourth-dimensional whole because there is an internal differentiation within the latter that is denied of the former (1994, 592–98). The question of timelessness in Parmenides is a matter of considerable controversy; it would mark the first reference to timelessness in Western literature. See Tarán (1965, 175–88); Guthrie (1962–81, 3:26–30, 45, 49); Kahn (1969, 716); Mourelatos (1970, 105–11); Stokes (1971, 128–30); Manchester (1979); Gallop (1984, 13–14); Cordero (2004, 171). Tarán believes that the apparent reference to timelessness in line 5—οὐδέ ποτ' ἦν οὐδ' ἔσται, ἐπεὶ νῦν ἔστιν ὁμοῦ πᾶν ("Nor was it ever nor will it be, since it is now, all together")—is incompatible with the words with which the sentence concludes in line 6, ἕν, συνεχές ("one, continuous") (1965, 177). But συνεχές literally means "holding together" and can be applied to what is timeless in the sense of "indivisible," as in B8.22 Parmenides says, "Nor is it divided, since it all is alike." Cf. Owen: "That συνεχές can have a temporal sense needs no arguing" (1975, 63). Tarán does not deny that Parmenides's doctrine *entails* atemporality; he merely denies that Parmenides was aware that it did: "The denial of difference makes all process impossible; the logical connection between time and process would require, if Parmenides was aware of it, that he deny duration, too" (1965, 175; cf. Tarán 1979, 43–53). Others have argued that Parmenides's use of the term *now* is incompatible with timelessness because *now* is a temporal term. See Mourelatos (1970, 103–11); Stokes (1971, 129–30); Miller (1978, 27). But *now* has been used throughout history to refer to timeless immediacy as well as to present time.

58. This sense of timelessness is difficult for us to understand, being "far from the beaten path of humans" (B1.27), but writers have spoken of it in all cultures and all ages, it is not limited to the "unsophisticated" beginnings of philosophy. The nineteenth-century English poet and literary critic John Addington Symonds, for example, describes his own experience of "a gradual but swiftly progressive obliteration of space, time, sensation, and the multitudinous factors of experience which seem to qualify what we are pleased to call our Self. . . . At last nothing remained but a pure, absolute, abstract Self. The universe became without form and void of content. It served to impress upon my growing nature the phantasmal unreality of all the circumstances which contribute to a merely

phenomenal consciousness" (Brown 1895, 29–31, cited by William James in James ([1901–2] 1929), Lecture 16). Also see Verdenius (1949, 124n46). In "Burnt Norton" T. S. Eliot similarly writes that we cannot sustain such an experience very long because "human kind / Cannot bear very much reality" (1.44–45). "I can only say, *there* we have been: but I cannot say where. / And I cannot say, how long, for that is to place it in time. . . . Time past and time future / Allow but a little consciousness. To be conscious is not to be in time" (2.22–39). This testimony, among countless others, shows Parmenides to be far from alone in the view that only the timeless, spaceless unity is fully real and that in its light the temporal world of becoming dims to something less than real without being nonexistent.

59. See note 38 above.

60. Cf. Scharfstein: "There has been much debate over whether or not Spinoza takes the attributes to have an objective existence. When he defines them as 'what the intellect perceives of substance as constituting its essence,' does his *if* mean *as if*? Does he mean that human limitations cause us to perceive God *as if* he was infinite matter and infinite thought rather than as simply Substance, without real attributes?" (1998, 396; also see the subsequent paragraph and footnote). I am inclined to agree with Scharfstein that this is the less natural reading, although, as he goes on to say, "No interpretation is without its difficulties."

61. AB §45. Cf. TC 2.1.1 in Shankara (1957–58, 1:288); VSC intro. in Shankara (1904, 9).

62. The ontological coequality of mind and body is not compromised by the epistemological priority of corporeal explanations (as in the previous example we understood "the idea of the stone" by reference to corporeal stones). On some views Spinoza's dual-aspect theory is no more than a smokescreen to conceal his materialism. I do not find this a convincing way of reading Spinoza, although I think such devices were employed by others such as Descartes (see Dorter 1973). For Spinoza it makes sense to argue from the visible to what is not visible.

63. Cf. VC §§75, 88, 97, 209, 280. Not only is superimposition the effect of karmic reincarnation, it is also the karmic cause of future reincarnation (§179). Liberation is the breaking of the circle.

64. Scharfstein suggests that just as in Spinoza the attributes are a bridge "between the metaphysical infinite and the finite objects and persons," in Shankara "name and form" (*namarupa*) provide a similar bridge (1998, 405–6). But "name and form" seem to me to belong to the realm of "finite objects and persons" rather than being intermediate between it and "the metaphysical infinite."

65. VC §551.

66. "The first meditative state: rapture and pleasure born from withdrawal, accompanied by thought and evaluation. With the stilling of thought and

evaluation, he enters and remains in the second meditative state: rapture and pleasure born of concentration, internal composure and unification of awareness free from thought and evaluation. With the fading of rapture he remains in equanimity, mindful and alert, physically sensitive of pleasure. He enters and remains in the third meditative state. With the abandoning of pleasure and pain— as with the earlier disappearance of elation and displeasure—he enters and remains in the fourth meditative state: purity of equanimity and mindfulness, neither pleasure nor pain" (*Maggasamyutta* 1.8, in Buddha 2000, 1528–29).

67. VSC 1.1.4 in Shankara (1904, 41). Cf. VC §§544–45: "Neither pleasure nor pain, nor good nor evil, ever touches this knower of Brahman, who always lives without the body-idea. Pleasure or pain, or good or evil, affects only him who has connections with the gross body etc., and identifies himself with these."

68. AB §46. Cf. AB §59; *Upadesha Sahasri* §§10–18 in Shankara (n.d.-b).

69. AB §§26, 30.

70. VC §483.

Chapter 3

1. Zhu Xi's concept of "principle" is closer to Plato's conception of form than to Aristotle's. He says, for example, "Before things existed, their principles of being had already existed. Only their principles existed, however, but not yet the things themselves" (*Complete Works* 495b–496a, in Zhu Xi 1963a, 637, §110), and "Before the existence of things and affairs their principles are already present" (*Chu Tzu yü-lei* 95:22a, in Zhu Xi 1967, 27). For Aristotle, on the other hand, one cannot say that the form is ontologically prior to the existence of any individual of that type. On the question of whether Zhu Xi's holism is a monism, see Chan (1963a, 634–35), as well as Chan (1989, 139–40); and Zhu Xi (1991, 38). Zhu Xi and neo-Confucianism generally also show parallels with Pythagoreanism; see Kim (2000, 75, 183, 278–79).

2. Something like the Platonic receptacle (*Timaeus* 49a) is suggested by such remarks as "Without the material force and concrete stuff of the universe, principle would have nothing in which to inhere" (*Chu Tzu yü-lei* 10a–b, in Zhu Xi 1967, 73) and "If the nature of heaven's endowment is lacking in material substance, then there is no place where it can be. It is like a spoonful of water: if there is nothing to hold it, then there is nowhere for the water to be" (*Further Reflections* 1.13, in Zhu Xi 1991, 60). But material force and the stuff of the universe are not ontologically independent of principle, as Plato's receptacle is ontologically independent of the forms. Stephanus numbers for Plato's works

correspond to the Burnet edition of the Oxford Classical Texts (Burnet 1900–1907). All translations from Plato are my own unless otherwise specified.

3. See Daniel Gardner in Zhu Xi (1990, 10–12). And yet elsewhere Zhu Xi can sound very much like the Buddhist he was in his youth: "After you become intimately familiar with moral principle, it alone will be your true standard. You'll view the myriad affairs of the world as confusing, enticing, and all part of a staged play—you'll find it truly unbearable to keep your eyes on them. He also said in response to a letter: The myriad affairs of the world might be transformed or extinguished in a split second. They should not become dear to us" (*Chu Tzu yü-lei* 8.17a.5, in Zhu Xi 1990, 114–15, slightly modified). Julia Ching writes that "the emphasis on stillness or tranquility was an older teaching of Chu's that he developed before he was thirty-nine" (2000, 122).

4. *Chin-ssu lu* 1.1, in Zhu Xi (1967, 5), slightly modified. The opening quotation is from the *Book of Odes*, 235. See Appendix 2 for Zhou Duyni's diagram.

5. Letter to Lu Chiu-shao, *Chu-tzu ta-ch'üan* 36:8b–9a, in Ching (2000, 48), insertion by Ching.

6. Or even a nonbeing in Zhu Xi's sense of differentiated "operations of heaven."

7. *Enneads* 5.1.10. Translations and line numbers from Plotinus are from A. H. Armstrong's translation (Plotinus 1966–88).

8. *Chu Tzu yü-lei* 125:12a, in Zhu Xi (1967, 286). However, it seem unfair for Zhu Xi to write, "Lao Tzu [Laozi] said that things come from being and being comes from nonbeing. Even principle is considered nonexistent. This is wrong" (*Chu Tzu yü-lei* 98:25b, in Zhu Xi 1967, 286). Laozi would not equate nonbeing with nonexistence any more than Zhu Xi would.

9. Commentary on the *T'ai-chi-t'u shuo*, in Zhu Xi (1967, 5).

10. *Chu Tzu yü-lei* 1.2b:12, in Zhu Xi (1990, 92), translating *qi* as "material force" rather than Gardner's "psychophysical stuff."

11. *Metaphysics* E1.1026a10–19, Barnes edition (Aristotle 1984). Unless otherwise stated, all translations from Aristotle are from this edition. Cf. Kosman (2000, 307–26). Bekker numbers for Aristotle correspond to the Oxford Classical Texts series (Oxford: Clarendon Press, various dates) except where otherwise noted.

12. *Metaphysics* Λ.7.1073a5–7. I leave aside the problem that Aristotle creates by having subordinate unmoved movers to account for the motions of the stars (*Metaphysics* Λ.8). He does not explain how if they are unmoved they can be unified under a single principle (*Generation and Corruption* 2.10.337a21). For a comprehensive survey of traditional discussion of this issue, see Elders (1972, 57–68). A more recent discussion may be found in G. E. R. Lloyd (2000, 245–74).

13. God is a pure thinking, since that is the highest state, and the highest thinking thinks only what is best, so God's thinking is a thinking on thinking (*Metaphysics* Λ9.1074b33–34). Hence, unlike other beings, in God subject and object are one (1074b28–1075a10). For an excellent discussion of what this implies, and in particular why it does not imply the reflexive self-knowledge that is sometimes ridiculed as narcissistic, see Kosman (2000, 315–25).

14. Cf. Plato, *Timaeus* 30a. Some scholars, however, believe that the temporal sequence of creation in the *Timaeus* is meant literally rather than as a metaphor for ontological priority.

15. See *Metaphysics* Λ.7.1072a26, 1072b3, and 1072b10–11, respectively.

16. *Metaphysics* Λ.9.1074b34–35. In this chapter, translations from Aristotle are my own unless otherwise noted.

17. *Metaphysics* Λ7.1072b14–19; *Nicomachean Ethics* 10.7; *Eudemian Ethics* 7.15.1249b16–23; *Politics* 7.3.1326b14–33. Ching believes that Aristotle differs from Zhu Xi because for the former our goal is self-fulfillment, while for the latter it is self-transcendence (2000, 105). But for Aristotle, as for Zhu Xi, self-fulfillment implies self-transcendence: "It is not in so far as he is man that he will live so, but in so far as something divine is present in him" (*Nicomachean Ethics* 10.7.1177b26–27).

18. "We must consider also in which of two ways the nature of the universe contains the good or the highest good, whether as something separate and by itself, or as the order of the parts. Probably in both ways, as an army does. For the good is found both in the order and in the leader, and more in the latter; for he does not depend on the order but it depends on him. And all things are ordered together somehow, but not all alike,—both fishes and fowls and plants; and the world is not such that one thing has nothing to do with another, but they are connected. For all are ordered together to one end. (But it is as in a house, where the freemen are least at liberty to act as they will, but all things or most things are already ordained for them, while the slaves and the beasts do little for the common good, and for the most part live at random; for this is the sort of principle that constitutes the nature of each)" (*Metaphysics* 1075a11–23).

19. This relationship provides a basis for an Aristotelian philosophy of ecology, but a very indirect basis compared to Zhu Xi. See Sim (2010, 77–92, esp. 85–91).

20. *Metaphysics* Λ.7.1072b13. Or in David Sedley's words, "The realization of form in natural processes expresses the 'desire' of matter for its divine object, form (*Physics* I.9)." Sedley also argues that the desire need not be directly for God but for an intermediate imitation of God: "The seasonal cycle of weather comes about 'in imitation of the cycle of the sun' (. . . *Meteor.* I.9.346b36). . . . So too in general, the four simple bodies by their cycle of intertransformations

'imitate' the eternal circular motion of the heavens (*De Gen. et Corr.* II.10.337a1 ff.) and indeed simply by their constant activity of change (with or without intertransformation) 'imitate' the imperishables" (*Met.* Θ 8.1050b28 ff.). Imitation is assumed to be somehow transitive. If A imitates B and B imitates C, there will be some sense in which A is imitating C" (2000, 333–34, 357–50). Also see Elders's (1972, 167, 175) notes on 1071a29 and 1072b3–4 and Charles Kahn's (1985, 183–205) discussion of the issues surrounding the creativity of the unmoved mover.

21. All translations from Plato are my own unless otherwise specified. Stephanus numbers correspond to the Burnet edition of the Oxford Classical Texts (Burnet 1900–1907). This line has been interpreted in a variety of different ways. See, for example, Rawson (1966, 111); White (1979, 181); Gadamer (1986, 84–101); Santas (2002); Gerson (2002); Gill (2002). For a fuller discussion, see Dorter (2006, 188–90).

22. Socrates goes on to say that when the highest kind of thinking, *noesis*, comes to know the Good itself it then "descends again to a conclusion, . . . moving from forms themselves, through forms, to them, it concludes in forms" (511b–c), which suggests that the forms to which the Good gives rise are hierarchically ordered in the way that emanationism requires.

23. Although he is described as good, the demiurge is not a personification of the Idea of the Good, because he creates only the world of becoming—including the sun and the soul (38c) which is the principle of motion (34b–c)—not the realm of eternal being that is known by reason. In fact, he looks to the latter for patterns to follow in making mortal things (28a–29a). For an argument to the contrary, see Seifert (2002, 413–18).

24. Soul is not a third principle independent of the other two but a transitional principle comprising the rationality of the intelligible realm and the otherwise disorderly flux of the corporeal (*Timaeus* 30a).

25. See *Chu Tzu yü-lei* 95:19a–b, in Zhu Xi (1967, 21), and Plotinus, *Enneads* 1.7.1.

26. Commentary on Zhang Zai's "Western Inscription" (*Chang Tzu ch'üan-shu*) 1.7a, in Zhu Xi (1967, 77). But see Chan's (1963a, 499–500) comment. For a more detailed correlation between the doctrines of Zhu Xi and Plotinus, see Blakeley (1996).

27. In these movements time and space are created as well. See Wittenborn, in Zhu Xi (1991, 15). The following account and quotations are by Zhou Dunyi, cited by Zhu Xi in Zhu Xi (1967, 6–7).

28. "The *ch'i* that constitutes 'heaven' . . . does not have physical form. . . . This formless *ch'i* acquires physical form through 'aggregation' (*chü*), and it is the aggregated *chi* [*sic*] . . . that constitutes men and things" (Kim 2000, 31).

29. *Chu Tzu yü-lei* 1.2b:12, in Zhu Xi (1990, 92), quoted above.

30. Thus too Joseph Needham describes yin and yang as "an ancient hypostatisation of the two sexes . . . which appeared [in science] as negative and positive electricity, which in our own age have proved to constitute, in such forms as protons and electrons, the components of all material particles" (1959–61, 2:467, cited in Ching 2000, 7; the insertion is Ching's).

31. *Enneads* 5.1.10.1–5, substituting "mind" for Armstrong's "intellect."

32. See the discussions in Chan (Zhu Xi 1967, 360), and Wittenborn (Zhu Xi 1991, 23–24).

33. "If, too, the making principle is prior to the matter, matter will be exactly as the making principle wills it to be in every way" (2.4.8.19–21).

34. For a fuller discussion, see Dorter (1994, 19–47). Cf. Dorter (1996).

35. *Chu Tzu yü-lei* 69:22a, in Zhu Xi 1967, 9). Again, "In talking to students, we can only teach them to act according to the teachings of sages. When after some effort they realize something within themselves, they will naturally understand what it really is to be a sage" (*Chu Tzu yü-lei* 93:10b, in Zhu Xi 1967, 204–5). On Chu Hsi as a dialectical thinker, see Ching (2000, 212), who says, "Chu Hsi's method tends to be dialectical, as he attempts to unite seemingly opposing sides, integrating them into a higher unity."

36. *Metaphysics* Z.1.1028b2–4. Also see Code (1984).

37. The first is cited by Kim (2000, 73), the second is from *Complete Works* 44:13a–b, in Zhu Xi (1963a, 630, §83); cf. *Chu Tzu yü-lei* 15:5a, in Zhu Xi (1967, 92). "Image" is Kim's translation of *hsiang*. The phrase "sudden release" is Chan's translation in both the *Complete Works* (Zhu Xi 1963a) and *Reflections on Things at Hand* (1967). But Chan (1989, 305–8) elsewhere argues *against* the translation of "sudden," on the grounds that it is overly influenced by Western mysticism. However, the concept of sudden enlightenment is traditional in Chinese philosophy as well, going back at least five hundred years before Zhu Xi, to Hui-neng, founder of the Southern School of Ch'an Buddhism. And in the end of his discussion Chan himself acknowledges that Zhu Xi "did not completely refrain from talking about sudden understanding" (1989, 308). The passages that Chan cites show that penetration did not come without being preceded by a gradual accumulation of knowledge, but they do not deny that when a certain point is reached the perceptual switch is an abrupt dislocation rather than one further increment like all the others. Cf. Ching, who says of Zhu Xi's concept of sudden illumination: "It may not be a mystical experience, if by this we refer to pure experience, that which goes beyond subject-object distinctions to the whole of reality. But we have no reason to think he rejects the mystical experience in itself. He just perceives the attainment of wisdom and sagehood as a task requiring much effort and struggle" (2000, 131).

38. Ho Lin, "Sung-ju te ssu-hsiang fang-fa" [The method of thinking of the Sung philosophers], in *Sung-shih yen-chiu chi* [Collected studies in Sung history] comp. Study Committee on Sung History (Taipei, 1964), 65–66, quoted in Ching (2000, 213). Similarly, in the *Republic* Socrates says that someone who has not been able to see the good itself, but only has opinions about it, is like someone still asleep and dreaming (7.533a and c, 534c).

39. Whether Plato's Second Letter is authentic is a matter of debate, but the following passage says succinctly what book 7 of the *Republic* says at length: "There are people, indeed many of them, who have the ability to understand what they hear, and to remember it, and to pass judgement after carefully examining it in every way, who are already old and have been hearing these things for not less than thirty years, and only now say that the doctrines that formerly seemed to them most uncertain now seem most certain and evident, while the ones that formerly seemed most certain now seem the opposite" (314a–b). Zhu Xi tells of Li Hsi-shan: "When Li talked to his students he told them to take the classics and study them again, and then again. If you reach a point where they seem meaningless you must think about them even more until, without eating or sleeping, all kinds of doubts rise up. Only then will you suddenly begin to advance" (*Further Reflections* 11.3, in Zhu Xi 1991, 151).

40. Cheng Hao, *I-shu* 2A:2a, in Chan (1963a, 530, §11).

41. As well as the distinctions between rational form and contingent corporeality, between rationality and mechanical necessity, and between reason and the prime matter that Plato calls the "receptacle" (e.g., *Phaedo* 66b–d, 80a–b; *Timaeus* 47e–53b).

42. See *Metaphysics* Θ7 and Λ.6.1071b3–22.

43. See *Metaphysics* Θ7.1049a1927; 1050b24–28; Λ.9; *Physics* 2.5.196b19–197a14. For Plato, see especially *Timaeus* 47e–53b.

44. *The Great Learning*, in Chan (1963a, 86); *Chu Tzu yü-lei* 95:28a, in Zhu Xi (1967, 40).

45. Cf. Ching (2000, 29): "The terms 'form' and 'matter' cannot accurately or adequately translate *li*ᵃ and *ch'i*ᵃ, since in Aristotle, form is active and matter passive. In Chu Hsi, it is rather *li*ᵃ that is passive and *ch'i*ᵃ that is active."

46. *Complete Works* 42:9b–10a, in Zhu Xi (1963a, 617, §45).

47. *Complete Works* 43:2b–3a, in Zhu Xi (1963a, 624, §62).

48. *Complete Works* 42:21b, in Zhu Xi (1963a, 619, §52).

49. Treatise on Ch'eng Ming-tao's (Ch'eng Hao's) *Discourse on Nature* (Zhu Xi 1963b, 598).

50. *Complete Works* 43:7a–b, in Zhu Xi (1963a, 625, §66). Zhu Xi proposed physical causes for these disparities: "When the sun and the moon are clear and bright, and the weather is harmonious and correct, and if a man is born and is

endowed with this *qi*, then it is clear, bright, complete, and thick *qi* and must make a good man. If the sun and the moon are dark, and the cold and hot weather is not normal, all this is the perverse *qi* of heaven and earth. If a man is endowed with this *qi*, then he becomes a bad man" (in Kim 2000, 208).

51. *Chu Tzu yü-lei* 55.10 (in Chan 1989, 282), and 12.7a:7 (in Zhu Xi 1990, 168), respectively. Zhu Xi was himself accused of this by Zhang Xi, who told Zhu Xi in a letter that he sometimes showed an "imbalance of material endowment" (*Nan-hsüan Hsien-sheng wen-chi* 20:8b, in Chan 1989, 398). In another letter he colorfully accused Zhu Xi of, on one occasion, giving "the impression of great anger to the point of causing one's hair to go through one's hat" (*Nan-hsüan Hsien-sheng wen-chi* 21:2b–3a, in Chan 1989, 398).

52. *Complete Works* 43:8a–b, in Zhu Xi (1963a, 625, §68). Throughout this chapter words within angle brackets are my insertions, while parentheses and square brackets are insertions by the translator.

53. See Plato's *Protagoras* 326a–b, *Republic* 443d, *Philebus* 25e–26b, and *Timaeus* 47d, as well as Plotinus's *Enneads* 1.2.1, 1.4.10, 3.6.2, 4.4.35, 4.7.12(8⁵ in MacKenna's enumeration).

54. *The Great Learning*, in Chan (1963a, 86). More fully: the way to rectify our mind is to make our will sincere, the way to make our will sincere is to extend our knowledge, and the way to extend our knowledge is through the investigation of things.

55. Zhu Xi, *Complete Works* 44:13a–b, in Zhu Xi (1963a, 630, §83).

56. This is also a question for Stoicism. See Hadot (1998, 77–82).

57. *Complete Works* 44:1b, in Zhu Xi (1963a, 628, §75). Again: "If heaven and earth have no mind, then probably oxen will give birth to horses and plum flowers will blossom on peach trees" (cited in Kim 2000, 116).

58. *Complete Works* 2:38b, in Zhu Xi (1963a, 608, §14).

59. *Complete Works* 42:31b–32a, in Zhu Xi (1963a, 623, §61).

60. Schopenhauer extends to everything that exists his distinction between the inner reality of will and its outward appearance as representation: "We shall therefore assume that as, on the one hand, they are representation, just like our body, and are in this respect homogeneous with it, so on the other hand, if we set aside their existence as the subject's representation, what still remains over must be, according to its inner nature, the same as what in ourselves we call *will*. . . . Besides the will and the representation there is absolutely nothing known or conceivable for us." "I therefore name the genus after its most important species, the direct knowledge of which lies nearest to us and leads to the indirect knowledge of all the others" (*World as Will and Representation* 2.19 and 2.22, in Schopenhauer 1969, 105, emphasis in original, and 111).

61. *Complete Works* 23b–24a, in Zhu Xi (1963a, 643, §127).

62. Thus, "If heavenly principle is preserved, human desire will disappear. If human desire should overcome it, heavenly principle will be extinguished. Never do heavenly principle and human desire permeate each other" (*Chu Tzu yü-lei* 7:9, in Zhu Xi 1990, 51).

63. *Complete Works* 24a, in Zhu Xi (1963a, 643, §128). Thus too: "To have no mind or feeling of one's own is the same as to respond spontaneously to all things as they come"; "The sage's mind is vacuous and clear. That is why he can [remember things without effort]. Ordinary people try to remember things but forget them because they are deliberate" (*Chu Tzu yü-lei* 95:28a, in Zhu Xi 1967, 40, and 96:2b, in Zhu Xi 1967, 133); "In doing something to prevent the bias [of one's natural character], the fact that you're trying to correct it, the less correct it will be. It is important for you simply to see the great principle of Tao distinctly and clearly, then your bias will naturally be understood" (*Further Reflections* 5.17, in Zhu Xi 1991, 107).

64. *Complete Works* 49:23b–24a, in Zhu Xi (1963a, 643, §127). The quotation from Ch'eng Hao is from *Ming-tao wen-chi* 3:1a. In this passage and the one cited in the previous note, Zhi Hsi seems to be using the concept of mind differently than when he said, "If heaven and earth have no mind, then probably oxen will give birth to horses and plum flowers will blossom on peach trees" (Kim 2000, 116). In the latter, "mind" refers to rationality; in the former, to something like willfulness.

65. The concept of seeking the lost mind means uncovering the original good mind within us that has become obscured by desires and false opinions. "If you know that it is lost and wish to find it, then you're at the point of knowing where to look for it. We don't have to wait and look for it somewhere else since the total substance and function of our minds is already right here" (*Further Reflections* 3.12, in Zhu Xi 1991, 89). Earlier he said, "If we can indeed empty our minds and ease our thoughts and gradually seek its truth in our daily affairs, then we will automatically grasp the greatness of its scope and the deep subtleties of its twists and turns" (*Further Reflections* 1.58, in Zhu Xi 1991, 68). He explains Mencius's conception of "finding the lost mind" as follows: "What appears in our daily affairs is mostly the good principle of Tao. All it needs is for people to recognize it" (*Further Reflections* 12.39, in Zhu Xi 1991, 163). For Plato's analogous concept of recollecting our lost knowledge, see, e.g., *Meno* 80d–81d.

66. *Complete Works* 45:19b, in Zhu Xi (1963a, 632, §94).

67. "If one does not understand this basis first and merely desires to take up [particular] events and to understand them, then even if one understands many curiosities, [they will] only add to much confusion and disorder" (cited in Kim 2000, 249; insertions in original).

68. *Complete Works* 3:8a, 3:8b, 3:12b, in Zhu Xi (1963, 609, §§20–22). Also in *Further Reflections* 2.14–15, in Zhu Xi (1991, 75). Cf. *Chu Tzu yü-lei* 95:35b on the relationship between rectifying moral principles and illuminating the Way: "There is no difference in time. They are like the folding of one's palms" (in Zhu Xi 1967, 57). Again: "If we do not take personal action but simply think that knowing is enough, then why did Confucius' seventy disciples follow him for so many years without leaving when everything could have been said in just a couple of days?" (*Further Reflections* 5.40, in Zhu Xi 1991, 111).

69. From the *Ta Hsüeh Chang-chü* [Commentary on the great learning], in Chan (1963a, 89). Cf. *Further Reflections* 2.20, in Zhu Xi (1991, 76): "Some people study books and become clear about moral principles, others discuss the ancients and distinguish right from wrong, while still others attend to things and events and deal with what is proper and what is not. All of these are the investigation of things." And Zhu Xi (*Further Reflections* 2.41, in Zhu Xi 1991, 79): "If we are to discuss the pursuit of learning . . . there are many things to consider, such as astronomy, geography and topography, proper rites and music, institutions, military affairs, and punishment and laws." Most of Zhu Xi's scientific writings are not available in English but are the focus of a comprehensive study by Kim (2000).

70. *Kan-ying* and *pien-hua*. See Kim (2000, 122–32).

71. *Further Reflections* 3.38, in Zhu Xi (1991, 93).

72. As an anonymous referee points out, "We cannot say what the philosopher and aesthetician do is also science simply because they also investigate the empirical things."

73. The active intellect of *De anima* 3.6. The activity of the active intellect is not inconsistent with the unchanging nature of Aristotle's God, since that activity is conceived not as change but as "a positive state like light" (430a15–16), which is constant and unchanging.

74. *Parts of Animals* 1.1.639b19–21, substituting "the purpose" for "that for the sake of which." Bekker numbers for *Parts of Animals* and *Generation and Corruption* (*Coming-to-Be and Passing-Away*) correspond to the Loeb edition (Aristotle 1955).

75. *Metaphysics* Λ7.1072b8–10, *Generation and Corruption* 2.11 337a1–2, *Physics* 8.9.

76. For example, astronomical questions in the first three tractates of the second Ennead, and questions related to the life-principle and perception in the first six tractates of the fourth.

77. For example, in the case of the first and simplest of these studies, arithmetic is "necessary for the philosophers because they have to rise out of becoming and grasp being" (525b).

78. "God invented and gave us sight in order for us to observe the revolutions of reason in the heavens and use them for the revolutions within us of our mind, which are akin to them although our revolutions can be disturbed while the others cannot. And so that by learning and partaking in reasoning that is correct by nature, and by imitating the absolutely unvarying revolutions of the God, we might stabilize the variable ones within ourselves" (*Timaeus* 47b–c).

79. Even if it is all that is necessary for the attainment of wisdom, it has been criticized as not doing what is necessary to make a contribution to the practical world. Zhu Xi writes, "Master Chou [Lien-hsi] considers tranquility to be fundamental, primarily because he wants people's minds to be tranquil and calm and he wants people to be their own master. Master Ch'eng [I], on the other hand, is afraid that if people merely seek tranquility they will not have anything to do with things and affairs. He therefore talks about seriousness" (*Chu Tzu yü-lei* 94:20a, in Zhu Xi 1967, 143). Elsewhere Zhu Xi criticizes Yang Chu for being too much like Laozi: "He did not care for people who devoted themselves to the affairs of the world. He cared only for himself" *Chu Tzu yü-lei* 55:15a, in Zhu Xi 1967, 280). For a discussion of these alternatives, see Dorter (2006, 219–22).

Chapter 4

1. Laozi, considered to be the founder of Daoist philosophy, lived in China either in the sixth or fourth century BCE, depending on which account we accept, while Heraclitus lived in Greece circa 535–475 BCE.

2. I have left the term *logos* untranslated because of the wide range of its meanings: word, argument, account, reason, speech, definition, et cetera. For interpretations of Heraclitus's "logos," see Kirk (1954, 37–40); Marcovich (1967, 8–9); Guthrie (1962–81, 1:419–34); Kahn (1979, 97–98); Robinson (1987, 74–76); Curd (1991, 532–35); Wilcox (1991, 627–30); Dilcher (1995, 29–49). Heidegger's distinctive interpretation can be found in Heidegger (1957, 97–102; 1954b, 207–29). For a postmodern interpretation, see Waugh (1991, esp. 616).

3. Thus Heidegger criticizes Eugen Fink for beginning his interpretation from a fragment that enables him to give disproportionate weight to the concept of light, namely B64: "The lightning bolt steers all" (Heidegger and Fink 1979, 135). It was only the prominence that Fink gave to this fragment that troubled Heidegger; Fink's interpretation of it derived from an essay by Heidegger himself (Heidegger 1954b, 222, 229). Heidegger's own point of departure was B1, which focuses on the concept of logos. The most ambitious attempt to order the fragments coherently is that of Kahn (1979), which results in a

plausible and illuminating arrangement. At the same time, Kahn's sensitivity to the systematic ambiguity and multiple implications of Heraclitus's style has the effect of making us aware that fragments that are grouped together by virtue of one of their implications could have been differently grouped by virtue of other implications.

4. Guthrie (1962–81, 1:427). Cf. Heidegger: "What would be achieved if one wished to reject [a certain interpretation] as simply incorrect? One could at best make it seem that the subsequent remarks believe themselves to hit upon Heraclitus' teaching in the one absolutely correct way. The task is limited to staying closer to the words of Heraclitus' saying." At the conclusion of his exegesis he writes: "Did Heraclitus intend his question in the way we just explicated? Does what is said through this explication stand within the field of his representations? Who can know or say? But perhaps the saying says it independently of Heraclitus' contemporary representational field" (1954a, 260, 279). Translations are my own unless otherwise indicated.

5. Isabelle Robinet points out that among the traditional commentators "One does not find the same degree of divergence as with the modern exegetes . . . [who] are influenced by modern preoccupations, be they linguistic or historical" (1999, 131). The chapters in the edited volume (Csikszentmihalyi and Ivanhoe 1999) that includes Robinet's essay give a good sense of the wide diversity of interpretations, both through the differences among the individual contributors and through the differences documented by the contributors in the literature they cite. To give one straightforward example, the first two lines of Laozi, chapter 2, are 天下皆知美之為美, 斯惡矣 (tianxia jie zhi mei zhi wei mei, si e yi). Tateno Masami translates: "Everyone in the world knows the beauty of what is beautiful only because there are things that are ugly" (1999, 176), while Bryan Van Norden translates the same lines as "When all under heaven know beauty as beauty, already there is ugliness," and comments, "In other words, I will not feel unattractive unless I compare myself to someone whom my community labels 'beautiful'" (1999, 191). Thus for Tateno the lines indicate that ugliness and beauty are natural properties, while for Van Norden the same lines indicate that the distinction is only conventional.

6. Except as noted, translations from Laozi are from Chan (1963b), occasionally modified. Parenthetical insertions are Chan's and are not always included; bracketed insertions are my own. For convenience I shall refer to the author of the *Daodejing* as Laozi despite uncertainties about the authorship and integrity of the text, especially after the discovery of the Guodian version in 1993. See, for example, Csikszentmihalyi and Ivanhoe (1999, 2–11); Henricks (2000, 2–11). Not everyone agrees that Laozi's paradoxes are expressions of ineffability. See, for example, Csikszentmihalyi (1999, 33–58). I am largely in

sympathy with LaFargue's proposal that the meaning of the aphorisms is not vague and that the aphorisms must be interpreted the way we interpret proverbs like "'A watched pot never boils.' Taken literally, it is clearly false. But we do not take it literally. . . . We ought to try first to devise an account of competence able to draw definite meanings from the words of the text, and only conclude that it is vague if this attempt fails. . . . Aphorisms are corrective, compensatory wisdom, designed to wake people up to a possibility they are overlooking" (1994, 135, 149, 153). If people need to be awakened to something, however, and not simply informed about it, does this not mean that a certain element of ineffability is inevitable—the event (awakening) cannot be reduced to concepts (information)? LaFargue prefers to avoid talk of ineffability in favor of a phenomenological-pragmatic-semiotic conception of goodness as independent of (objective) truth: "Well-foundedness in worldviews is a basically a moral rather than a metaphysical issue" (269), and "All worldviews are essentially semiotic systems of *mutually defining elements*" (289, emphasis in original).

7. Substituting "is" for Chan's interpretive insertion ("arises the recognition of") and removing the colon after "Therefore."

8. For a discussion of Laozi's critique of language in a wide-ranging study, see Scharfstein (1993).

9. 道可道, 非常道 (Dao ke Dao, fei chang Dao). Peter Boodberg's attempt at an etymologically literal translation, whatever its virtues, does not make the text less recalcitrant: "Lodehead lodehead-brooking: no forewonted lodehead" (1957, 618).

10. Cf. Heraclitus fragments 1, 2, 50, 72, 108, 115.

11. Cf. Chan (1963a, 139n11).

12. A different punctuation gives "The two are produced by the same source, / But they have different names" (see Chan 1963a, 139n12). The following interpretation can be defended on either translation.

13. There is a certain correspondence between this and Kant's discussion of "The Transcendental Ideal" (*Critique of Pure Reason* A571–83/B599–611), however different the emphasis.

14. On its being the book's opening, see Aristotle, *Rhetoric* 3.5.1407b16–17, and Sextus Empiricus, *Adversus mathematicos* 7.132.

15. Thus Aristotle: "We imagine the sun to be a foot in diameter though we are convinced that it is larger than the inhabited part of the earth" (*De anima* 2.428b3–4). Cf. Robinson (1987, *ad loc.*): "From Aristotle (see Kahn, n193) we can infer that the phrase 'the sun is a foot wide' was a standard examples of deceptive appearance (like 'sticks look bent in water')." This seems to be his point also in quoting the children's riddle: "All we saw and grasped we have left behind, but all we neither saw nor grasped we bring with us" (B56), the answer to

which is "lice." For Heraclitus the significance of the riddle would be that, like the lice, the reality that we now see will be left behind when we see the logos, while the unseen reality—the nature that loves to hide—is always with us. Also see Rethy (1987).

16. Julius Moravcsik (1991, 551–54) reminds us that this insight was already present in another way in religious thinking.

17. McKirahan (1994), after Kirk, has "Wisdom is one thing, to be skilled in true judgment, how all things are steered through all things." See Kirk (1954, 286–91), but also Gregory Vlastos's (1955, 352–53) reply to Kirk. For other discussions, see Kahn (1979, 170–72), and Robinson (1987, 107–8).

18. Exactly how verbatim Porphyry's quotation is in B102 is a matter of debate. Kahn suggests that the wording "is that of some anonymous Homeric commentator, perhaps a Stoic, and we cannot know how well it reflects what Heraclitus said" (1979, 183), but cf. Robinson: "Most modern commentators see no reason for not accepting it as fairly exact" (1987, 149). In any case, the same basic point is evident in other fragments as well: B1 tells us that all things happen in accordance with the logos; B41 says that all things are steered through all things by an intelligence; B4, B9, and B61 point out that things that are bad to us are good to other forms of life; B67 identifies God with night, winter, war, and hunger, as well as with day, summer, peace, and satiety; and B106 rebukes Hesiod for considering some days good and others bad (although the authenticity of this fragment has been questioned).

19. For a discussion of the identity of opposites in Heraclitus, see Guthrie (1962–81, 1:445–46).

20. My translation. McKirahan (1994) does not consider it authentic.

21. *Nicomachean Ethics* 7.1177b26–27, Barnes edition (Aristotle 1984). Unless otherwise stated, all translations from Aristotle are from this edition. Bekker numbers for Aristotle correspond to the Oxford Classical Texts series (Oxford: Clarendon Press, various dates) except where otherwise noted. For the suggestion that Heraclitus is referring to the divine within us in these passages I am indebted to Enrique Hülsz.

22. Cf. "What we see when awake is death, what we see asleep is sleep" (B21). To be asleep is to see nothing of the world but only sleep itself, and even when we are awake we see only the mortal world of things that are constantly passing away. But as B1 and B2 show, there is one further step: beyond the sleep that we see when asleep, and the death or transience we see when awake, there is also something eternal that we can awaken to in another sense. The same analogy appears again in B26: "A person in the night kindles [ἅπτεται] a light for himself when his sight is extinguished. While living, he approximates to [ἅπτεται] a dead man during sleep; while awake, he approximates to [ἅπτεται] one who

sleeps" (the translation of the second sentence is Kathleen Freeman's [1956, 26]). The point of the second sentence is similar to what we have just seen: not only do we resemble someone dead when we are asleep, but when we are awake we normally resemble someone asleep. The first sentence implies this through a different metaphor: just as we kindle a light for ourselves in the literal darkness of night, we need to kindle a different kind of light for ourselves in the metaphorical darkness of our waking life. Heraclitus often uses word play to establish connections, as in B1 (λανθάνει, ἐπιλανθάνονται), B5 (μιαινόμενοι, μαίεσθαι), B25 (μόροι, μοίρας), B45 (λόγος), B48 (βίος, βιός), and B114 (ξὺν νόῳ, ξυνῷ). In this case the term ἅπτεται, which originally means "to touch," is used in the extended senses of "to kindle" (touch fire to fuel) and "to approximate." Taking ἅπτεται more literally, as "touch," gives no clear sense of the whole, even by the standards of "Heraclitus the Obscure." Thus Heidegger, who interprets ἅπτεται in the literal sense of "touch," confesses that "everything that follows ἑαυτῷ [i.e., everything after the words "A person in the night kindles a light for himself"] is puzzling to me. I do not see the thrust of the fragment" (Heidegger and Fink, 1979, 131); Kahn calls it "a thicket of riddles" (1979, 215); and Robinson agrees that it "is one of the most puzzling of the fragments" (1987, 93). Burnet translates quite differently: "Man kindles a light for himself in the night-time, when he has died but is alive. The sleeper, whose vision has been put out, lights up from the dead; he that is awake lights up from the sleeping" ([1930] 1957, *ad loc.*) Also see Fink (Heidegger and Fink, 1979, 127–31), and Gadamer (2002, 74–77). A similar point is implied when B15 says that "Hades and Dionysus are the same," if Martha Nussbaum (1972, 1–16, 153–70, 159) is right to identify Dionysus with self-indulgence. In that case we can take it to mean that a life devoted to our individual appetites, instead of what is common to all, is a kind of living death. For other appearances of the sleeping/waking metaphor, see fragments B73, B75, B88, and B89.

23. There is a word play between ξὺν νόῳ ("with understanding") and ξυνῷ ("common to all").

24. The kindling and extinction of individuals and the kindling and extinction of fire are inversely related: "All things are an exchange for fire and fire for all things" (90); "Fire will advance and judge and convict all things" (66). I agree with Guthrie (1962–81, 1:455; cf. 458) that the phrase "ever living" implies a continual exchange at the level of parts rather than a periodic conflagration of the whole in which the world is destroyed. Also see Kirk (1954, 315–24); Kahn (1979, 134–38); Robinson (1987, 96–97).

25. B113 has been interpreted in widely different ways: from Kirk's (1954, 55–56, 63) dismissal of it as a paraphrase of B2, to Kahn's interpretation of it as panpsychism, to Schindler's proposal to take it as meaning "I cannot think by myself alone" (2003, 425).

26. 自然 *ziran*, that is, spontaneity, naturalness, what is so of itself.

27. Liu Xiaogan tries to dissolve the apparent paradox of chapter 25 by taking "Dao models itself after naturalness" to mean, not that naturalness is not identical with the Way, but that "the lofty position of honor occupied by the Way comes to it naturally" (X. Liu 1999, 211–37, 219). Nevertheless, the symmetry of the last four lines encourages the paradoxical reading of Dao and *ziran* as not identical: "Man models himself after Earth, Earth models itself after Heaven. Heaven models itself after Dao. And Dao models itself after *ziran*." Since man is not identical with earth, earth with heaven, or heaven with Dao, we would expect that neither is Dao identical here with *ziran*. Thus too Wang Bi (Wang Pi) (1979, 78).

28. See, for example, Charles Wei-hsun Fu (1973, 372–79).

29. Thus Girardot writes: "The Tao is called the 'mother' (*mu*) of the world, which is reflective of numerous mythologies where creation involves a cosmic ancestral giant, animal, or Great Mother that spawns a male and a female off-spring who in turn incestuously engender the human world. Another frequent mythological form of this idea of the Tao's motherhood, and one that appears close to the intention of the Taoist texts, is the idea of a primal ancestral bird, snake, or fish that lays a cosmic egg that subsequently splits open, giving rise the dual principle of the cosmos" (1983, 51).

30. *Chu Tzu yü-lei* 1.2b:12, in Zhu Xi (1990, 92).

31. Fung (1948, 96). So too Chan (1963b, 7–8); LaFargue (1994, 255–56). On the other hand, Wang Bi (Pi) (1979, 1) takes it to be a temporal process: see his comment on 1.4.

32. For a different view, see Girardot (1983, 65). An excellent survey of these issues may be found in Robinet (1999).

33. Chan (1963b, 150n60) translates *jing* as "essence" but mentions "life-force" as another of its meanings. Ames and Hall (2003) have "seminal concentrations of *qi*," LaFargue (1994) "vital energy," Ellen Chen (1989) "life seed," Wing (1984) "Life Force," and Waley (1958) "force."

34. Ames and Hall write: "The Chinese tradition does not have the separation between time and entities that would allow for either time without entities, or entities without time" (2003, 15). It follows that there was never a moment when Dao was and things in general were not yet.

35. Cf. Fu (1973): "They are not categories but perspectives" (373); "The ontologically non-differentiated and the ontologically differentiated are but two aspects of the same Tao" (378).

36. "Being and non-being produce each other" (2.5). The sage "causes his people to be without knowledge" (3.9). "Dao is empty . . . [but] never ex-hausted" (4.1–2). "While vacuous, it is never exhausted" (5.6). "Concentrate

your *qi* and achieve the highest degree of weakness" (10.2). "It is on its non-being that the utility of the carriage [and utensil and room] depends" (11.2,4,6). "How much difference is there between yes and no? . . . Mine is indeed the mind of an ignorant man" (20.2 modified, 20.13). "To be empty is to be full" (22.3). "A well-tied knot needs no rope and yet none can untie it" (27.4). The sage "returns to the state of the Ultimate of Non-being" (28.10). "In order to weaken it is necessary first to strengthen" (36.3–4). "Dao invariably takes no action, and yet there is nothing left undone" (37.1). "Enumerate all the parts of a chariot as you may, and you still have no chariot" (39.26). "Being comes from non-being" (40.4). "Great form has no shape" (41.20). "What is most full seems to be empty" (45.3).

37. *Mulamadhyamakakarika* 22.11 (Nagarjuna 1995, 61).

38. "Treatise on the Two Levels of Truth," in Chan (1963a, 360). The parenthetical expansion is Chan's.

39. For Laozi, by contrast, form is within the formlessness of the Dao rather than something extrinsic to it: "The thing that is called Dao is eluding and vague. Vague and eluding, there is in it the form" (21.2–3).

40. Cf. Leibniz:

> Look at a very beautiful picture, then cover up all but a small part. What will be evident in it, no matter how closely you look at it, but some confused chaos of colours, without selection, without art; indeed, the more you look at it the more chaotic it will seem. And yet when the covering is removed, you will see the whole picture from an appropriate position, and then you will see that what seemed to be thoughtlessly smeared on the canvas was in fact accomplished with the greatest skill by the author of the work. What the eyes discern in a painting is also what the ears discern in music. Indeed, distinguished masters of composition often mix dissonances with consonances so that a listener may be aroused and pricked, as it were, and as if anxious about the outcome, be so much more joyful when all is then restored to order. It is much like our taking delight in small dangers, or in the experience of misfortunes, our delight coming from the very sense of our own power or happiness or the act of showing off. Or it is like when we delight in the spectacle of tightrope-walking or sword-dancing because of the very fears that that they inspire, and we laughingly half-let go of children as if we were going to throw them away. . . . On the same principle it is insipid to constantly eat sweet things; sharp, sour, and even bitter things should be mixed in to excite the taste. He who has not tasted the bitter does not deserve the sweet, nor will he appreciate it in fact. This is the very law of enjoyment,

that pleasure does not come from a uniform course, for this produces disgust and makes us dull, not joyful. (Leibniz [1697] 2014)

A similar translation may found in Leibniz (1951, 352–53).

41. Removing Chan's quotation marks around the terms *good* and *evil*.

42. *Huainanzi* 18.6a. This retelling is condensed from H. Smith (1964, 188–89).

43. Cf. LaFargue: "Since the *Tao Te Ching* is such a brief work, however, some of the special terms are used too seldom in it to give us good contextual evidence as to what connotations they had for Laoists. This deficiency of the *Tao Te Ching* can be partly made up for by first examining some passages in the *Chuang Tzu*, which uses many of the same special terms used in *Tao Te Ching* and often gives us better contextual clues as to what the terms might have meant to those involved in self-cultivation" (1994, 201). In the present case LaFargue cites the *Nei Yeh*: "Life then thought, thought then knowledge, knowledge then stop" (1994, 479).

44. Chap. 2, Watson translation (Zhuangzi 2013, 41), numbers added. Since the comparison is with Chan's translation of Laozi, here is the same passage from Zhuangzi in Chan's translation: "The knowledge of the ancients was perfect. In what way was it perfect? There were those who believed that nothing existed. Such knowledge is indeed perfect and ultimate and cannot be improved. The next were those who believed there were things but there was no distinction between them. Still the next were those who believed there was distinction but there was neither right nor wrong. When the distinction between right and wrong became prominent, Dao was thereby reduced" (Chan 1963a, 185).

45. There is a long tradition of reading the Bible allegorically. Chapter 2 of Genesis admits of a reading parallel to these texts from Laozi and Zhuangzi: "Out of the ground the Lord God formed every beast of the field and every bird of the air, and brought them to Adam to see what he would call them; and *whatever Adam called every living creature, that was its name*" (Gen. 2:19, New King James Version, emphasis added). "And the Lord God commanded Adam, saying, 'You may freely eat of every tree of the garden; but of the tree of the knowledge *of good and evil* you shall not eat, for in the day that you eat of it you shall die'" (2:16–17). So puzzling is this passage that it is usually incompletely recalled as saying that we are forbidden to eat of the tree of knowledge, not the tree of the knowledge "of good and evil." The mistake is understandable because it is easier to think of religion as being anti-intellectual than being antimoral. But in view of what we have seen in the Daoists, Genesis may be making a subtle and important point about the danger of distinguishing things as good or evil (stage 4 in Zhuangzi), while still permitting "naming," that is, recognizing the boundaries between things (stage 3).

46. "The good man is the teacher of the bad" (27.9, cf. 27.1–3, 6–7, 10). "The good ruler when at home honors the left (symbolic of good omens)" (31.4). "I treat those who are good with goodness, / And I also treat those who are not good with goodness. / Thus goodness is attained" 49.3–5). "To patch up great hatred is surely to leave some hatred behind. / How can this be regarded as good? . . . 'The Way of Heaven has no favorites. / It is always with the good man'" (79.1–2, 7–8). "A good man does not argue. / He who argues is not a good man" (81.3–4).

47. Cf.: "The sage . . . accomplishes without any action" (47.6); "The sage says: I take no action" (57.15); "The sage takes no action" (64.12, cf. 64.19).

48. For "One who is good," Chan (1963b) has "A good (general)."

49. The same ideas are presented in chaps. 10 (10.6, 8–9) and 77 (77.11–12). Chapter 51 makes a similar point about the Dao itself (51.12–13). For further discussion of *wuwei*, see X. Liu (1999) and Ivanhoe (1999, 247–50).

50. Freedom from desire is a recurring theme in Laozi: "Have few desires" (19.12); the Dao is "always without desires" (34.6); "Being free of desires, it is tranquil" (37.6); "Shut the doors (of . . . desire)" (52.9, 56.4); "The sage says: . . . I have no desires" (57.14, 18); "The sage desires to have no desire" (64.16).

51. Cf. 3.1, 8.12, 22.13, 24.1–6, 30.5–11, 66.11, 68.5, 73.6, 77.12.

52. Corresponding views appear in other traditions. A particularly eloquent example in the Confucian tradition appears in Wang Yang-ming's *Inquiry on "The Great Learning"*:

> [Each person forms] one body with Heaven, Earth, and the myriad things. Therefore when he sees a child about to fall into a well, he cannot help a feeling of alarm and commiseration. This shows that his humanity forms one body with the child. It may be objected that [this is not one body with Heaven, Earth, and the myriad things because] the child belongs to the same species. Again, when he observes the pitiful cries and frightened appearance of birds and animals about to be slaughtered, he cannot help feeling an inability to bear their suffering. This shows that his humanity forms one body with birds and animals. It may be objected that birds and animals are sentient beings as he is. But when he sees plants broken and destroyed, he cannot help a feeling of pity. This shows that his humanity forms one body with plants. It may be said that plants are living things as he is. Yet even when he sees tiles and stones shattered and crushed, he cannot help a feeling of regret. This shows that his humanity forms one body with tiles and stones. This means that even the mind of the ordinary man necessarily has the humanity that forms one body with all. (Wang Yang-ming 1963a, 659–60)

The most famous Western example is by the seventeenth-century Anglican priest John Donne: "No man is an island entire of itself; every man is a piece of the continent, a part of the main; if a clod be washed away by the sea, Europe is the less, as well as if a promontory were, as well as any manner of thy friends or of thine own were; any man's death diminishes me, because I am involved in mankind. And therefore never send to know for whom the bell tolls; it tolls for thee" (Meditation 17 of "Devotions upon Emergent Occasions," spelling modernized; in Donne 1952, 441).

53. The translation of 同其塵 (*tong qi chen*, also at 4.7) as "Become one with the dusty world" is Chan's. Others have "All dust smoothed" (Waley 1958), "Make identical the dust" (Chen 1989), "Identify with the ways of the world" (Wing 1984), "Make the dust merge together" (LaFargue 1994), "Bring things together on the same track" (Ames and Hall 2003), "Become one with your dust" (Alquiros 2002), "Settles the dust" (Henricks 2000).

54. Cf. Wang Bi's (Wang Pi's) comment on the contrast between the Way of Heaven and the Way of Man in chap. 77: "Only by not clinging to one's own body and not keeping Nature for oneself can one be identified with the virtue of Heaven and Earth" (1979).

55. "Lost" is Chen's translation (1989, 103). Chan has "wearied."

56. Cf. 22.11–12, 24.5–6, 30.7–9, 77.12.

57. Substituting "flavorless" for Chan's "tasteless," which is ambiguous.

58. The need to know things through themselves is illustrated by "How do I know that the beginnings of all things are so? / Through this" (21.9–10); and "How do I know this to be the case in the world? / Through this" (54.14–15).

59. Cf. 35.5–10, quoted above.

60. "Reversal is the action of Dao" (40.1, replacing Chan's "reversion"). Harold Roth argues that in Zhuangzi there are two modes of mystical experience. In the first mode "The adept achieves complete union with the *Dao*." In the second "The adept returns to the world and retains, amidst the flow of daily life, a profound sense of the unity previously experienced." He continues, "While evidence for its presence is not as strong in the *Laozi* as in the *Zhuangzi*, it is, as we shall see, most certainly there" (1999, 66).

61. Cf. 27.1–10, 31.1–7, 49.2–4, 79.2,8, 81.3–4.

62. "*Wuwei* . . . involves the absence of any course of action that interferes with the particular focus (*de*) of those things contained within one's field of influence" (Ames and Hall 2003, 39, cf. 32, 67). "The variations on *wuwei* are modes of selfless experience, experience that is extremely efficacious precisely because it is selfless. It comes from the Way and not the individual self" (Roth 1999, 80). "*Wuwei* . . . is well illustrated here by the field. The field appears to do nothing; all of this happens 'by nature' (*ziran*—'it is so on its own')" (Henricks

2000, 165). "*Wu-wei* [means] . . . taking no action, living in nonaction: loving tranquillity, engaging in no activity, and having no desires—which leads to natural transformation, correctness, prosperity, and simplicity" (S. Liu 1998, 345–60). "*Wuwei* [unlike *ziran,* naturalness], . . . while still preserving the emphasis on naturalness nevertheless imposes restrictions upon certain types of spontaneous actions—for instance those motivated by desire for and pursuit of fame or profit" (X. Liu 1999, 214). "*Chuang Tzu 5.*(13/2–10) speaks of *wu wei* as an inner state: '*hsü*/Empty, *ching*/Still, limpid, silent, not-doing (*wu wei*)" (LaFargue 1994, 215–16). "The Taoist allows events to unfold according to their inner rhythms; he acts by non-action (*wu-wei*), which is acting with, not against, the inner rhythms of things" (Chen 1989, 41, cf. 169). "The important idea of *wu-wei* represents the individual Taoist's identification with, and emulation of, the cosmic life of spontaneity and naturalness (*tzu-jan*) of the Tao" (Girardot 1983, 56). "Taking no action (*wu-wei*) does not mean to be 'dry wood and dead ashes,' to use the metaphors of Chuang Tzu. Rather, it means taking no artificial action, noninterference, or letting things take their own course" (Chan 1963b, 8).

63. For example *Nicomachean Ethics* 1.8. In one place Aristotle compares our acquired character to our inborn nature (7.3.1147a22). For those whose character is virtuous, doing what is good comes "naturally."

64. For a comprehensive comparison of Confucius and Aristotle on these matters, see Yu (2007, 96–139).

65. Cf. 18.1–4, 19.1–2, 20.1, 64.13, chap. 65.

66. Also see 57.14–18, 63.9–10, 72.6–7.

67. Moreover, for Kant it is not a question of purifying our desires by learning, self-control, and habituation—as in Confucius and Aristotle—but rather of regarding our desires as simply irrelevant if not inimical to moral questions. The moral person should simply attend to impersonal duty, should "desire to have no desires." But there is nothing like the effortless spontaneity of *wuwei*. On the contrary, every moral action is a result of the most deliberate effort of rational calculation. The difference between Laozi and Kant is the difference between "superior virtue" and "superior humanity": "The man of superior virtue takes no action, but has no ulterior motive to do so. . . . The man of superior humanity takes action, but has no ulterior motive for doing so" (38.5, 7).

68. Cf. Nietzsche's *Also sprach Zarathustra* (Vorrede, §5). "Must one first smash their ears so that they learn to hear with their eyes?" (1963a, my translation).

69. Stephanus numbers for Plato's works correspond to the Burnet edition of the Oxford Classical Texts (Burnet 1900–1907). Translations from Plato are my own unless otherwise specified. The metaphor occurs also in B12, B49a, and B91. Whether these were originally independent statements or whether one or more is

a paraphrase or misquotation of the other(s) is a matter of dispute. The same idea seems implied by B21: "What we see when awake is death," i.e., everything is always passing away. Similarly, even "The sun is new each day" (6)—although others take this to be a more literal scientific claim (see Kirk 1954, 265–79, and Robinson 1987, 79). Some readers doubt that the flux doctrine was meant to apply universally. Kirk, for example, writes that Heraclitus "believed strongly in the value of sense-perception, providing that it is interpreted intelligently. . . . Our observation tells us that this table or that rock are *not* changing at every instant" (1954, 376). But observation told the atomists and other pre-Socratics that rock and other solids did slowly erode. Aristotle says (before refuting it), "The view is actually held by some that not merely some things but all things in the world are in motion and always in motion, though we cannot apprehend the fact by sense-perception. . . . The theory resembles that about the stone being worn away by the drop of water or split by plants growing out of it" (*Physics* 8.3.253b10–15). As Guthrie writes in response to Kirk, "That the rock is changing every instant we cannot see with our eyes, but it is what their evidence suggests if we apply 'minds that understand the language.'. . . The continuous imperceptible change is a natural inference from the observation" (1962–81, 1:451).

70. *Metaphysics* Γ.5.1010a12–15.

71. Dilcher (1995, 67–69, 90–96) is especially alert to the microcosm-macrocosm theme.

72. Here *logos* has the double meaning of measure and the principle of the universe.

73. E.g., "The pursuit of learning is to increase day after day. The pursuit of Dao is to decrease day after day" (48.1–2), or "A wise man has no extensive knowledge; He who has extensive knowledge is not a wise man" (81.5–6).

74. *Barbaros* means someone who does not speak Greek. Also see Kahn (1979, 106–7), and Dilcher (1995, 80). Joel Wilcox argues for taking "*barbaros*" in its more colloquial sense of "foreigner": "Eyes and ears are bad witnesses for those whose *psychai* are foreign to the *logos*" (1991, 633). Nussbaum takes it to refer to linguistic incompetence more generally (1972, 9–12).

75. And so do their material elements. The material basis of all things is the mixture in different proportions of the same four elements, fire, water, earth, and air (B76a). So all things, no matter how diverse, are to be understood not only in terms of common species but also in terms of the four elements common to all things. The goal of wisdom is to become acquainted not simply with the multitude of individual things themselves but with what lies behind them, that "by which all things are steered through all things" (B41).

76. The idea of the same things being transformed not only from life to death but also from death back to life, and not only from young to old but also from

old back to young, is often taken to be a reference to reincarnation, which it may be, but it may also be a reference to the material elements that alternate between living and dead bodies, and in the same way between old and young ones.

77. Emphasis added. "Fire" is McKirahan's (1994) insertion based on Diels's conjecture. Oil, air, water, and wine have been other proposals. "Fire" has the advantage of alluding to Heraclitus's conception of fire as the elemental universe as a whole (B69), but the point is the same with any of the conjectures.

78. Some fifty years earlier Anaximander had written: "The things that are perish . . . according to necessity, for they pay penalty and retribution to each other for their injustice in accordance with the ordering of time" (Anaximander B1). Taking the perfumes to refer to moments in time is not open to the objection Kahn raises against interpreting the metaphor as fire and incense, namely that unlike the whole and its parts "the altar flame is of course distinct from the incense or spices that are thrown upon it" (1979, 280). Kahn offers an alternative reading of the fragment.

79. A different kind of interpretation has been suggested by Reinhardt (1942, 228–35). Also see Kirk (1954, 294–305), and Kahn (1979, 155–56).

Chapter 5

1. The last of the great neo-Confucianists, Wang (1472–1529 CE) came near the end of the tradition founded two thousand years earlier by Confucius (551–479 BCE), revitalized as neo-Confucianism by Zhou Dunyi (Chou Tun-i 1017–73 CE), and given an idealistic interpretation by Cheng Hao (1032–85 CE) and Lu Xiangshan (1139–93 CE).

2. For a careful discussion of the late twentieth-century literature surrounding this issue, coupled with a defense of the claim that knowledge can be virtue, see Little (1997). For the relevance of Wang Yangming's arguments to contemporary Western action research, see Tickle (2005).

3. E.g., Bailey (2010).

4. Pioneers in this field include Alfred Adler; Ellis (1962); and Beck (1976). Also see Gilbert (1988); Carmin and Dowd (1988); and Wessler (1988).

5. John Burnet and A. E. Taylor believe that the Socrates of Plato's "Socratic dialogues" is a reliable portrait of the historical Socrates. Taylor agrees with Burnet that "Plato's historical sense forbade him to make Socrates the expositor of philosophical and scientific interests and doctrines which Plato well knew to be his own and those of his contemporaries. . . . We may infer that Plato was at least unconscious of any departure from historical verisimilitude in the picture drawn of Socrates in the more numerous dialogues where that philosopher

is the central figure" ([1933] 1952, 28–29, cf. 11–36). Burnet writes, "I do not regard the dialogues of Plato as records of actual conversations, though I think it probable that there are such embedded in them" ([1914] 1964, 121), and Taylor acknowledges that the "Socrates of history and the Platonic Socrates are two and not one" (1917, 96). Also see de Stryker (1966, 431); Taylor ([1933] 1952, 11–36); Guthrie (1962–81, 3:325–75); Lacey (1971); Vlastos (1991, 21–106); Kahn (1996, 71–100); McPherran (1996, 12–19); Brickhouse and Smith (2000, 11–52); Nails (2002, 263–69; 2009). For a recent discussion, see Nails (2014). I agree with Kahn (1996) that even the early Platonic dialogues, with the possible exception of the *Apology*, are Platonic and not merely Socratic.

6. Cf. McPherran (1996, 202): It is one of "several propositions that Socrates relies on and seems absolutely confident of, and we never see them subjected to the *elenchos*."

7. Stephanus numbers for Plato's works correspond to the Burnet edition of the Oxford Classical Texts (Burnet 1900–1907). All translations from Plato are my own unless otherwise specified. Bekker numbers for Aristotle correspond to the Oxford Classical Texts series (Oxford: Clarendon Press, various dates) except where otherwise noted.

8. Unless otherwise stated, all translations from Aristotle are from the Barnes edition (Aristotle 1984).

9. Also see Guthrie (1962–81, 3:450–62).

10. Euripides, *Hippolytus* 380–83, trans. David Grene. Socrates lived from about 470 to 399 BCE, Euripides from 480 to 406 BCE.

11. *Magna moralia* 1182a20–25, with "virtues" substituted for "excellences."

12. *Nicomachean Ethics* 7.2.1145b21–29, my translation.

13. For recent investigations into *akrasia* or weakness, see McKie (1994), which cites five studies as showing that "sincerely expressed moral beliefs are often not reflected in action" (27).

14. In other supposedly early dialogues as well, Socrates seems committed to moral intellectualism, the view that whether we are virtuous depends solely on our intellect and has nothing to do with the strength or weakness of a will that is distinct from the intellect.

15. *Nicomachean Ethics* 7.2.1145b31–35, my translation, emphasis added.

16. Gerasimos Santas has disputed that any distinction between knowledge and opinion can help us explicate the "Virtue is knowledge" equation:

> It cannot be taken for granted that Plato means to exclude the view that true *belief* (as distinct from knowledge) is sufficient for acting justly. Though he uses *sofia, episteme, mathesis* (all usually translated "knowledge"), which he distinguishes from *pistis* or *doxa* (belief, opinion),

in stating the moral paradox, he nevertheless contrasts these with ignorance of false belief (never with true belief) when he argues for the
moral paradox [*Prot.* 360b–c, 360d1–2]. It is reasonable to suppose that
he would accept the view that true belief . . . if it is a firm conviction,
would be sufficient for acting justly. (1964, 162)

Throughout this argument Santas speaks not of "being just" but of "acting
justly." However, the *Republic*, at least, never defines justice in terms of particular kinds of actions, but rather in terms of the inward state of the soul (443c–
444a). Assuming that the same is true for Socrates, as I believe it is, Santas's
conclusion does not follow unless he can show that on this view when we have
a firmly held true opinion the state of our soul is not significantly different from
when we have knowledge, and that would be a difficult position to defend. At
least in the case of Plato, as the *Phaedo* shows, even certain kinds of *false* beliefs
are sufficient for *acting* justly, but the resulting actions are not instances of justice, only of what the many *call* justice (68d–e, 82a–b).

17. *Nicomachean Ethics* 7.3.1147b6–16, emphasis added.

18. σωφροσύνη is often translated as "temperance" or "moderation," but for
the present purpose I prefer a translation that captures something of σωφροσύνη's
connotation of a subject that holds firm against corrosive influences. σωφροσύνη
comes from σῶς, "safe and sound" and φρήν, "mind," and thus points to a subject, the mind, that is "safe and sound" rather than eroded by irrational elements.
Analogously if not quite accurately, Aristotle derives it from σώζω and φρόνησις:
"preserving wisdom" (*Nicomachean Ethics* 6.5.1140b11–12). Although the elements of the term *self-control* do not parallel those of σωφροσύνη, it nevertheless conveys in its own way the sense of a subject that has preserved itself from
the influence of irrational elements. *Moderation*, on the other hand, comes from
modus, "measure," and "temperance" from *temper*, "to mix in proper measure,"
so they are closer to Greek words like μέτριος ("moderate") that come from the
word for measure.

19. Lloyd Gerson and Glenn Lesses both take Plato to be talking about
akrasia there; Guthrie on the other hand thinks that throughout the *Republic*
"the Socratic 'Virtue is knowledge' was still [Plato's] guide." See Gerson (1986,
359); Lesses (1987, 148); and Guthrie (1962–81, 4:435–36).

20. Someone who rules according to the knowledge of ruling, for example,
can never err because at the moment he errs he no longer actively possesses that
knowledge (*Republic* 1.340c–e).

21. Plato's Seventh Letter gives a famous description of how conversion can
be effected by a teacher: "It cannot be expressed in speech like other kinds of
knowledge, but after a long attendance upon the matter itself, and communion

with it, then suddenly—as a blaze is kindled from a leaping spark—it is born in the soul and at once becomes self-nourishing" (341c–342a). Cf. his Second Letter 314a–c. The authenticity of Plato's letters is a never-ending source of debate, but it need not concern us here.

22. E.g., Emile de Stryker: "The Socratic insight [*phronesis*], which is virtue, is not the conclusion of a merely intellectual demonstration, it is not some knowledge which may be separated from the ends for which we strive, it is a caring for some definite things more than for others. In other words, it is a choice, by which we concretely and effectively put that which is objectively more valuable *above* other things which might also attract us. . . . Insight into the good and love for the good are one, and it is precisely in this unity that the typical fullness of the human person, that virtue (*arete*) consists" (1966, 440–41). In support of this de Strycker refers to *Republic* 10.617e, where Socrates says (in de Stryker's translation), "As man does *value* virtue more or less, he will possess more or less of it" (444). Similarly, Samuel Scolnicov writes, "Moral excellence is knowledge and no one does evil willingly, because the soul is essentially one and it is impossible to separate between its cognition and its volition. True knowledge is, in itself, a motive power" (1978, 45; cf. Scolnicov 1988, 102, 112). Julia Annas makes a similar point in connection with knowledge of the forms: "Plato always connects Forms with recognizing and valuing what is good, not just with having the capacity to follow an argument. . . . It is thus a change of heart more than a mere sharpening of the wits that is needed to make one realize that there are Forms" (1981, 237).

23. See, for example, Irwin (1974, 755); Sprague, who takes justice to be equivalent to the craft of ruling (1976, 66, 74); Parry (1983, 1996); Nussbaum (1986, 298); McKie (1994, 20, 26); Annas (1995).

24. This problem is not addressed by Richard Parry when he tries to assimilate self-control to knowledge by making justice, conceived in terms of self-control, into a craft. Parry argues that in Socrates's description of justice as the application of self-control to the wise and courageous individual soul at 443c–444a, "Justice . . . is compared to a craft. . . . The words for 'disposing,' 'ordering,' and 'harmonizing' are the same—or derivatives of the—craft words used at *Gorgias* 503e5–504a4: *kosmeo, harmozo, tithemi* [order, harmonize, dispose]. . . . Finally, just and fine action (*praxis*) is any action which preserves and helps finish (*sunapergazetai*) the order . . . and *sunapergazetai* is clearly a craft word" (1983, 26). But if the self-control element of justice is a craft, then, since a craft need not be put into practice, we get the absurd result that we can have self-control without actually being in control of ourselves. Laurence Houlgate formulates the difficulty succinctly: "To say that A has an ability to do X does not imply that A will do X when the circumstances and the opportunity arise. . . . A man

may fail to do what is virtuous even where he has knowledge of virtue, and this is true regardless of whether we conceive 'knowledge of virtue' as like knowledge of a definition or as analogous to possession of a skill or technique" (1970, 148). We still need something like willpower. However much Socrates may attribute some aspects of crafts to justice and self-control, he never attributes to them the teachable rules of crafts.

25. Cf. Cross and Woozley (1964, 13–16); Strauss (1964, 72); Annas (1981, 24–28); Reeve (1988, 8). On the other hand, in his debate with Thrasymachus Socrates argues that craft is always unselfish (341c–342e and 346c–347a), which undermines the claim that if justice were a craft it could also be the craft of stealing. But then he reverses himself again by calling moneymaking a craft despite its being avowedly selfish (346c). It is a puzzling move, since moneymaking is no more a craft than justice (we make money *in exchange* for crafts), and calling it a craft needlessly subverts the premise that all crafts are unselfish. The move salvages his earlier argument against Polemarchus but at the expense of his present argument against Thrasymachus. By calling both justice and moneymaking crafts, while at the same time showing that they cannot be crafts, Socrates creates a certain parallel between them that, if nothing else, prefigures their future complementarity as the poles (reason and appetite) between which the dialogue will eventually play itself out.

26. See Sprague (1976, 63–66); Parry (1996, 88, 96); and Irwin (1995, 69, 171, 377n14).

27. Especially since the weak sense of *techne* is more or less synonymous with *episteme*. Aristotle uses them virtually interchangeably in the passage quoted above, and Plato often does so as well (at least in the early dialogues; see Parry 1996, 15).

28. See, for example, Nivison (1973, 136–37). For an extensive analytical examination of Wang's doctrine, see Cua (1982). For his philosophy as a whole, see Ching (1976).

29. *Analects* 1.12. "If you keep pursuing harmony just because you know harmony, and do not use the rituals to regulate it, it will not work." Unless otherwise stated, all references to the *Analects* are to Huang's translation and numbering (Confucius 1997).

2.4. "At forty I was free from delusion; . . . at seventy, I was able to follow my heart's desire without overstepping the rules of propriety."

4.23. "Those who err through self-restraint are rare indeed."

6.20. "Those who know it are not comparable to those who love it; those who love it are not comparable to those who delight in it."

12.1. When Yan Yuan asked about humanity, the Master said: "To restrain oneself and return to the rituals constitutes humanity." For some criticisms from the standpoint of the "contemporary Confucian philosopher," see Cua (1993, 635–37).

30. According to Marcus Aurelius, "These three principles you must have in readiness. In the things which you do do nothing either inconsiderately or otherwise than as justice herself would act; but with respect to what may happen to you from without, consider that it happens either by chance or according to Providence, and you must neither blame chance nor accuse Providence. Second, consider what every being is from the seed to the time of its receiving a soul, and from the reception of a soul to the giving back of the same, and of what things every being is compounded and into what things it is resolved. Third, if you should suddenly be raised up above the earth, and should look down on human things, and observe the variety of them how great it is, and at the same time also should see at a glance how great is the number of beings who dwell around in the air and the aether, consider that as often as you should be raised up, you would see the same things, sameness of form and shortness of duration. Are these things to be proud of?" *Meditations* 12.24 (George Long translation [Marcus Aurelius 1862], modernized). Cf. 3.10–11, 4.3, 4.24, 8.29, 9.1, 11.18. In general, Marcus Aurelius had no hesitation in continuing to defend the claim that virtue is knowledge. See 2.1, 6.27, 7.26, 8.14, 11.1, 185.26. According to Locke, "For the removing of the pains we feel, and are at present pressed with, being the getting out of misery, and consequently the first thing to be done in order to happiness, absent good, though thought on, confessed, and appearing to be good, not making any part of this unhappiness in its absence, is justled out, to make way for the removal of those uneasinesses we feel; till due and repeated contemplation has brought it nearer to our mind, given some relish of it, and raised in us some desire: which then . . . comes in turn to determine the will" (*Essay Concerning Human Understanding* 2.21.46, in Locke [1894] 1959, 344). According to Leibniz, "When one is occupied with a very strong passion . . . it is then necessary for the mind to be prepared in advance, and to find itself already in process of going from thought to thought, in order not to hesitate too much at a slippery and dangerous step. . . . And for this purpose it is well from time to time to accustom ourselves to collect our thoughts and to raise ourselves above the present tumult of impressions, to go forth, so to speak, from the place where we are, to say to ourselves: 'Why are we here? consider the end, where are we then? or let us come to the purpose, let us come to the point.' . . . Now being once in a condition to stop the effect of our desires and passions, *i.e.* to suspend (their) action, we can find means to combat them, whether by contrary desires or inclinations or by diversions, *i.e.* by occupations of another nature. It is by these methods and artifices that we become as it were masters of ourselves." (*New Essays on Human Understanding* 2.21.47, in Leibniz 1949, 202–3).

According to Spinoza, "Through the ability to arrange and associate rightly the affections of the body we can bring it about that we are not easily affected by bad emotions. . . . Therefore the best course we can adopt, as long as we do not have perfect knowledge of our emotions, is to conceive a right method of living, or fixed rules of life, and to commit them to memory and continually apply them to particular situations that are frequently encountered in life, so that our casual thinking is thoroughly permeated by them and they are always ready to hand" (*Ethics*, pt. 5, prop. 10, scholium, in Spinoza 1992, 207–8). For Spinoza, however, Plato's more direct equation in the knowledge that he calls conversion is present in the knowledge that Spinoza calls intuition as described in *Ethics* 5, props. 37–42.

31. *Wang Wen-ch'eng kung ch'üan-shu* 6:215a, quoted in Ching (1976, 69). For Wang's advocacy of meditation, see Wang Yang-ming's *Instructions for Practical Living* 1.17 (in Wang 1963b, 26), 1.39 (in Wang 1963b, 35), 3.204 (in Wang 1963b, 192), 3.256 (in Wang 1963b, 214), 3.262 (in Wang 1963b, 217), 3.279 (in Wang 1963b, 223–24). There is no record that Socrates taught tranquility through meditation, unless one interprets in that way the ambiguous passage in the *Symposium* about Socrates's habit of withdrawing into himself for extended periods of time (175a–c). On this occasion although his absence lasted until halfway through dinner it is described as "not a long time" (175c).

32. "What is meant by 'making the will sincere' is allowing no self-deception, as when we hate a bad smell or love a beautiful color" (*Commentary on "The Great Learning"* §6, in Wang 1963a, 89).

33. Thus Taylor writes, "The miscalculation is not one of 'amounts of pleasure,' but of values of good. This is the real point of the argument in Plato's *Protagoras*" ([1933] 1952, 143, 143n).

34. Compare John Stuart Mill: "Of two pleasures, if . . . one of the two is, *by those who are competently acquainted* with both, placed so far above the other that they prefer it, even knowing it to be attended with a greater amount of discontent, . . . we are justified in ascribing to the preferred enjoyment a superiority" (1979, 8, emphasis added).

35. John Kelly makes a related point: "The goods of the soul, as they are usually referred to, can only be achieved through the soul's standing in the proper relationship to a reality external to itself as a result of living a certain kind of life. Thus, the virtuous life is required to engender the virtuous soul, while the soul seeks its fulfilment and perfection through living such a life" (1989, 203).

36. There is no explicit evidence that this "doctrine of recollection" is Socratic as well as Platonic, but it has been suggested that it is implicit in Socrates's teachings even if the implication was never explicitly recognized by Socrates

himself. Vlastos writes: "Since Socrates does expect to discover truth by this method, he must be making an exceedingly bold assumption which he never states and, if he had stated it, would have been in no position to defend, namely that side by side with all their false beliefs, his interlocutors always carry truth somewhere or other in their belief system" (1991, 113–14). Cf. A. E. Taylor: "There is one fundamental desire which is ineradicable in all of us: the desire for *good* or *happiness*. . . . To say that vice is involuntary means, therefore, that it never brings the vicious man that on which his heart, whether he knows it or not, . . . is really set. . . . Thus, if a man really knew as assured and certain truth, of which he can no more doubt than he can doubt of his own existence, that the so-called 'goods' of body and 'estate' are as nothing in comparison with the good of the soul, and know what the good of the soul is, nothing would ever tempt him to do evil" ([1933] 1952, 142–43). In a similar spirit Guthrie writes with respect to the theory of forms (which implies something like recollection): "The justification, then, in Plato's mind for putting a doctrine into Socrates's mouth was not that the doctrine *tel quel*, in its complete form, had been taught by Socrates, but that it could appear to Plato to be based on one of Socrates's fundamental convictions" (1962–81, 3:353).

37. Thus Irwin argues that Plato's conception of virtue requires the doctrine of recollection (1974, 760, 768, 771). However, whereas we have taken this to be an elucidation of Socrates's previous equation of virtue with knowledge, Irwin takes it to be a rejection of that doctrine. He rightly notes that recollection is different from the empirical knowledge characteristic of crafts, but he also claims that the identification of virtue with knowledge requires that virtue "will be a craft; several of Socrates' arguments require us to take this claim seriously, as more than a loose analogy" (755). Although it is true that more than a loose analogy is involved, it is also true that the dialogues that make this claim end in perplexity. A standard way of explaining that perplexity has been to suppose that it is Plato's way of provoking us to see that the craft analogy is an inadequate model of knowledge. See, for example, de Stryker (1966): "Thus the dialogue [*Hippias Minor*, one of the dialogues cited by Irwin] ends in an *aporia*; but this *aporia* possesses a clear meaning: Plato wishes to show that we were wrong when we identified the knowledge which is basic for virtue with the technical knowledge of the expert" (432). De Stryker refers to previous defenses of this view by Hirshberger, Kuhn, and Goldschmidt (432n14).

38. Translation by Chan (Wang 1963a, 58). Lau's translation of "strayed heart" (Lau 1970, 167) instead of "lost mind" has not been as influential. Also see Nivison (1973, 126). Although it is not relevant to our present concern, I see no reason to doubt that Mencius, if pressed, would account in the same

way for our innate but implicit ability to learn mathematics and other matters, as demonstrated in Plato's *Meno*. But he would have to expand the statement that "humanity [humaneness] is man's mind" to something more inclusive. For Wang Yangming's allusions to the lost mind, see, e.g., *Instructions for Practical Living* 1.79 (in Wang 1963b, 53), 1.118 (in Wang 1963b, 76), and 2.134 (in Wang 1963b, 95).

39. "Innate knowledge of the good" is Chan's translation of *liang chih* (Wang 1963a, 656), followed by Liu Shu-Hsien, who adds that it "refers to metaphysical or moral insights which cannot be established in terms of empirical knowledge through seeing and hearing" (S. Liu 1998, 346). Nivison translates it as "pure intuitive knowing" (1973, 125), while Ching has "going right to the heart of the matter" (1976, 43) but also "the principle of their originally good human nature" (47). According to Cua, who gives an extended discussion of the concept (1993, 627–34), the phrase is "a binomial involving *chih* (knowledge) as a component . . . [and] clearly implies *liang* in the sense of innateness, though it also conveys some sense of goodness that cannot be understood apart from Wang's vision" (1993, 628–30). Cua, however, denies that Wang is an ethical intuitionist (1982, 91). If ethical intuitionism is taken to mean not only that we have an innate ability to discover moral truths, which cannot be reduced to what comes to us through the senses, but also that we are born knowing ethical facts, then Cua's denial is surely correct.

40. *Inquiry on "The Great Learning,"* in Wang (1963a, 272–73), emphasis added.

41. *Instructions for Practical Living* §222, in Wang (1963a, 200). Cf. Ching (1976): "The issue is thus not so much one of the correctness of certain intellectual propositions, than of wisdom, which concerns insights into the whole of life, of man and his place in the universe, the knowledge of which must be accompanied by virtuous behavior" (xiii, cf. 46); see also Cua (1982, 51–53).

42. *Phaedrus* 275c, 277a. Cf. Vlastos (1971a, 13–14). Cf. Plato's Seventh Letter, previously quoted in chapter 1: "There is no way of putting [the object of philosophy] into words like other studies. Acquaintance with it must come rather after a long period of attendance on instruction in the subject itself and of close companionship, when, suddenly, like a blaze kindled by a leaping spark, it is generated in the soul and at once becomes self-sustaining" (341c–d).

43. Nivison (1973, 123n10). Thus Nivison writes that Wang "tries to guide his students to think out moral problems afresh for themselves, feel out for themselves their inner moral responsiveness as persons, and does not point to established doctrine and say simply 'accept this'" (1973, 133). Vlastos (among others) makes a similar point about Socrates: see, e.g., Vlastos (1971a, 14).

Chapter 6

1. See Chichung Huang's note on the function of the bell in his translation of the *Analects* 3.24n4 (Confucius 1997, 66), and Chan's explanation in Chan (1963a, 25). Unless otherwise stated, all references to the *Analects* are to Huang's translation and numbering (Confucius 1997). Huang's hyphenation of some names has been dropped.

2. Confucius calls it "a sublime virtue indeed" (*Analects* 6.29). I see no reason to follow Huang (Confucius 1997) in limiting the mean to the exact observance of the rituals. Huang considers the best clue to the nature of the mean to be the passage in *Analects* 11.16, in which Confucius says that Shi goes too far and Shang not far enough and that both are equally wrong. After pointing to a similar story in the *Records of the Rituals*, where Zigong asks, "What constitutes the mean here?" and Confucius replies, "The rituals," Huang concludes that "what the constant mean signifies is following the rituals to the letter, no more and no less" (25). However, since Zigong asks, "What constitutes the mean *here*," Confucius's answer applies only to this one example, not to every instance of the mean. Moreover, there are other analects that are just as much illustrations of the mean as the story about Shi and Shang and that do not refer to the rituals. According to 7.37, "Confucius is affable but dignified, austere but not harsh, polite but completely at ease." Chan seems justified in calling this "the Confucian mean in practice" (1963a, 33). Also see 11.21 and 13.21.

3. *Laws* 691c; cf. *Statesman* 283d–284d. Stephanus numbers for Plato's works correspond to the Burnet edition of the Oxford Classical Texts (Burnet 1900–1907). All translations from Plato are my own unless otherwise specified.

4. *Apology* 31d. "The usual prophetic voice of the divinity in previous times always spoke to me very frequently and opposed me even in very trivial matters, if I was about to do something that was not right. . . . It could not be the case that the usual sign would not have opposed me if I was not about to do something good." (*Apology* 40a–c; cf. *Euthydemus* 272e, *Phaedrus* 242b).

5. *Analects* 11.20. Cf. 11.16: "Zigong asked: 'Between Shi and Shang, which is the worthier?' The Master said: 'Shi goes beyond whereas Shang falls short.' Zigong said: 'Then Shi is the superior?' The Master said, 'To go beyond is the same as to fall short.'"

6. Likewise, the Eleatic visitor concedes the necessity of supplementing teaching with marriage between the two opposed temperaments (*Statesman* 310a–e).

7. See, for example, Gallop (1998).

8. *Analects* 15.24, modified. "What you do not wish for yourself do not impose on others" appears also in 12.2, where Huang writes that it is "believed to be an old proverb" (Confucius 1997, 126n4).

9. Chap. 10, p. 92, in Chan (1963a). All references to *The Great Learning* are to this edition.

10. Wang Yangming, *Commentary on "The Great Learning,"* §6, in Wang (1963a, 89–90).

11. Cf. Mencius: "If he does not understand goodness he cannot be sincere with himself" (4A.12). The same statement appears in *The Doctrine of the Mean*, chap. 20, in Chan (1963a, 107). All references to *The Doctrine of the Mean* are to this edition and are given by chapter and page. Unless otherwise stated, all translations from Mencius are from D. C. Lau's *Mencius* (Lau 1970). In this case I have substituted Chan's (1963a) "sincere with himself" for Lau's "true to himself."

12. Whether or not the discrepancy in Plato is only contextual—following from the contexts of two very different dialogues—will not concern us here, since our discussion of Plato will focus primary on the *Republic*.

13. *Doctrine of the Mean*, chap. 1, p. 98. In the *Republic* there is a comparable distinction. It is possible to achieve a state of simplicity where the whole soul together is turned toward the good so that emotions never arise in opposition to reason (518c–d, 519b) and where any behavior that is not good is unthinkable (516d). But when the soul is not at one with itself and the good, and when the appetitive and spirited emotions arise in opposition to the dictates of reason about what is good, then virtue can still be achieved by means of a "harmony" of the three elements, if each is permitted to perform its own proper function without interference from the others (cf. "Each and all attain due measure and degree"; 443d–444a).

14. *Republic* 618b–619b. The term translated as "mean" is μέσον (Aristotle uses both μέσον and μεσότης), whereas the *Statesman* and *Laws* use μέτριον.

15. I have omitted Young Socrates's responses without indicating the omissions by ellipses. The ellipsis marks refer to the Eleatic visitor's words.

16. For the *Republic*'s conception of ruling as a techne, see 341d–342e, 374e, 466e, 488d–489a, 493d; cf. *Statesman* 284a. I have discussed in detail the *Republic*'s treatment of techne, education, justice, and the mean in Dorter (2001, 2006).

17. Even justice is at one place said to be a techne (332d), but the *reductio ad absurdum* that follows makes it clear that that designation is not intended to be taken seriously.

18. Later, Socrates extends the prohibition in a most un-Confucian way to families, so that every guardian will have the same relationship to all members of the opposite sex in common and to all children in common, "to prevent them from tearing the city apart by applying the word 'mine' not to the same things, but each to something different" (457b–c).

19. According to Mencius (5B.1, in Chan 1963a, 150), "Confucius was the sage whose actions were timely," i.e., *kairotic*.

20. Zhu Xi's respect for Chen Yi leads him in one place to speak of meditation in a conciliatory way: "Chen Yi sometimes also taught people sitting in meditation. But from Confucius and Mencius upward, there was no such doctrine. We must search and investigate on a higher plane and see that sitting in meditation and the examination of principle do not interfere with each other, and then it will be correct" (*Complete Works* 2:44a–b, in Chan 1963a, 608). By "examination of principle" he means a primarily empirical kind of investigation, however, and he does not speak tolerantly of types of meditation that lead away from such investigation: "To be serious does not mean to sit still like a blockhead, with the ear hearing nothing, the eye seeing nothing, and the mind thinking of nothing" (2:22a, in Chan 1963a, 607); and "As soon as they open their eyes from meditation, what they try to get hold of is again gone from them as before" (60:21a–b, in Chan 1963a, 650).

Chapter 7

1. These colophons are (1) The depression of Arjuna; (2) The yoga of theory (*samkhyayogo*); (3) The yoga of actions (*karmayogo*); (4) The yoga of knowledge (*jñanayogo*); (5) The yoga of renunciation of action (*karmasamnyasayogo*); (6) The yoga of meditation (*dhyanayogo*); (7) The yoga of knowledge and wisdom (*jñanavijñanayogo*); (8) The yoga of the imperishable absolute (*aksarabrahmayogo*); (9) The yoga of sovereign knowledge and sovereign mystery (*rajavidyarajaguhyayogo*); (10) The yoga of manifestation (*vibhutiyogo*); (11) The vision of the cosmic form; (12) The yoga of devotion (*bhaktiyogo*); (13) The yoga of the distinction between the field and the knower (*ksetraksetrajñanavibhagayogo*); (14) The yoga of the differentiation of the three modes (*gunatrayavibhagayogo*); (15) The yoga of the supreme person (*purusottamayogo*); (16) The yoga of the distinction between the divine and the demoniac endowments (*daivasurasampadvibhagayogo*); (17) The yoga of the threefold division of faith (*sraddhatrayavibhagayogo*); and (18) The yoga of release by renunciation (*moksasamnyasayogo*).

2. Cf. A. Sharma (1986, xii–xvi).

3. Cf. Radhakrishnan (1948, 28): "The boundless universe in an endless space and time rests in Him and not He in it."

4. Unless otherwise specified, all translations from the Bhagavad Gita (with occasional modifications) are from Radhakrishnan (1948). Parentheses within the quotations are the translator's amplifications; mine are within brackets. For an exploration of Krishna's injunction here, see Sartwell (1993).

5. "One who sets fires, gives poison, attacks with weapon in hand, plunders the property, dispossesses of the territory as well as of women—these six are *atatayinah*" (*Vasisthasmrti* 3.16). Cited in Upadhyaya (1969, 164). Upadhyaya points out that the Kauravas "committed not one but all the six heinous crimes" (1969, 164).

6. In the first of the preliminary arguments, Krishna chides Arjuna for a faintheartedness that will lead to his disgrace, an argument that does nothing to shake Arjuna's scruples about killing members of his clan (2.2–9). In the second, Krishna argues that since the true self cannot be killed Arjuna's scruples are irrelevant (2.11–30), but this does nothing to dispel Arjuna's worries about destroying the family dharma.

7. The kingly warrior caste: "Heroism, vigor, steadiness, resourcefulness, not fleeing even in a battle, generosity and leadership, these are the action [*karma*] of a Kshatriya born of his nature" (18.43).

8. The Gita is often critical of the Vedas:

> The undiscerning who rejoice in the letter of the Veda, who contend that there is nothing else, whose nature is desire and who are intent on heaven, proclaim these flowery words that result in rebirth as the fruit of actions and (lay down) various specialized rites for the attainment of enjoyment and power. The intelligence which is to be trained, of those who are devoted to enjoyment and power and whose minds are carried away by these words (of the Veda) is not well-established in the Self. (2.42–44)

> The seeker after the knowledge of *yoga* goes beyond the Vedic rule. (6.44)

> They speak of the imperishable peepal tree as having its root above and branches below. Its leaves are the Vedas and he who knows this is the knower of the Vedas. Its branches extend below and above, nourished by the modes, with sense objects for its twigs; and below, in the world of men, stretch forth the roots resulting in actions. Its real form is not thus perceived here, nor its end nor beginning nor its foundation. . . . Cut off this firm-rooted peepal tree with the strong sword of non-attachment. (15.1–3)

The comparison of the Vedas to the leaves suggests that the Vedas are the most remote and extrinsic expressions of truth, dependent on sense objects (the twigs), although Shankara (1991, 593) interprets the metaphor more favorably to the Vedas ("As leaves serve as protectors of a tree, so the Vedas serve as the protectors of the world"; cf. Radhakrishnan and Moore 1957, 150n). This is not to deny that the Vedas have an important function. When Krishna says, "As is the use of a pond in a place flooded with water everywhere, so is that of all the Vedas for the Brahmin who understands" (2.46), the implication is that although the Vedas are superfluous for those who can achieve an inner apprehension of the truth, they are important for those whose inner resources are more limited. Also see 17.1–5, 17.14–19.

9. In the text Radhakrishnan translates this as "not brought about in regular causal sequence," but in his notes he leaves out the word *causal*.

10. Shankara (1977, on 3.5) removes the paradox by taking Krishna to be referring only to the unenlightened.

11. On Shankara's interpretation (1977, on 4.18) it is only the unenlightened who perceive *karma* in *akarma* —the way to someone on a moving boat the motionless trees appear to be moving—while the enlightened perceive *akarma* in *karma* because they recognize that *karma* is only a superimposition on *akarma*.

12. "And yet, inconsistently as it seems at first sight, the soul is spoken of as experiencing pleasure and pain, which result from material contacts and processes. . . . The key to the seeming inconsistency . . . [is that] it is only because the soul is associated with matter . . . that it *seems* to 'enjoy' material processes . . . due to the confusion caused by the organ of self-consciousness, the 'I-faculty,' which is a product of material nature and really quite disconnected with the soul" (Edgerton 1968, 143; cf. 141 for the role of the I-faculty, *ahamkara*).

13. Radhakrishnan's translation is: "Though I am its creator, know me to be incapable of action or change," which I modified to bring out the opposition between *kartaram* and *akartaram*, as does Radhakrishnan himself when he paraphrases the passage as "He is the doer of works who yet is not the doer, *kartaram, akartaram*" (1948, 72).

14. All translations from the Upaniṣads are taken from *The Thirteen Principal Upaniṣads*, translated by Robert Hume (Upaniṣads [1877] rev. 1931), modernized.

15. Arvind Sharma quotes Raynor Johnson: "There is no fate, circumstance or even[t] which in the last analysis we do not or have not created for ourselves" (A. Sharma 1979, 536). On Herbert Fingarette's view, "The *Gita* by-passes, and in an important sense undercuts, the traditional Western preoccupation with free will and determinism" (1984, 364). James Sellmann (1987) argues in quasi-Kantian terms that although from an empirical point of view the Gita's determinism cannot be refuted, there is an absolute ineffable sense of freedom that exists together with it. For a more recent discussion, see Stansell (2008, 76–78).

16. The clearest example of knowledge bestowed by grace is in chapter 11: "But thou canst not behold Me with this (human) eye of yours; I will bestow on thee the supernatural eye" (11.8). And later, "By My grace, through My divine power, O Arjuna, was shown to thee this supreme form" (11.47). Cf. 18.56, 18.58, 18.62.

17. Cf. Radhakrishnan (1948, 375–76).

18. This is a simplification of the five factors mentioned by Krishna: "The seat of action and likewise the agent, the instruments of various sorts, the many kinds of efforts and [divine] providence being the fifth" (18.14). For discussion of this passage, including the implications for human freedom and responsibility, see MacKenzie (2001).

19. "The boundless universe in an endless space and time rests in Him and not He in it" (Radhakrishnan 1948, 28). "God has control over time because He is outside of it" (280).

20. *Timaeus* 37d. Cf. Radhakrishnan: "Time derives from eternity and finds fulfillment in it" (1948, 38).

21. For a subtle phenomenological exploration of how this appears within our consciousness, see Teschner (1992, 65–68, 76–77). Teschner also argues that "it is particularly difficult for Western philosophy to understand the importance and centrality of action in the interpretation of Asian thought . . . [because] for Indian philosophy of mind, thought is a species of action and behaviour. . . . However, for Western philosophy, the causality of thought and action are different. A reason for this is to be found in the concept of mind which Western thinkers have inherited from the G[r]eek and Christian traditions" (74–75). But Krishna has to convince Arjuna that *prakriti*, and not Arjuna's intentions, is the agency of events, which suggests that Arjuna's attitude, and that of his culture, is not very different from ours.

22. Cf. *Meditations* 2.10, 3.16, 6.16, 7.33, 7.64, 7.68, 8.10, 9.7, 9.40, 11.3. All quotations from Marcus Aurelius are from the George Long translation (Marcus Aurelius 1862); I have modernized and often considerably abridged them here to narrow the focus to the issue at hand.

23. Marcus Aurelius's mind-body dichotomy can be mapped fairly comfortably onto Samkhya's *sattva-rajas-tamas* (truth-passion-dullness) triad by taking *rajas* and *tamas* to be two aspects of the body. Where he adopts Plato's tripartite division, as at 6.51, spiritedness and appetite together are equivalent to *rajas*, while *tamas* would correspond to a privation of the force of the three Platonic motivations.

24. Cf. *Meditations* 4.33, 6.22, 6.26, 7.13, 7.36, 7.44, 7.45, 7.70, 8.27.

25. Cf. *Meditations* 2.5, 7.43, 9.35, 11.11.

26. Parenthetic insertions in quotes from this edition are the translator's.

27. *Dhyana* is not normally accorded the same status by scholars, but it seems to be on an equal footing in the Gita. Chapter 3 recognizes only two yogas: "A twofold way of life has been taught of yore by Me, the path of knowledge [*jñanayogena*] for men of contemplation [*samkhyanam*] and that of actions [*karmayogena*] for men of action [*yoginam*]" (3.3). *Bhakti* does not appear as an

additional path until chapter 9. In between, Krishna says, "Earth, water, fire, air, ether, mind and understanding and self-sense—this is the eightfold division of my nature [*prakrtir*]. This is My lower nature. Know My other and higher nature which is the soul [*jiva*], by which this world is upheld" (7.4 and 5). Although the terminology differs, the distinction between Krishna's lower and higher nature appears to anticipate the subsequent distinction in chapter 13 between *prakriti* and *puruṣa*. If *dhyana* can be considered a fourth principal yoga here, it is possible that the transition from two yogas to four is because the distinction between *prakriti* and *puruṣa* cuts across that between contemplation (*samkhya*) and action (*yoga*): action focused on *prakriti* is *karma* yoga, and focused on *puruṣa* is *bhakti* yoga, while contemplation focused on *prakriti* is *jñana* yoga, and focused on *puruṣa* is *dhyana* yoga. In any case, nothing in my overall reading turns on the relative status of *dhyana*.

28. Cf. *Meditations* 6.7, 7.13, 8.1, 8.8, 8.26, 8.27, 8.56, 9.16. Pierre Hadot writes, "Orthodox Stoics [as opposed to Aristo], while they recognized that the things which do not depend on us are indifferent, nevertheless admitted that we could attribute to them a moral value, by conceding the existence of political, social, and family obligations" (1998, 72).

29. The same point is made in the titles of the anonymous *Cloud of Unknowing* and Nicolas of Cusa's *De docta ignorantia*.

30. τὸν κοινὸν θεοῖς καὶ ἀνθρώποις λόγον.

31. ὁ διοικῶν λόγος οἶδε πῶς διακείμενος.

32. ὁ ἑκάστου νοῦς θεὸς καὶ ἐκεῖθεν ἐρρύηκεν.

33. "To the rational animal the same act is according to nature and according to reason" (7.11). Again, nature, like reason, is said to govern the whole (7.25).

34. "Did nature herself design to do evil to the things which are parts of herself?" (10.7). Cf. 6.1.

35. μία ψυχή, κἂν φύσεσι διείργηται μυρίαις καὶ ἰδίαις περιγραφαῖς. μία νοερὰ ψυχή, κἂν διακεκρίσθαι δοκῇ.

36. Epictetus, *Discourses* 3.22. Also see Marcus Aurelius, *Meditations* 3.6, 5.29, 7.68, 8.16, 8.56.

37. Cf. *Meditations* 2.3, 4.9–10, 4.34, 5.21, 5.32, 7.41, 7.55, 7.57, 7.68.

38. Radhakrishnan writes, "We must divest our minds of all sensual desires, abstract our attention from all external objects and absorb it in the object of meditation. See Gita XVIII, 72, where the teacher asks Arjuna whether he heard his teaching with his mind fixed to one point" (1948, 193). Radhakrishnan even titles chapter 6 of the Gita, which is devoted to meditation, "The True *Yoga*."

39. For further details about the contradictions and their reception, see A. Sharma (1986, xxiii–xxx).

40. E.g., Hiriyanna ([1932] 1993, 118). Shankara, on the other hand, is at pains to reject this conclusion.

41. Shankara refers to a similar sentiment at 3.1—"If thou deemest that (the path of) understanding [*buddhir*] is more excellent than (the path of) action [*karmanas*]"—as evidence that the path of understanding takes absolute precedence over the path of action (Shankara 1991 following 2.10, 3.1, and passim). But other passages show the issue to be less straightforward, as we shall see. Radhakrishnan translates *jñane* and *jñanena* here as "wisdom." Throughout, he translates forms of *jñana* as either "knowledge" or "wisdom" depending on context. I substitute "knowledge" for "wisdom" here and elsewhere in order to emphasize with terminological consistency where *jñana* yoga is implied.

42. Cf. 2.52: "When thy intelligence shall cross the whirl of delusion, then shalt thou become indifferent to what has been heard and what is yet to be heard [*srotavyasya srutasya*]."

43. Thus Shankara on 12.9: "Practice [*abhyasa*] consists in repeatedly fixing the mind on a single object by withdrawing it from everything else" (1991, 481). In the next quotation (12.10), Radhakrishnan translates *abhyase* by "practice" instead of "the practice of concentration" as here. I expand it to the previous rendering to indicate that the same term is being used.

44. Cited in Shankara (1977, 309n"*").

45. "Yet others, ignorant of this, hearing [*srutva*] from others, worship; they too cross beyond death by their devotion to what they have heard [*sruti*]." Cf. Gambhirananda: "*Practice [abhyasat]*—repeated effort to ascertain the true meaning of Vedic texts, in order to acquire knowledge" (in Shankara 1991, 483n3).

46. Baghavad Gita 13.15. Radhakrishnan translates, "He is too subtle to be known." Cf. 7.26: "Me [Krishna] no one knows [*veda*]." As an avatar of God, Krishna refers to God sometimes in the third and sometimes in the first person.

47. Cf. C. Sharma (1960, 33–37). Chandrahar Sharma concludes, however, that *jñana* is the most important and that *karma* and *bhakti* "are only manifestations of *jñana*" (37). In accordance with the usual practice he is concerned only with *bhakti*, *karma*, and *jñana* yogas and not with *dhyana*.

48. Cf. Rauf Mazari: "Love is a way to truth, to knowledge, to action. But only those who know of real love can approach these things by means of love. The others have misunderstood certain other feelings for those of real love. . . . Truth is a way to love, knowledge, to action. But only those who can follow real truth can follow its path as a way. . . . What [others] call truth is something less. Knowledge is a way to action, to love, to truth. But since it is not the kind of knowledge that people hold it to be, they do not benefit from it. It is everywhere, but they cannot see it, and call out for it while it is beside them all the time. Action, too, is a way.

It is a way to love, to truth, to knowledge. But . . . [people] will generally be so immersed in action of another kind that [they] will not be able to perform the right action which [they] need." Quoted in Shah (1974, 285).

49. Arvind Sharma suggests that these contradictory passages can be seen as differences in emphasis and that Krishna's point is that "Arjuna should fight no matter from which angle the issue was viewed—whether of *Jñana*, *Bhakti* or *Karma*" (1986, xxiii, xxvi). Also see Minor (1980, 346–51).

50. Edgerton (1968, 147–48), italics and parentheses in the original.

51. Thus too in the Bible's book of Genesis we are commanded not to eat from the tree of the knowledge of good and evil but at the same time are required to know and to do the good commanded by God and avoid the evil forbidden by God (Gen. 2:17). The tree of the knowledge of good and evil makes us sinful because it makes us be like God (3:5). What pleases and displeases God is good and evil absolutely, but for us to equate our own pleasure and displeasure with goodness and evil is to become self-willed and sinful.

52. "Self-control and calmness; pleasure and pain, existence and non-existence, fear and fearlessness. Non-violence, equal-mindedness, . . . fame and ill-fame, the different states of being proceed from me alone" (10.4–5). Cf. 13.7, 16.2, 17.14. I use the popular translation of *ahimsa* as "nonviolence," although "not harming" is more literal.

53. But Krishna would not go as far as Kant in saying that an action in accord with duty should be independent of our inclination. For the virtue ethics of the Gita, unlike Kant's deontology, it is necessary to bring our inclinations as well as our decisions into agreement with the good rather than with self-interest.

54. For an extended discussion of this issue, see the chapter "Nonutopian Observations on Machiavellism," in Scharfstein (2014, 152–91).

55. Cf. *Meditations* 3.4, 6.44, 8.51, 8.57, 10.9.

56. On the Stoic conception of becoming the equal of God, cf. Hadot (1998, 76).

Conclusion

1. Stephanus numbers for Plato's works correspond to the Burnet edition of the Oxford Classical Texts (Burnet 1900–1907).

2. Spinoza, *Ethics*, part IV, proposition 37 and scholium 1, and part IV, proposition 27, both in Spinoza (1994).

3. *Atma Bodha*, §14, in Shankara (n.d.-a).

BIBLIOGRAPHY

Allinson, Robert. 1989. *Chuang-Tzu for Spiritual Transformation*. Albany: SUNY Press.

Alquiros, Hilmar. 2002. "Lǎozǐ, *Dàodéjīng*" [Lao Tzu, *Tao Te Ching*]. www.tao-te-king.org/.

Ames, Roger. 2005. "Getting Past the Eclipse of Philosophy in World Sinology: A Response to Eske Møllgaard." *Dao* 4:347–52.

Ames, Roger, and David Hall. 2003. *Dao De Jing: A Philosophical Translation*. New York: Ballantine.

Annas, Julia. 1981. *An Introduction to Plato's "Republic."* Oxford: Clarendon Press.

———. 1995. "Virtue as a Skill." *International Journal of Philosophical Studies* 3:227–43.

Aristotle. 1894. *Ethica Nicomachea*. Edited by Ingram Bywater. Oxford Classical Texts. Oxford: Clarendon Press.

———. 1937. *Parts of Animals*. Loeb Classical Library. Cambridge, MA: Harvard University Press; London: Heineman.

———. 1955. *Generation and Corruption*. Loeb Classical Library. Cambridge, MA: Harvard University Press; London: Heineman.

———. 1956a. *De anima*. Edited by W. D. Ross. Oxford Classical Texts. Oxford: Clarendon Press.

———. 1956b. *Physica*. Edited by W. D. Ross. Oxford Classical Texts. Oxford: Clarendon Press.

———. 1957. *Metaphysica*. Edited by Werner Jaeger. Oxford Classical Texts. Oxford: Clarendon Press.

———. 1984. *The Complete Works of Aristotle: The Revised Oxford Translation*. Edited by Jonathan Barnes. Princeton, NJ: Princeton University Press.

Bailey, Olivia. 2010. "What Knowledge Is Necessary for Virtue?" *Journal of Ethics and Social Philosophy* 4:1–17.

Beck, Aaron T. 1976. *Cognitive Therapy and the Emotional Disorders*. New York: International Universities Press.

Benjamin, Walter. 1968. "The Task of the Translator." In *Illuminations*. New York: Harcourt, Brace, Jovanovich.

Bennett, Jonathan. 1984. *A Study of Spinoza's Ethics*. Indianapolis: Hackett.

Bergson, Henri. 1911. *Laughter: An Essay on the Meaning of the Comic*. Translated by C. Brereton and F. Rothwell. New York: Macmillan.

Blakeley, Donald. 1996. "Cultivation of Self in Chu Hsi and Plotinus." *Journal of Chinese Philosophy* 23:385–413.

Blocker, Gene. 1999. *World Philosophy: An East-West Comparative Introduction to Philosophy*. Upper Saddle River, NJ: Prentice-Hall.

Boodberg, Peter. 1957. "Philological Notes on Chapter One of the Lao Tzu." *Harvard Journal of Asiatic Studies* 20:598–618.

Bormann, Karl. 1979. "Simplicius on Parmenides." *Monist* 62:30–42.

Bowra, C. M. 1937. "The Proem of Parmenides." *Classical Philology* 32:97–112.

Brickhouse, T., and N. Smith. 2000. *The Philosophy of Socrates*. Boulder, CO: Westview Press.

Brown, H. F. 1895. *J. A. Symonds, a Biography*. London.

Buddha. 2000. *The Connected Discourses of the Buddha: A Translation of the Samyutta Nikaya*. Translated from the Pali by Bhikkhu Bodhi. Boston: Wisdom Publications.

Burik, Steven. 2009. *The End of Comparative Philosophy and the Task of Comparative Philosophy: Heidegger, Derrida, and Daoism*. Albany: SUNY Press.

Burnet, John, ed. 1900–1907. *Platonis opera*. 5 vols. Oxford: Clarendon Press.

———. [1914] 1964. *Greek Philosophy: Thales to Plato*. London: Macmillan.

———. [1930] 1957. *Early Greek Philosophy*. 4th ed. London: Macmillan.

Carmin, C. N., and E. T. Dowd. 1988. "Paradigms in Cognitive Therapy." In Dryden and Trower 1988, 1–22.

Chan, Wing-tsit. 1963a. *A Source Book in Chinese Philosophy*. Princeton, NJ: Princeton University Press.

———. 1963b. *The Way of Lao Tzu*. Indianapolis: Bobbs-Merrill.

———. 1989. *Chu Hsi: New Studies*. Honolulu: University of Hawaii Press.

Chen, Ellen. 1989. *The Tao Te Ching: A New Translation and Commentary*. New York: Paragon.

Ching, Julia. 1976. *To Acquire Wisdom: The Way of Wang Yang-ming*. New York: Columbia University Press.

———. 2000. *The Religious Thought of Chu Hsi*. Oxford: Oxford University Press.

Chinn, Ewing. 2007. "The Relativist Challenge to Comparative Philosophy." *International Philosophical Quarterly* 47:451–66.

Code, Alan. 1984. "An Aporematic Approach to Primary Being in *Metaphysics Z*." *Canadian Journal of Philosophy*, suppl. 10:1–20.

Confucius. 1979. *The Analects*. Translated by Dim Cheuk Lau. Harmondsworth: Penguin.

———. 1997. *The Analects*. Translated by Chichung Huang. Oxford: Oxford
University Press.

Cook, Scott. 2003. "Harmony and Cacophony in the Panpipes of Heaven." In
Hiding the World in the World: Uneven Discourses on the Zhuangzi, edited by
Scott Cook, 64–87. Albany: SUNY Press.

Cordero, Néstor-Luis. 2004. *By Being, It Is: The Thesis of Parmenides*. Las Vegas,
NV: Parmenides.

Cornford, F. M. 1939. *Plato and Parmenides*. London: Routledge.

Cross, R. C., and A. D. Woozley. 1964. *Plato's "Republic": A Philosophical Commentary*. London: Macmillan.

Csikszentmihalyi, Mark. 1999. "Mysticism and Apophatic Discourse in the
Laozi." In Csikszentmihalyi and Ivanhoe 1999, 33–58.

Csikszentmihalyi, Mark, and Philip Ivanhoe, eds. 1999. *Religious and Philosophical Aspects of the Laozi*. Albany: SUNY Press.

Cua, A. S. 1982. *The Unity of Knowledge and Action: A Study in Wang Yang-ming's
Moral Psychology*. Honolulu: University of Hawaii Press.

———. 1993. "Between Commitment and Realization: Wang Yang-Ming's
Vision of the Universe as a Moral Community." *Philosophy East and West*
43:611–47.

Curd, Patricia. 1991. "Knowledge and Unity in Heraclitus." *Monist* 74:531–49.

———. 2004. *The Legacy of Parmenides*. Las Vegas, NV: Parmenides.

Curley, Edwin. 1988. *Behind the Geometrical Method: A Reading of Spinoza's
"Ethics."* Princeton, NJ: Princeton University Press.

Davidson, Donald. 1973–74. "On the Very Idea of a Conceptual Scheme."
Proceedings and Addresses of the American Philosophical Association
47:5–20.

Della Rocca, Michael. 2008. *Spinoza*. London: Routledge.

de Stryker, Emile. 1966. "The Unity of Knowledge and Love in Socrates' Conception of Virtue." *International Philosophical Quarterly* 6:428–44.

Diels, Hermann, and Walther Kranz, eds. 1966. *Die Fragmente der Vorsokratike*.
12th ed. Zurich: Weidmann.

Dilcher, Roman. 1995. *Studies in Heraclitus*. Hildesheim: Georg Olms

Doctrine of the Mean, The. In Chan 1963a, 98–114.

Donagan, Alan. 1989. *Spinoza*. Chicago: University of Chicago Press.

Donne, John. 1952. *The Complete Poetry and Selected Prose*. New York: Modern
Library.

Dorter, Kenneth. 1973. "Science and Religion in Descartes' *Meditations*."
Thomist 37:313–40.

———. 1994. *Form and Good in Plato's Eleatic Dialogues: The Parmenides, Theaetetus, Sophist, and Statesman*. Berkeley: University of California Press.

———. 1996. "Three Disappearing Ladders in Plato." *Philosophy and Rhetoric* 29:279–99.

———. 2001. "Philosopher-Rulers: How Contemplation Becomes Action." *Ancient Philosophy* 21:335–56.

———. 2006. *The Transformation of Plato's "Republic."* Lanham, MD: Lexington Books.

———. 2010. "Plato's Use of the Dialogue Form: Skepticism and Insemination." In *Literary Form, Philosophical Content: Historical Studies of Philosophical Genres*, edited by J. Lavery and L. Groarke, 41–52. Madison, NJ: Fairleigh Dickinson University Press.

———. 2012a. "Being and Appearance in Parmenides." In *Metaphysics*, edited by Mark Pestana, 45–64. Rijeka, Croatia: InTech. www.intechopen.com /books/metaphysics/being-and-appearance-in-parmenides.

———. 2012b. "A Dialectical Interpretation of the *Bhagavad-Gita*." *Asian Philosophy* 22:307–26.

Dryden, Windy, and Peter Trower, eds. 1988. *Developments in Cognitive Psychotherapy*. London: Sage Publications.

Edgerton, Franklin. 1968. *The Bhagavad Gita*. New York: Harper and Row.

Elders, Leo. 1972. *Aristotle's Theology: A Commentary on Book Λ of the Metaphysics*. Assen: Van Gorcum.

Ellis, Albert. 1962. *Reason and Emotion in Psychotherapy*. New York: Lyle Stuart, 1962.

Euripides. 1958. *Hippolytus*. Translated by David Grene. In *Complete Greek Tragedies*, edited by David Grene and Richmond Lattimore, vol. 3. Chicago: University of Chicago Press.

Feuer, Lewis. 1958. *Spinoza and the Rise of Liberalism*. Boston: Beacon Press.

Fingarette, Herbert. 1984. "Action and Suffering in the *Bhagavadgita*." *Philosophy East and West* 34:357–69.

Finkelberg, Aryeh. 1986. "The Cosmology of Parmenides." *American Journal of Philosophy* 107:303–17.

———. 1999. "Being, Truth and Opinion in Parmenides." *Archiv für Geschichte der Philosophie* 81:233–48.

Frede, Michael, and David Charles, eds. 2000. *Aristotle's Metaphysics Lambda: Symposium Aristotelicum*. Oxford: Clarendon Press.

Freeman, Kathleen. 1956. *Ancilla to the Presocratic Philosophers*. Oxford: Blackwell.

Froese, Katrin. 2013. "Humour as the Playful Sidekick to Language in the Zhuangzi." *Asian Philosophy* 23:137–52.

Fu, Charles Wei-hsun. 1973. "Lao-Tzu's Conception of Tao." *Inquiry* 16:367–94.

Fung, Yu-lan. 1948. *A Short History of Chinese Philosophy*. New York: Macmillan.

Gadamer, Hans-Georg. 1972. *Wahrheit und Methode*. 3rd ed. Tübingen: J. C. B. Mohr.

———. 1975. *Truth and Method*. Anonymous translator. New York: Seabury.

———. 1986. *The Idea of the Good in Platonic-Aristotelian Philosophy*. New Haven, CT: Yale University Press.

———. 2002. "Heraclitus Studies." In *The Beginning of Knowledge*, 33–81. New York: Continuum.

Gallop, David. 1979. "'Is' or 'Is Not'?" *Monist* 62:61–80.

———. 1984. *Parmenides of Elea*. Toronto: University of Toronto Press.

———. 1998. "Socrates, Injustice, and the Law: A Response to Plato's *Crito*." *Ancient Philosophy* 18:251–65.

Geldard, Richard. 2007. *Parmenides and the Way of Truth*. Rhinebeck, NY: Monkfish.

Gemelli Marciano, M. Laura. 2008. "Images and Experience: At the Roots of Parmenides' *Aletheia*." *Ancient Philosophy* 28:21–48.

George Victor, P. 2002. *Life and Teachings of Adi Sankaracarya*. New Delhi: D. K. Printworld.

Gerson, Lloyd. 1986. "Platonic Dualism." *Monist* 69:352–69.

———. 2002. "The Development of the Doctrine of the Good and Plato's Development." In Reale and Scolnicov 2002, 379–91.

Gilbert, Paul. 1988. "Emotional Disorders, Brain State and Psychosocial Evolution." In Dryden and Trower 1988, 41–70.

Gill, Christopher. 2002. "A Critical Response to the Hermeneutic Approach from an Analytic Perspective." In Reale and Scolnicov 2002, 211–22. Sankt Augustin: Academia Verlag.

Girardot, N. J. 1983. *Myth and Meaning in Early Taoism*. Berkeley: University of California Press.

Graham, A. C. 1981. *Chuang-tzu: The Seven Inner Chapters and Other Writings*. London: George Allen and Unwin.

Granger, Herbert. 2008. "The Proem of Parmenides' Poem." *Ancient Philosophy* 28:1–20.

———. 2010. "Parmenides of Elea: Rationalist or Dogmatist?" *Ancient Philosophy* 30:15–38.

Great Learning, The. 1963. In Chan 1963a, 86–94.

Guthrie, W. K. C. 1962–81. *A History of Greek Philosophy*. 5 vols. Cambridge: Cambridge University Press.

Hadot, Pierre. 1998. *The Inner Citadel: The Meditations of Marcus Aurelius*. Translated by Michael Chase. Cambridge, MA: Harvard University Press.

Hegel, G. W. F. 1988. *Introduction to the Philosophy of History*. Translated by Leo Rauch. Indianapolis: Hackett.

Heidegger, Martin. 1954a. "Aletheia (Heraklit, Fragment 16)." In Heidegger 1954d, 257–82.

———. 1954b. "Logos (Heraklit, Fragment 50)." In Heidegger 1954d, 207–29.

———. 1954c. "Moira (Parmenides VIII, 34–41)." In Heidegger 1954d, 231–56.

———. 1954d. *Vorträge und Aufsätze*. Pfullingen: Neske.

———. 1957. *Einführung in die Metaphysik*. 2nd ed. Tübingen: Max Niemeyer.

———. 1966. *Discourse on Thinking*. Translated by John M. Anderson and E. Hans Freund. New York: Harper Perennial. Originally published as *Gelassenheit* (Pfullingen: Neske, 1959).

———. 1975. "The Origin of the Work of Art." In *Poetry, Language, Thought*, translated by Albert Hofstadter, 17–87. New York: Harper and Row.

———. 2000. *Introduction to Metaphysics*. Translated by Gregory Fried and Richard Polt. New Haven, CT: Yale University Press.

Heidegger, Martin, and Eugen Fink. 1979. *Heraclitus Seminar 1966/67*. Mobile: University of Alabama Press.

Henricks, Robert. 2000. *Lao Tzu's Tao Te Ching: A Translation of the Startling New Documents Found at Guodian*. New York: Columbia University Press.

Heraclitus. 1966. *Die Fragmente der Vorsokratike*. Edited by Hermann Diels and Walther Kranz. 12th ed. Zurich: Weidmann.

Hiriyanna, Mysore. [1932] 1993. *Outlines of Indian Philosophy*. Delhi: Motilal Banarsidass.

Hirst, Jacqueline Suthren. 2005. *Samkara's Advaita Vedanta: A Way of Teaching*. London: RoutledgeCurzon.

Hölscher, Uvo. 1968. *Anfängliches Fragen: Studien zur frühen griechischen Philosophie*. Göttingen: Vandenhoeck und Ruprecht.

Houlgate, Laurence. 1970. "Virtue Is Knowledge." *Monist* 54:142–53.

Hoy, Ronald. 1994. "Parmenides' Complete Rejection of Time." *Journal of Philosophy* 91:573–98.

Hsü Ai. 1965. Preface to *Wang Wen-ch'eng Kung ch'üan shu* [Complete works of Wang Yangming]. Ssu-pu Ts'ung-k'an ed. Taipei.

Huainanzi. N.d. Szu-pu ts'ung-k'an (SPTK) ed. Shanghai: Commercial Press.

Huang, Chichung, trans. 1997. *The Analects of Confucius*. Oxford: Oxford University Press.

Huxley, Aldous. [1944] 1970. *The Perennial Philosophy*. New York: Harper and Row.

Irwin, Terence. 1974. "Recollection and Plato's Moral Theory." *Review of Metaphysics* 27:752–72.

———. 1995. *Plato's Ethics*. Oxford: Oxford University Press.

Isayeva, Natalia. 1993. *Shankara and Indian Philosophy*. Albany: SUNY Press.

Ivanhoe, Philip. 1999. "The Concept of *de* ('Virtue') in the Laozi." In Csikszent-mihalyi and Ivanhoe 1999, 239–57.

Izutsu, Toshihiko. 2004. *The Absolute and the Perfect Man in Taoism*. Colombo: Sri Lanka Institute of Traditional Studies.

James, William. [1901–2] 1929. *The Varieties of Religious Experience*. New York: Modern Library.

Kahn, Charles. 1969. "The Thesis of Parmenides." *Review of Metaphysics* 22:700–724.

———. 1979. *The Thought and Art of Heraclitus*. Cambridge: Cambridge University Press.

———. 1985. "The Place of the Prime Mover in Aristotle's Teleology." In *Aristotle on Nature and Living Things*, edited by Allan Gotthelf, 183–205. Cambridge: Cambridge University Press. 1985.

———. 1996. *Plato and the Socratic Dialogue: The Philosophical Use of a Literary Form*. Cambridge: Cambridge University Press.

Kelly, John. 1989. "Virtue and Inwardness in Plato's *Republic*." *Ancient Philosophy* 9:189–205.

Kierkegaard, Søren. 1941. *Concluding Unscientific Postscript*. Translated by D. Swenson and W. Lowrie. Princeton, NJ: Princeton University Press.

Kim, Yung Sik. 2000. *The Natural Philosophy of Chu Hsi*. Philadelphia: American Philosophical Society.

Kingsley, Peter. 1999. *In the Dark Places of Wisdom*. Inverness, CA: Golden Sufi Center.

———. 2003. *Reality*. Inverness, CA: Golden Sufi Center.

Kirk, G. S. 1954. *Heraclitus: The Cosmic Fragments*. Cambridge: Cambridge University Press.

Kohn, Livia. 2011. *Chuang-tzu: The Tao of Perfect Happiness*. Woodstock, VT: SkyLight Paths.

Kosman, Aryeh. 2000. "*Metaphysics* Λ 9: Divine Thought." In Frede and Charles 2000, 307–26.

Kupperman, Joel. 1989. "Not in So Many Words: Chuang Tzu's Strategies of Communication." *Philosophy East and West* 39:311–17.

———. 1999. *Learning from Asian Philosophy*. New York: Oxford University Press.

———. 2007. *Classic Asian Philosophy: A Guide to the Essential Texts*. 2nd ed. New York: Oxford University Press.

———. 2010. "Why Ethical Philosophy Needs to Be Comparative." *Philosophy* 85:185–200.

Lacey, A. R. 1971. "Our Knowledge of Socrates." In Vlastos 1971b, 22–49.

LaFargue, Michael. 1994. *Tao and Method: A Reasoned Approach to the Tao Te Ching*. Albany: SUNY Press.

Lagan, William. 1982. "Parmenides and Mystical Reason: A Metaphysical Dilemma." *Modern Schoolman* 60:30–47.

Lau, D. C., trans. 1970. *Mencius*. Harmondsworth: Penguin Books.

Leibniz, Gottfried Wilhelm. [1697] 2014. "On the Ultimate Origin of Things." Translated by Lloyd Strickland. www.leibniz-translations.com/ultimateorigination.htm.

———. 1949. *New Essays on Human Understanding*. Translated by Alfred Gideon Langley. 2nd ed. La Salle, IL: Open Court.

———. 1951. *Leibniz Selections*. Edited by Philip Weiner. New York: Scribner's.

Lesses, Glenn. 1987. "Weakness, Reason, and the Divided Soul in Plato's *Republic*." *History of Philosophy Quarterly* 4:147–61.

Lewis, Frank. 2009. "Parmenides' Modal Fallacy." *Phronesis* 54:1–8.

Little, Margaret Olivia. 1997. "Virtue as Knowledge: Objections from the Philosophy of Mind." *Nous* 31:59–79.

Liu, Shu-Hsien. 1998. "On the Final Views of Wang Yang-ming." *Journal of Chinese Philosophy* 25:345–60.

Liu, Xiaogan. 1999. "The Core Value of Laozi's Philosophy." In Csikszentmihalyi and Ivanhoe 1999, 211–37.

Lloyd, Genevieve. 1994. *Part of Nature: Self-Knowledge in Spinoza's "Ethics."* Ithaca, NY: Cornell University Press.

Lloyd, G. E. R. 2000. "*Metaphysics Λ* 8." In Frede and Charles 2000, 245–74.

Locke, John. [1894] 1959. *Essay Concerning Human Understanding*. Edited by Alexander Campbell Fraser. New York: Dover.

Long, A. A. 1975. "The Principles of Parmenides' Cosmology." In *Studies in Presocratic Philosophy*, edited by R. E. Allen and David Furley, vol. 2, 82–101. London: Routledge and Kegan Paul.

Ma, Lin, and Jaap van Brakel. 2013. "On the Conditions of Possibility for Comparative and Intercultural Philosophy." *Dao* 12:297–312.

———. 2016. *Fundamentals of Comparative and Intercultural Philosophy*. Albany: SUNY Press.

MacKenzie, Matthew. 2001. "The Five Factors of Action and the Decentring of Agency in the *Bhagavad Gita*." *Asian Philosophy* 11:141–50.

Manchester, P. B. 1979. "Parmenides and the Need for Eternity." *Monist* 62:81–106.

Marcovich, M. 1967. *Heraclitus*. Merida, Venezuela: Los Andes University Press.

Marcus Aurelius. 1862. *Meditations*. Translated by George Long. Modernized by K. Dorter. http://classics.mit.edu/Antoninus/meditations.html.

McKie, John. 1994. "Linguistic Competence and Moral Development: Some Parallels." *Philosophical Inquiry* 16:20–31.

McKirahan, Richard. 1994. *Philosophy before Socrates.* Indianapolis: Hackett.

McLeod, Alexus. 2016. *Theories of Truth in Chinese Philosophy: A Comparative Approach.* London: Rowman and Littlefield.

McPherran, Mark. 1996. *The Religion of Socrates.* University Park: Pennsylvania State University Press.

Melamed, S. M. 1933. *Spinoza and Buddha: Visions of a Dead God.* Chicago: University of Chicago Press.

Mencius. 1970. Translated by Dim Cheuk Lau. Harmondsworth: Penguin.

Merton, Thomas. [1965] 1997. *The Way of Chuang Tzu.* New York: New Directions.

Mill, John Stuart. 1979. *Utilitarianism.* Indianapolis: Hackett.

Miller, Mitchell. 1978. "Parmenides and the Disclosure of Being." *Apeiron* 13:12–35.

Minor, Robert. 1980. "The *Gita*'s Way as the Only Way." *Philosophy East and West* 30:339–59.

Møllgaard, Eske. 2007. *An Introduction to Daoist Thought: Action, Language and Ethics in Zhuangzi.* New York: Routledge.

Moravcsik, Julius. 1991. "Appearance and Reality in Heraclitus' Philosophy." *Monist* 74:551–67.

Mourelatos, Alexander. 1970. *The Route of Parmenides: A Study of Word, Image, and Argument in the Fragments.* New Haven, CT: Yale University Press.

Nadler, Steven. 2006. *Spinoza's "Ethics": An Introduction.* Cambridge: Cambridge University Press.

Nagarjuna. 1995. *The Fundamental Wisdom of the Middle Way: Nagarjuna's Mulamadhyamakakarika.* Translated with a commentary by Jay Garfield. Oxford: Oxford University Press.

Nails, Debra. 2002. *The People of Plato.* Indianapolis: Hackett.

———. 2009. "The Trial and Death of Socrates." In *A Companion to Greek and Roman Political Thought,* edited by Ryan Balot, 323–38. Oxford: Blackwell.

———. 2014. "Socrates." Revised version. In *The Stanford Encyclopedia of Philosophy.* http://plato.stanford.edu/entries/socrates/.

Needham, Joseph. 1959–61. *Science and Civilisation in China.* 2 vols. Cambridge: Cambridge University Press.

Nehamas, Alexander. 2002. "Parmenidean Being / Heraclitean Fire." In *Presocratic Philosophy: Essays in Honour of Alexander Mourelatos,* edited by V. Caston and D. Graham. Burlington, VT: Ashgate.

Neville, Robert Cummings. 2016. "Turns of the Dao." *Dao* 15:499–510.

Nietzsche, Friedrich. 1963a. *Also sprach Zarathustra.* In *Werke,* edited by Karl Schlechta. Munich: Hanser.

———. 1963b. *Zur Genealogie der Moral.* In *Werke,* edited by Karl Schlechta. Munich: Hanser.

———. 1969. *On the Genealogy of Morals.* Translated by Walter Kaufmann and R. J. Hollingdale. New York: Vintage.

Nivison, David. 1973. "Moral Decision in Wang Yang-ming: The Problem of Chinese 'Existentialism.'" *Philosophy East and West* 23:121–37.

Nussbaum, Martha. 1972. "ΨΥΧΗ in Heraclitus," I and II. *Phronesis* 17.

———. 1986. *The Fragility of Goodness.* Cambridge: Cambridge University Press.

Owen, G. E. L. 1975. "Eleatic Questions." In *Studies in Presocratic Philosophy,* edited by R. E. Allen and David Furley, vol. 2. London: Routledge and Kegan Paul.

Owens, Joseph. 1979. "Knowledge and *Katabasis* in Parmenides." *Monist* 62:15–29.

Palmer, John. 2008. "Parmenides." In *Stanford Encyclopedia of Philosophy,* http://plato.stanford.edu/entries/parmenides/.

Parry, Richard. 1983. "The Craft of Justice." *Canadian Journal of Philosophy,* suppl. 9:19–38.

———. 1996. *Plato's Craft of Justice.* Albany: SUNY Press.

Plotinus. 1966–88. *Enneads.* Translated by A. H. Armstrong. 7 vols. Loeb Classical Library. Cambridge, MA: Harvard University Press; London: Heineman.

Radhakrishnan, Sarvepalli, ed. 1948. *The Bhagavadgita; With an Introductory Essay, Sanskrit Text, English Translation and Notes.* New York: Harper.

Radhakrishnan, Sarvepalli, and Charles Moore. 1957. *A Source Book in Indian Philosophy.* Princeton, NJ: Princeton University Press.

Rawson, Glenn. 1966. "Knowledge and Desire of the Good in Plato's *Republic.*" *Southwest Philosophy Review* 12:103–15.

Reale, Giovanni, and Samuel Scolnicov, eds. *New Images of Plato: Dialogues on the Idea of the Good.* Sankt Augustin: Academia Verlag.

Reeve, C. D. C. 1988. *Philosopher-Kings: The Argument of Plato's "Republic."* Princeton, NJ: Princeton University Press.

Reinhardt, Karl. [1916] 1977. *Parmenides und die Geschichte der griechischen Philosophie.* 3rd ed. Frankfurt: Klostermann.

———. 1942. "Heraclitea." *Hermes* 77:225–48.

Rethy, R. 1987. "Heraclitus Fragment 56." *Ancient Philosophy* 7:1–7.

Robinet, Isabelle. 1999. "The Diverse Interpretations of the Laozi." In Csik-szentmihalyi and Ivanhoe 1999, 127–59.

Robinson, T. M. 1987. *Heraclitus*. Toronto: University of Toronto Press.

Roth, Harold. 1999. "Early Daoist Mystical Praxis." In Csikszentmihalyi and Ivanhoe 1999, 59–96.

———. 2003. "Bimodal Mystical Experience in the 'Qiwulun' Chapter of the *Zhuangzi*." In *Hiding the World in the World: Uneven Discourses on the Zhuangzi*, edited by Scott Cook, 15–32. Albany: SUNY Press.

Santas, Gerasimos. 1964. "The Socratic Paradoxes." *Philosophical Review* 73:147–64.

———. 2002. "Plato's Idea of the Good." In Reale and Scolnicov 2002, 359–78.

Sartwell, Crispin. 1993. "Art and War: Paradox of the *Bhagavad Gita*." *Asian Philosophy* 3:95–102.

Scharfstein, Ben-Ami. 1993. *Ineffability: The Failure of Words in Philosophy and Religion*. Albany: SUNY Press.

———. 1998. *A Comparative History of World Philosophy: From the Upanishads to Kant*. Albany: SUNY Press.

———. 2009. *Art without Borders: A Philosophical Exploration of Art and Humanity*. Chicago: University of Chicago Press.

———. 2014. *The Nonsense of Kant and Lewis Carroll: Unexpected Essays on Philosophy, Art, Life, and Death*. Chicago: University of Chicago Press.

Schindler, D. C. 2003. "The Community of the One and the Many: Heraclitus on Reason." *Inquiry* 46:413–48.

Schopenhauer, Arthur. 1969. *The World as Will and Representation*. Translated by E. F. J. Payne. 2 vols. New York: Dover.

Scolnicov, Samuel. 1978. "Reason and Passion in the Platonic Soul." *Dionysus* 2:35–49.

———. 1988. *Plato's Metaphysics of Education*. London: Routledge.

Sedley, David. 2000. "*Metaphysics Λ* 10." In Frede and Charles 2000, 357–50.

Seifert, Josef. 2002. "The Idea of the Good as the Sum Total of Pure Perfections: A New Personalist Reading of *Republic* VI and VII." In Reale and Scolnicov 2002, 407–24.

Sellmann, James. 1987. "Free Will and Non-attachment in the *Bhagavad Gita*." *Indian Philosophical Quarterly* 14:375–88.

Sextus Empiricus. 1960–61. *Adversus mathematicos*. In *Sextus Empiricus*, translated by R. G. Bury. Cambridge, MA: Harvard University Press

Shah, Idries. 1974. *The Way of the Sufi*. London: Penguin.

Shankara. 1904. *Vedânta-Sûtras with the Commentary by Sankarâkârya*. Translated by George Thibaut. Sacred Books of the East 34. Oxford: Clarendon Press.

———. 1957–58. *Eight Upanisads with the Commentary of Sankaracarya*. 2 vols. Translated by Swami Gambhirananda. Calcutta: Advaita Ashrama.

————. 1977. *The Bhagavad Gita with the Commentary of Sri Sankaracharya.* Translated with notes by Alladi Mahadeva Sastry. Madras: Samata.

————. 1991. *Bhagavadgita with the Commentary of Sankaracarya.* Translated with notes by Swami Gambhirananda. 2nd ed. Calcutta: Advaita Ashrama.

————. N.d.-a. *Atma Bodha.* Translated by Swami Chinmayananda. Mumbai: Chinmaya Mission. www.geocities.com/advaitavedant/atmabodha.htm.

————. N.d.-b. *Upadesha Sahasri.* Translated by Swami Jagadananda. Chennai: Sri Ramakrishna Math. www.celextel.org/adisankara.html.

————. N.d.-c. *Vivekachudamani.* Translated by Swami Madhavananda. Calcutta: Advaita Ashram. www.celextel.org/adisankara.html.

Sharma, Arvind. 1979. "Fate and Free Will in the *Bhagavadgita.*" *Religious Studies* 15:531–37.

————. 1986. *The Hindu Gita.* LaSalle, IL: Open Court.

Sharma, Chandrahar. 1960. *A Critical Survey of Indian Philosophy.* Delhi: Motilal Banarsidass.

Sim, May. 2010. "From Metaphysics to Environmental Ethics: Aristotle or Zhu Xi." In *Democracy, Ecological Integrity and International Law*, edited by J. R. Engle, Laura Westra, and Klaus Bosselmann, 77–92. Newcastle upon Tyne: Cambridge Scholars.

Smid, Robert. 2009. *Methodologies of Comparative Philosophy: The Pragmatist and Process Traditions.* Albany: SUNY Press.

Smith, Huston. 1964. *The Religions of Man.* New York: Harper Colophon Books.

Smith, Steven. 2003. *Spinoza's Book of Life: Freedom and Redemption in the Ethics.* New Haven, CT: Yale.

Spinoza, Baruch. 1905. *The Principles of Descartes' Philosophy.* Translated by Halbert Hains Britan. Chicago: Open Court.

————. 1992. *Ethics.* Translated by Samuel Shirley. Indianapolis: Hackett.

————. 1994. *A Spinoza Reader: The Ethics and Other Works.* Edited and translated by Edwin Curley. Princeton, NJ: Princeton University Press.

Sprague, Rosamond Kent. 1976. *Plato's Philosopher-King.* Columbia: University of South Carolina Press.

Stansell, Ellen. 2008. "The *Guna* Theory of the Bhagavad Gita." *Journal of the Indian Council of Philosophic Research* 25:61–78.

Stokes, Michael. 1971. *One and Many in Presocratic Philosophy.* Washington, DC: Center for Hellenic Studies.

Strauss, Leo. 1964. *The City and Man.* Chicago: Rand McNally.

Swabey, Marie. 1961. *Comic Laughter.* New Haven, CT: Yale University Press.

Tarán, Leonardo. 1965. *Parmenides: A Text with Translation, Commentary, and Critical Essays.* Princeton, NJ: Princeton University Press.

————. 1979. "Perpetual Duration and Atemporal Eternity." *Monist* 62:43–53.

Tateno Masami. 1999. "The Laozi from an Ontological Perspective." In Csik-szentmihalyi and Ivanhoe 1999, 175–85.

Taylor, A. E. 1917. *Plato's Biography of Socrates*. London: British Academy.

———. [1933] 1952. *Socrates*. Garden City, NY: Anchor.

Teschner, George. 1992. "Anxiety, Anger, and the Concept of Agency and Action in the *Bhagavad Gita*." *Asian Philosophy* 2:61–77.

Tickle, Les. 2005. "Learning from Wang Yang-ming: Exploring Oriental Contributions to Understanding Action Research." *Educational Action Research* 13:595–606.

Upadhyaya, K. N. 1969. "The Bhagavad Gita on War and Peace." *Philosophy East and West* 19:159–69.

Upaniṣads. [1877] 1931. *The Thirteen Principal Upaniṣads*. 2nd, rev. ed. Translated by Robert Hume. London: Oxford University Press.

Van Norden, Bryan. 1999. "Method in the Madness of the Laozi." In Csikszent-mihalyi and Ivanhoe 1999, 187–210.

Verdenius, W. J. [1942] 1964. *Parmenides: Some Comments on His Poem*. Amsterdam: Hakkert.

———. 1949. "Parmenides' Conception of Light." *Mnemosyne*, 4th ser., 2:116–31.

Vlastos, Gregory. 1955. "On Heraclitus." *American Journal of Philology* 76:337–68.

———. 1971a. "The Paradox of Socrates." In Vlastos 1971b, 1–21.

———, ed. 1971b. *The Philosophy of Socrates: A Collection of Critical Essays*. Garden City, NY: Anchor Books.

———. 1991. *Socrates, Ironist and Moral Philosopher*. Ithaca, NY: Cornell University Press.

Waley, Arthur, trans. 1958. *The Way and Its Power*. New York: Evergreen.

Wang Pi. 1979. *Commentary on the Lao Tzu*. Translated by Ariane Rump. Honolulu: University of Hawaii Press.

Wang Yang-ming. 1963a. *Inquiry on "The Great Learning."* In Chan 1963a, 659–67.

———. 1963b. *Instructions for Practical Living and Other Neo-Confucian Writings by Wang Yang-ming*. Edited and translated by Wing-tsit Chan. New York: Columbia University Press

Waugh, Joanne. 1991. "Heraclitus: The Postmodern Presocratic?" *Monist* 74:605–23.

Wessler, R. L. 1988. "Affect and Nonconscious Processes in Cognitive Psychotherapy." In Dryden and Trower 1988, 23–40.

White, Nicholas. 1979. *A Companion to Plato's "Republic."* Indianapolis: Hackett.

Wilcox, Joel. 1991. "Barbarian *Psyche* in Heraclitus." *Monist* 74:624–37.

Wing, R. L. 1984. *The Tao of Power*. New York: Doubleday/Dolphin.

Wolfson, Harry. 1934. *The Philosophy of Spinoza: Unfolding the Latent Processes of His Reasoning*. Cambridge, MA: Harvard University Press.

Wu, Kuang-ming. 1982. *Chuang Tzu: World Philosopher at Play*. New York: Crossroad; Chico, CA: Scholars Press.

———. 1990. *The Butterfly as Companion: Meditations on the First Three Chapters of the Chuang Tzu*. Albany: SUNY Press.

Yu, Jiyuan. 2007. *The Ethics of Confucius and Aristotle*. New York: Routledge.

Zhu Xi. 1963a. *Complete Works of Chu Hsi* [Chu Tzu ch'üan-shu]. Selected and translated in Chan 1963a, 605–53. Despite the title the book is not the complete works but a collection of passages from *The Collection of Literary Works by Master Chu* [Chu Tzu wen-chi] and *The Classified Conversations of Master Chu* [Chu Tzu yü-lei]. See Chan 1963a, 592n7.

———. 1963b. "Treatise on Ch'eng Ming-tao's (Ch'eng Hao's) *Discourse on Nature*." In Chan 1963a, 597–99.

———. 1967. *Reflections of Things at Hand* (*Chin-ssu-lu*). Translated by Wing-tsit Chan. New York: Columbia University Press. Although Zhu Xi only edited this book and did not contribute to it, Chan's translation includes selections from Zhu Xi's commentaries on various passages.

———. 1990. *Learning to Be a Sage: Selections from the Conversations of Master Chu, Arranged Topically*. Translated with a commentary by Daniel K. Gardner. Berkeley: University of California Press.

———. 1991. *"Further Reflections of Things at Hand," by Chu Hsi* [Chu Tzu hsu chin-ssu-lu]. Translated by Allen Wittenborn. Lanham, MD: University Press of America.

Zhuangzi. [1933] 1964. *Chuang Tzu*. Translated by Yu-Lan Fung. 2nd ed. New York: Paragon.

———. 1968. *The Complete Works of Chuang Tzu*. Translated by Burton Watson. New York: Columbia University Press.

———. 1996. *The Book of Chuang Tzu*. Translated by Martin Palmer. London: Penguin.

———. 2009. *Zhuangzi: The Essential Writings*. Translated by Brook Ziporyn. Indianapolis: Hackett.

———. 2013. *The Complete Works of Zhuangzi*. Translated by Burton Watson. New York: Columbia University Press.

Zong, D. 2010. "A New Framework for Comparative Study of Philosophy." *Dao* 9:445–59.

INDEX

Kenneth Dorter is a professor of philosophy at the University of Guelph. He has published three books on Plato and has written on various areas of philosophy.

www.ingramcontent.com/pod-product-compliance
Lightning Source LLC
Chambersburg PA
CBHW060329100426
42812CB00003B/926